PRAISE FOR THE BLACK BOOK ON CORPORATE SECURITY

W9-AMC-011

"This book is unique in that it provides practical knowledge, guidance and direction from the top thought leaders in the information security community. The authors have had "hands on" experience in all facets of information security and the content is useful to all levels of a company, from the boardroom to business and operations management. This is definitely a book that will be kept close at hand, with chapters being read more than once."

— *Steve Katz, Former CISO, Citigroup*

"The Black Book on Corporate Security provides an in-depth examination of many of the current cybersecurity issues confronting us today, and establishes a blueprint for addressing those issues. This body of work from subject matter experts has a broad application that can extend to the technical staff as well as the corporate board room."

— *William F. Pelgrin, Director, NYS Office of Cyber Security and Critical Infrastructure*

"The Black Book is spot-on in its approach to information security. It's often said that security is a process, not a product. But the fact is it's actually both... and much more. The authors of this work embrace that reality by boiling down security's complexities and offering a clear picture of the not-too-distant future, when security will be less about bolt-on technologies and more about operational risk."

— *Andrew Briney, Publisher, Information Security Magazine*

"CISO/CSOs and corporate security professionals continue to take the lead in creating the mosaic of security. The Black Book on Corporate Security will be one that significantly adds to the body of knowledge, effectively communicating the real struggles faced on a daily basis by the top practitioners in the industry."

— *Howard A. Schmidt, former Chairman - President's Critical Infrastructure Protection Board, White House*

"The Black Book on Corporate Security will become the teaching aid for the future. When will the Black Book for Government Security become available to the government security decision makers of the future?"

— *Edward Tyler, Publisher/President, GSN: Government Security News - A World Business Media, LLC Publication*

"Compelling and comprehensive, The Black Book on Corporate Security should have a place on every infosecurity practitioner's bookshelf."

— *Timothy Garon, Founder and former publisher of Information Security Magazine*

CORPORATE SECURITY

by Tony Alagna, Eva Chen, Maria Cirino, Colin Elliott, Rami Elron, Stephen W. Foster, Dr. Jim Kennedy, Mehrzad Mahdavi, George G. McBride, Ron Moritz, Jim Nisbet, Jim Porell, Howard Schmidt, Joseph C. Seanor, Somesh Singh, Prof. Salvatore Stolfo and Michael Xie

Published by:
Larstan Publishing Inc.
10604 Outpost Dr., N. Potomac, MD 20878
301-637-4591
orders@blackbooksecurity.com   www.larstan.com

PRINTED IN THE UNITED STATES OF AMERICA

Design by Rob Hudgins & 5050Design.com

ISBN, Print Edition 0-9764266-1-7
First Edition

LARSTAN'S THE BLACK BOOK™ ON CORPORATE SECURITY

TONY ALAGNA
EVA CHEN
MARIA CIRINO
COLIN ELLIOTT
RAMI ELRON
STEPHEN W. FOSTER
DR. JIM KENNEDY
MEHRZAD MAHDAVI
GEORGE G. MCBRIDE

- RON MORITZ
- JIM NISBET
- JIM PORELL
- HOWARD SCHMIDT
- JOSEPH C. SEANOR
- SOMESH SINGH
- PROF. SALVATORE STOLFO
- MICHAEL XIE

LARSTAN
PUBLISHING

WASHINGTON D.C. ■ PHILADELPHIA

TABLE OF CONTENTS

ACKNOWLEDGEMENTS

Without question, the excellence of this book is largely derived from its outstanding authors. However, this book could not have been possible without the hard work, expertise and creativity of the many people associated with it. I would like to give a very special thank you to **Howard Schmidt**, who from the beginning, when this book was merely an idea, trusted my judgement and integrity. He generously put his clout and knowledge behind our efforts in creating *The Black Book on Corporate Security*.

Our editorial advisory board members, **Robert L. Bush**, **Marcus Ranum**, and **Steve Katz** also saw fit to join us at the very beginning. As we shouldered this long and arduous process, we were bolstered by the wisdom and frankness of Bob; the deep-rooted security acumen of Marcus; and the pioneering insights of the first CISO ever, Steve Katz. We would not have made it across the finish line without each and every one of them.

Larstan's editorial team is one of the best in the business. Our Editorial Director **Lane Cooper** was the guiding light behind the book's editorial plan; Managing Editor **David Evancha** spent long hours working with the book's busy authors; and Publisher **John Persinos** exerted his considerable literary talents to full effect in editing and polishing all of the chapters.

A special thanks to **Rob Hudgins**, our talented art director who designed this book, and **Sherrie Saldana**, the most patient production manager on earth. Others who were instrumental in helping us behind the scenes include **Susan Aluise**, **Yi Gu**, **Jonathan Holasek**, **Michael Morin**, **Gregg Siegel**, and **Martin Zook**.

The Black Book Series was created and brought to life by Larstan CEO **Larry Genkin** and Group Publisher **Mike Wiebner**. Their hard work and innovation — combined with an unwavering belief in the market's need for an advanced-level series of books written by industry insiders — will benefit readers in many industries and, most near and dear to me, the security industry, for a long time to come. Furthermore, their support of this book was invaluable; without Larry and Mike there would be no Black Book Series. Thank you.

And last but certainly not least, a special thanks to my wife, **Lindsey**. When the Black Book on Corporate Security was a new and untested idea, it was Lindsey who made me realize that undertaking this book was the right thing to do. I hope the readers, authors and the security industry as a whole all benefit from the results.

— Eric S. Green
Publisher
The Black Book on Corporate Security

THE TEAM

Managing Editor | David Evancha
Contributing Editors | Susan Aluise, Yi Gu, Jonathan Holasek, Michael Morin,
      Gregg Siegel and Martin Zook
Publisher | John Persinos

Creative Director | Rob Hudgins
Production Manager | Sherrie Saldana

Publisher, The Black Book on Corporate Security | Eric S. Green
Group Publisher, The Black Book Series | Mike Wiebner
COO | Stan Genkin
CEO | Larry Genkin

DEDICATIONS

First, I would like to thank Dave Lemley and Luca Loiodice for their direct contributions to my chapter in this book. I would also like to thank all of those who have believed in and took a chance on me. I feel so privileged to have such wonderful mentors, colleagues, and investors in my professional life. A quick word to those who matter most, my family, I love you all very much. *—Tony Alagna*

I would like to dedicate this to all Trend Micro engineers that have been working with me for the past 15 years in security and antivirus technology. *—Eva Chen*

I dedicate this work to my wife — Angela, mother — Linda, and all women in their fight to conquer breast cancer. To Susan Morgan, Claude Baudoin, and Benoit Barbier for their constant support, mentorship, and friendship. And to my father for teaching me to always strive to do all that I can. Thank you. *—Colin Elliott*

I would like to express my gratitude to all my colleagues at BMC Software who have lent their critical eyes and encouragement to this project. I am especially grateful to Doron Cohen, whose comments provided important guidance and material, and to Cindy Sterling for her exceptional advice and help throughout this endeavor. Many thanks to Larstan Publishing for making this project a high quality experience. Finally, special thanks to my family, for love, inspiration and understanding beyond understanding. *—Rami Elron*

I would like to dedicate my chapter to my wife Karen and my children Brian and Kristin whose lives have enriched mine so much and who have helped me to achieve so many goals. *—Dr. Jim Kennedy*

I would like to dedicate my contribution to my father, General Nasser Mahdavi, who encouraged me to be a leader and to do everything I do with a passion. *—Mehrzad Mahdavi*

I'd like to dedicate my chapter to my wife Robin and my two sons Joshua and Timothy whose encouragement, support, and ceaseless energy always push me to reach for new challenges, and to my mother whose hard work and dedication to her career and family have hopefully rubbed off on me. —*George G. McBride*

To Pamela, Avital, Noa, Barak, and Yonatan, for providing real security, untethered and unencumbered, everyday, through their love and devotion.

—*Ron Moritz*

I'd like to thank my Tablus colleagues Jim, Aaron, Amol and Charley for their help in creating information security solutions. They work tirelessly, to understand and solve very challenging security problems. They have allowed me to share many of their insights in this chapter. I'd also like to acknowledge Leah and Jesse for their help in reviewing the content security information contained in this book. —*Jim Nisbet*

To Maureen, Beth and John for their vigilance in watching over me; my children for adding joy to my life; my parents for inspiring me to excel and to Tim, Rich, John, Mark, Walt, Linda, Phil, Dick and Ronn for making security infrastructure such an important part of my work.

—*Jim Porell*

My contribution to this book is dedicated to my wife Raemarie, a longstanding leader in R&D and the teaching of computer forensics, and to my son Kyle, who serves as a computer crime detective. Both work hard everyday, making the online world more secure, and they have supported me in my work. I also dedicate this to the men and women in the information security business. These dedicated professionals accomplish wonderful things with scarce resources, often working long hours and with little respect for their work. After disaster strikes, they keep the lights on, fresh water available, and money and goods moving. Through their commitment and knowledge, they make our way of life better and more secure.

—*Howard Schmidt*

This is dedicated to all who have supported me, my wife, my kids, my co-workers and my parents. —*Joseph C. Seanor*

The list of my colleagues at BMC software and our customers and partners who have been instrumental in developing Identity Aware business service management concepts and bringing it to fruition is too long to thank by name, but I am indebted to their wisdom and their critical thinking. During the process of writing this book, I do not know what we would have done without the coordination, communication and editing skills of my colleague Cindy Sterling. My heartfelt thanks go to Cindy. —*Somesh Singh*

I dedicate the chapter on "collaboration" to my wife Joanne and children Diana, Emily and David...who have taught me what collaboration truly means in life. —*Prof. Salvatore Stolfo*

This chapter is dedicated to the team of innovators fighting a rising tide of so-called "content-based" network attacks, such as viruses, worms and Trojans that are being introduced into organizations via seemingly innocuous activities such as web browsing. Throughout my career in computer network security I have continued to be impressed with advances in software development, ASIC computing power and rapid rise in system functionality. This trend is expected to continue as organizations turn increasingly to real-time communications, like web applications and instant messaging, as the means to remain responsive and competitive. —*Michael Xie*

FOREWORD

By Howard A. Schmidt

The overall mission of this book, and the reason why it is important, is that it bridges the gaps that separate security experts, technology experts, business experts and strategic planners. We hope that you see this book as such a bridge and that you use it as a way to increase your organization's understanding of the full dimension of e-threats.

Keep in mind, security must now be part of your core day-to-day business processes. Corporate security has been an important topic in business news for well over a decade. However, in the last two to three years, there has been a bewildering change in how companies protect important information assets. Threats have grown more complicated, and so have the solutions.

Technology enabled business strategies have become the standard. These have continuously manifested themselves in a proliferation of web-enabled business strategies that have opened up enterprise networks to not only close business partners, like suppliers and key customers, but now to the global online market. This has increasingly put a company's important information assets at a level of risk that did not exist in the past.

In the previous generation, the approach taken to protect critical assets was similar to the bricks and mortar approach — companies would "build a wall around it." Therefore, a company would construct a perimeter security, manned by technologies such as firewalls and intrusion detection systems, all with the goal to keep people out. But new threats and business technology strategies are emerging between and within corporations, spawning initiatives to enhance collaboration and interconnectivity. These initiatives highlight the need to knock down "silos" of protection and implement policies, procedures and technologies that protect the creation of, the sharing of and the access to data. Rather than building walls around data and applications, top managers are now looking at business processes and trying to secure them. That has made security much more of an interdisciplinary and operational issue for the global enterprise.

In the past, it was common to have security deployed as a reaction to an event or almost as an afterthought. The Chief Operating Officer (COO) would get the strategic direction from the Chief Executive Officer (CEO) and then work with the Chief Information Officer (CIO) to implement a technology infrastructure to support the new business processes. The Chief Security Officer (CSO)/Chief Information Security Officer (CISO) would then come in and do what he or she could do to protect the infrastructure. Well, that's no longer a viable technique.

As new processes develop and new technologies are introduced to the enterprise, the CSO/CISO must be involved at the beginning to ensure that the vulnerabilities and security threats associated with those technologies are identified and mitigated. Protecting data is now a considerably more dynamic situation for corporate America, elevating security to an important strategic issue that requires attention from senior management.

In the past, management may have been accustomed to handing security off to a CSO/CISO as a reactive function. Now, it needs to get the "business of security" built into the business process and understand the security implications of their business strategies, as well as that of the technology roadmap that they decide to follow over the next few years. They must adopt greater and earlier security awareness, as part of their strategic thinking.

Simultaneously, the skill sets associated with securing these business processes must respond and evolve. Before, security departments would have silo expertise, e.g., security professionals who were experts at implementing firewalls, or at patch management or at vulnerability assessments. That fragmented approach to point security is no longer viable for all the reasons previously stated.

There is a growing need within security to integrate its pool of activities and to understand the impact of those security activities on business processes. Not only must security professionals be more interdisciplinary within the field of security, but they must also be able to understand the business objectives. This requires innovative ways to protect technology, data, and business processes in an integrated manner.

Because threats continue to evolve and the originators of these threats are akin to terrorists, the threat does not have to be coordinated. There are many different people that are active in a variety of areas trying to develop and implement different types of threats. They don't have to coordinate with other attackers to do damage to an enterprise; they just have to succeed once. The situation now exists where corporate security officers must have a full understanding of not only what security technology does, but also the business imperatives of their company, and be able to prioritize the allocation of resources to those priorities.

You can't secure everything 100%, so you must understand what needs to be secured the most, and prioritize accordingly. Then, at the same time, you must have a growing understanding of the new types of threats that are launched on a daily basis. This is a big challenge for the corporate security community.

Important is effective communication among the CSO/CISO and the other senior executives in the organization. The CFOs who must underwrite and fund these initiatives, the COO who is implementing new business processes, and the CEO who is looking for a new direction, must all understand whether the new directions are viable from a security standpoint.

In the pages of this *Black Book on Corporate Security,* many of these dimensions are explored in great depth. They are also validated with a series of surveys that were conducted to identify what the market is saying about corporate security and what the experts, who are developing new responses to threats, are saying about these threats.

[1]
BUILDING A SECURE CORPORATE ENVIRONMENT FROM THE GROUND UP

Your company needs a secure data infrastructure, but how, exactly, do you set one up from scratch? Here, a former FBI agent who now serves as an information security officer reveals the best methods for creating a system that takes control of your information.

> "THERE'S A WAR OUT THERE, AND IT'S ALL ABOUT WHO CONTROLS THE INFORMATION. IT'S ALL ABOUT THE INFORMATION."
>
> - Cosmo, in the movie *Sneakers*

by STEPHEN W. FOSTER

I'm a battle-hardened veteran of DMZ skirmishes. No, I'm not talking about the "demilitarized zone" imposed between North and South Korea following the Korean War in the early 1950s.

Among information security officers such as myself, a DMZ is the euphemism for a computer host or small network inserted as a neutral buffer that separates a company's private network and the outside

SECURITY I.T. PERSONNEL NEED TO REALIZE THAT THEY DON'T OWN THE INFORMATION SYSTEMS. THEY ARE IN A SUPPORTIVE ROLE AND ARE A RESOURCE TO THE BUSINESS; SECURITY MUST BE BUILT INTO THE PRODUCT LIFE CYCLE.

public network. It stops outside users from obtaining direct access to a server that contains company data.

As you attempt to tailor a secure network to a company's overall business strategy, crucial and sometimes controversial issues such as DMZs emerge and they must be dealt with in a forthright manner. That's why building a secure corporate environment starts with communication.

Building a new information security team is no easy task and will be fraught with many obstacles. The building effort begins during the CISO's interview process, which will provide him/her with a window into senior management's philosophy on information security. The support they provide is essential to your success.

The first order of business in building any new program is the discovery phase. The CISO must get out of his office and meet other business managers face to face. Reaching out and developing a personal relationship is vital to your success. Today, too many managers rely exclusively on conference calls and email. The information security team should also educate key managers within the company as to how security can partner with them to help enable their business solutions. CISOs should continually demonstrate to the business that the information security team is an integral part of the business process.

For example: Business unit XYZ requests that a risk assessment be conducted for a new DMZ they want to build. This DMZ will be used for outsourcing services to their external customers. The initial security assessment reveals numerous high-risk exposures. The business unit becomes very defensive, insisting that the security team is creating obstacles that will prevent them from being successful and meeting their deadlines. At this point some important hand-holding is definitely required. This should include detailed discussions explaining what the security team is trying to accomplish, and how it will eventually enable their business goals. It should be made clear that the DMZ is going to be certified for operation and the security team is going to help them overcome any imposed security requirements. Once they understand that the security team is a full partner in the solution, attitudes will quickly change and compromises will become realities. A success story in the making.

It is imperative for anyone creating a security program to understand the needs of their internal and external customers. The CISO must understand the background and history of the company as well as each viable business unit. What are the company's products and services? What are the business environments they compete in? Who are their competitors? What are the company's strategic plans? How can information security be a value added and a market differentiator?

CISOs must also understand that the information security team does not own the computer systems, but are internal security consultants to the businesses who provide an important but supportive role.

CISOs should also understand the industry their company is competing in as well as the company's proprietary products and processes. How does the company work with its customers and contractors in this industry? Many of your information systems may be dependent on these proprietary processes and the level of protection that is required. Understanding the critical assets of the company is another key goal and will drive the allocation of limited funding. Finally, you should identify industry peers that you can call on to leverage experience and ideas.

> **Insider Notes:** It is imperative for anyone creating a security program to understand the needs of their internal and external customers. They must learn the background and history of the organization as well as each business unit.

INFORMATION SECURITY IS NOT A REVENUE PRODUCER; AS SUCH, THE SECURITY PROGRAM IS ALWAYS ON THIN ICE WITH THE CLIENT. NEVER PROVIDE UNREALISTIC EXPECTATIONS.

INDEPENDENT ASSESSMENT

A good way to obtain an independent view of your organization's information security posture is to conduct a full scale security review (such as ISO-17799) by a third party security consultant as soon as possible. Also review prior assessments, internal IT audits and SAS 70s for a comprehensive understanding of your companys IT security environment. By identifying the companys risk exposures and deficiencies you can begin to develop your new information security "road map" for success.

SERVICE LEVEL AGREEMENTS

Another important step is to conduct a full-scale review of existing Service Level Agreements (SLA) and contracts for internal and external customers, as well as your security vendors. Ensure that they make good business sense and are in alignment with business strategies. Do your vendors provide a timely response? Are they giving your company the support it requires? Are your internal customers pleased with support from your antivirus team? When viruses impact the network are they detected and cleaned within agreed SLA time lines?

SETTING EXPECTATIONS

Ensure that your organization issues a corporate-wide communication announcing the new CISOs arrival, your role, reporting structure and support by senior management. This communication is vital to your future success.

You should also define the organizational structure for your department. This will include:
- Develop your vision statement
- Develop your mission statement
- Develop your organizational chart

- Develop function work streams to meet you goals
- Define expected roles, responsibilities and functions
- Define information security processes

During the CISOs interview process he/she should have negotiated the reporting structure for this new and critical role. Current industry trends support the CISO reporting to the chief legal council, chief financial officer and/or the chief auditor. This is an important step towards maintaining independence (eGovernance) between senior IT managers, who often have different project priorities and funding requirements.

Another area for discussion is whether physical security should report to the CISO. The decision to incorporate all security into one reporting line may be simply based on the company's culture. There are many pros and cons on this subject and as such should be discussed in a chapter of its own.

In essence, these are the basic building blocks required to build an information security team. Remember that your organization exists to support the business and therefore your information security team should reflect all strategic and tactical goals of the business.

BUILDING THE SECURITY ROADMAP

Once you have compiled and digested all of this information, organizational planning can begin. Again it is imperative for this plan to be in sync with the long-term business strategy of the company as well as its short-term tactical needs. Use nimbus maps, or flow-charting, but somewhere you need to get it all on paper. You should also consider hiring a project manager to coordinate and plan these activities.

Develop a program that will allow your team to demonstrate immediate progress to senior management. This can be accomplished by developing a

Insider Notes: No other security program will hit a home run quicker then the Information Security Awareness program. By communicating to the global user community this program will also help you brand your new organization.

DATA SNAPSHOT

What level of support do you need to build your security organization

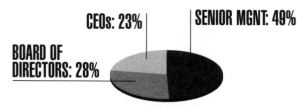

CEOs: 23%

SENIOR MGNT: 49%

BOARD OF DIRECTORS: 28%

Download the complete research study for free at www.blackbooksecurity.com/research
Source: 2005 Larstan / Reed Infosecurity Survey

project plan that incorporates incremental steps to achieve your goals. Hit some home runs quickly. Your "road map" should also drive the information security budget plan ensuring that all designated priorities are properly identified and funded.

ESTABLISH ACHIEVABLE GOALS

Remember that your security "road map" should never advance unrealistic goals and objectives. Do not promise something you cannot deliver in order to impress your new boss. Once you lose your credibility it will be hard to recover. Credibility is central to your continued success, especially with senior management.

If you are going to effectively challenge senior management, especially if their demands are unrealistic, you must always maintain confidence in yourself and your program. Information security is not considered a revenue producer and the information security program will only be important when there are serious risk exposures and/or compliance issues at hand. What happens when your information security team delivers a secure environment? Will the company continue to fund your team? Will it outsource or downsize? Start thinking about your second and third year strategic plans if you want to keep your program alive.

IMPLEMENTATION STEPS — SETTING MILESTONES FOR SUCCESS

Behind any good initiative there should be a well thought out strategy and detailed project plan. This includes tasking and ownership for deliverables. Tracking is essential thereby providing regular status reports and metrics for all levels of management. All good project plans are going to have milestones and by creating incremental change, you not only demonstrate early success-es, but also reduce risk exposures. An early success story that can provide company-wide exposure is a comprehensive security awareness program.

SECURITY AWARENESS PROGRAM

The biggest bang for your planning efforts will be the creation of a security awareness program. The security awareness program will help you to brand your new organization and communicate throughout the global enterprise. Part of this branding effort involves educating the user community about the difference between IT security and the information security team. It sounds like a small issue, but you don't want the IT organization taking credit for all your hard work. Below are some easy winners:

- Create a security web page on your company intranet with links from the company's Intranet home page.
- Display pictures of your team and define their security functions, roles and responsibilities.
- Begin weekly articles on your security website concerning information security tips and security topics that you want to socialize with your organization.
- Buy information security posters and display them at strategic locations around the company.
- Periodically deploy telephone message announcements concerning important security issues.

That's a success! Senior executives will walk out of their offices and see your posters. They will also surf the Intranet and see information about your organization as well as read weekly security articles.

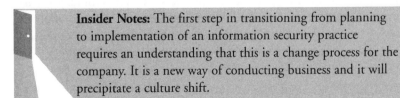

Insider Notes: The first step in transitioning from planning to implementation of an information security practice requires an understanding that this is a change process for the company. It is a new way of conducting business and it will precipitate a culture shift.

Once employees understand that there's a new security team in place they will want to work with that team. At that point you should begin to develop and publish your security policies to the greater user community. After a strong start, just keep the momentum going.

THE STEPS TO IMPLEMENTATION

This section is devoted to constructing your security department. Beginning with the planning phase discussed above, this section details how those plans are best put into action.

COMMUNICATIONS ARE THE KEY TO IMPLEMENTATION

Transitioning from planning to implementation involves a major culture shift for the company. Intra-company communications and your awareness program will become essential factors when trying to change company habits, especially in a global environment. It is important to make sure that everyone is aware of the paradigm shift and becomes part of the solution and not the problem. There will be many partners in this process, especially since information security touches all areas of the company. In order to ensure success, management, company employees, business partners and consultants must be educated and trained.

The optimal place to start your security "road show" is to educate management on the goals and projects of your security program (including the vice president and director levels). Make every effort to meet them personally because you will need them to champion your security work efforts. Be sure that your presentation is concise and to the point - providing scope, objectives and an executive summary. Support from this level of management will ensure that the entire user community will cooperate with your strategic security goals and projects.

Draw on the expertise of the corporate communication and public relations teams. They will be critical to the success of your communications campaign. Your communications campaign should detail information security expectations for all users in terms of both compliance and cooperation. Your objective is to make them feel part of the team and the solution process.

THE IMPORTANCE OF GOAL SETTING AND CREATING GOOD PUBLIC RELATIONS

Precise goals and realistic milestones need to be established. It is important to build in some early successes. Some quick wins will demonstrate to the company that a return on their security investment is in progress.

As previously indicated your security awareness program can be a quick success story. Weekly security messages and articles not only educate your users, but also give your team broad exposure. Employees will begin to observe information security posters on the wall or company bulletin boards. Information security screen savers should be installed on desktops and laptops. These quick security successes provide good public relations for security, get senior management's attention and also move you to a higher level of security.

Employees will begin to recognize that there are new security processes and this will help change the culture in a cost-effective, painless and transparent mode.

DEFINING YOUR SECURITY MATURITY MODEL

Everyone knows there is no such thing as 100% security, and as such there will always be risk exposures. So what is a "best-in-class" security model? This will depend on your industry, business practices and management culture. You should generally drive towards developing an enhanced security model that has multiple layers of good security practices. Don't be confused with trying to define the perfect security model known as "best-in-class". Your new security model will help you balance managing risk exposures with good cost-effective practices.

As referenced in the planning stage, you should engage an independent third party security consultant to review and assess your IT environment

Insider Notes: To ensure buy-in, the new organization needs to build both a road show and an awareness and communication program to get the word out. The optimal place to start the road show is at the next tier down from the CEO staff, the line vice presidents and director.

from top to bottom. This will highlight your primary risk exposures and what steps require attention in order to develop an enhanced security model. Your information security program should also be in alignment with current and future business strategies. Third party assessments should evaluate security processes, network processes, application processes and businesses processes as an integrated solution.

An ISO 17799 assessment will evaluate your overall information security environment and will also guide you to ISO compliance for your industry. With both of these assessments complete, your company will have its security framework and roadmap for the next couple of years. Now you can begin to map required security projects to the necessary funding required. This will form the basis of your security business case, and should be presented to senior management for approval.

PITFALLS TO AVOID

The two big pitfalls to avoid are not challenging unrealistic expectations and not surfacing jeopardies in real time. It is key to determine expectations, timelines, resources and funding for your security projects. There is also nothing worse than letting a problem linger for days or weeks. Recognize mistakes, take ownership and come up with a plan to remediate.

Overcoming your setbacks is about taking ownership (leadership), developing a new plan and executing. On the other hand, don't sidestep difficult issues — accept the challenge, that's what leadership is all about.

What are some of the most important characteristics of a security product vendor?

There is no absolute set of questions to ask vendors, but below are recommended questions to consider when evaluating a new technology purchase:

❶ Do you have a dedicated team to assess and respond to security vulnerability reports concerning your product?

❷ What is your vulnerability response process and track record?

❸ What process improvements have you made as a result of past vulnerabilities reported in your software?

❹ What is your release strategy (are they grouped or individual releases)?

In other words, how long do we have to wait for fixes to known software problems?

❺ What training does your development and test organization receive on application information security matters?

❻ What percent of your team is focused just on security issues?

❼ Does your company monitor the latest attack trends in the underground (Cracker) community and consider how those trends affect your software?

❽ Do you patch all currently supported vulnerable versions of your application/platforms at the same time (or are they released as needed)?

❾ Has a third party conducted an independent security review (code review) and what are the results?

❿ Can you provide independent references that are using this product?

⓫ Application RFPs should contain the following:

  a. The terms and period of your security support agreements
  b. Proof of security testing and vulnerability assessments during deployment
  c. Review vendors Common Criteria certifications or any other software certifications
  d. Review application patch records (quality and quantity)
  e. Future upgrades should be dependent on vendors' security records

When evaluating any new technology, all company stakeholders should be included in the process. Remember that there will be many cross dependencies and you need all parties involved if you want the project to be successful.

BUILDING A SECURITY ORGANIZATION

This section discusses in detail the measuring process employed when constructing a secured environment.

> **Insider Notes:** The two biggest pitfalls to avoid are providing unrealistic expectations and not revealing dangers in real time. Set expectations for both time and funding, with time being the most important.

AFTER 25 FAILED ATTEMPTS, THERE'S NO REASON TO THINK THAT HACKERS HAVE GONE AWAY. MAYBE THE 26TH TIME, THEY GOT IN. SECURITY DEPARTMENTS NEED TO PROACTIVELY LOOK AT THESE METRICS AND MAKE RECOMMENDATIONS TO SENIOR MANAGEMENT, SO CORRECTIVE ACTION CAN BE TAKEN.

UNDERSTANDING METRICS

A successful security organization is constructed on a foundation of four pillars: policy, awareness, risk and metrics. The policy development, awareness and risk assessment programs required have already been discussed earlier. This section will deal specifically with your security scorecard.

Your metrics should be designed to support business objectives, security operations, security projects and to measure overall progress. These metrics will be necessary to support four primary areas: on-going security operations, new security projects, supporting internal users and risk assessments.

INFORMATION COLLECTION

The key to good metrics is good information, and the key to good information is a good method for collecting and evaluating that information. The information collection process starts by identifying all information security work streams, functions and processes. Policy, systems, users and other resources are the drivers that will most impact your metrics. The ultimate goal is to develop the capability to automatically collect and track information that will help your team tell the information security story to senior management. Automation of the information collection process is essential if you want accurate and timely information.

Information security metrics are driven by two primary factors: the number of systems in the IT environment and the number of users who use those systems. A good Security Information Management (SIM) tool is a useful technology, which allows collection of logs from server and network devices to monitor, track and review compliance matters. It can also be leveraged to provide your information security dashboard, which will allow your team to build and compile better metrics, thereby giving management more flexibility to make cost-effective decisions.

Collecting and developing metrics is meaningless without a correlation of events and an action plan. Cleaning viruses as they impact your network is a necessary work effort, but understanding how viruses get through your gateway and why they were able to infect so many systems is even more important. Enterprise correlation of information from many sources is the key to effective security management. By reviewing events from various systems and devices such as intrusion detection alerts, antivirus gateway logs, firewall logs, system logs, etc. you will develop a clear picture of how the virus entered your environment and was able to propagate itself. By making better use of reporting capabilities and correlating security events you will be more effective at deploying your limited resources to mitigate risk exposures.

THE IMPORTANCE OF BEING PROACTIVE

Get out in front of your primary risk exposures. To be proactive, an organization must not only be able to collect systems and device logs real time, but collate them into meaningful reports and take action on them. By collecting these logs and sorting them into meaningful reports you may discover 25 failed logon attempts to your active directory. This should set off alarms and an investigation should be initiated to find out what took place. Maybe the twenty-sixth time the user was successful. Security departments need to be proactively looking at security metrics and making recommendations to senior management so corrective action can be taken. A process to collect metrics can be developed, but it does little good if it isn't reviewed and acted upon.

Insider Notes: When researching these technologies, all stakeholders should be given a "say," from the network architects and engineers, to the risk people. If it involves a security management product, a decision should not be made in a silo.

EVEN WITH ALL OF THE BEST HARDENING STANDARDS, BUILT TO SPECIFICATION, YOU MUST CONDUCT FREQUENT NETWORK SCANS TO FIND OUT IF ALL THE HARDENING YOU HAVE DONE IS STILL THERE WHEN YOU PUT THE SYSTEM INTO PRODUCTION.

For example, one indication of a problem might be having a high number of password resets. You can usually predict that your call center, depending on whether it is in-house or outsourced, is probably receiving a lot of calls. This costs money. You should be asking why are we having so many password resets? Is it that passwords are too complex and people can't remember them? Is it because employees are just forgetful, lazy or not paying attention to their work? What is driving the password resets? You may have to employ a security awareness program to educate and train users on password usage, which is much more cost-effective than burdening the helpdesk with a deluge of calls.

Another example: Correlation of internal maintenance scans reveals that a number of servers have high vulnerabilities. Your team has worked hard to develop good hardening standards, but you know there is always going to be the human factor to consider. IT organizations are always making changes to production, and new security patches are always being announced. Investigation of these vulnerabilities may indicate a poor patch management process or maybe a breakdown in your change control process. Regardless, metrics are not just for gathering information and generating reports, they are tools to solve security problems and reduce costs.

WHEN ARE METRICS SUCCESSFUL?

Developing a security dashboard and measuring your success through good quality metrics is another step towards achieving your information security maturity model. Achieving a full level of maturity is probably not possible since conditions will constantly change and the same is true about metrics. Probably the best measure of success is your ability to solve security problems and empower business processes through good metrics.

In order for senior management to understand the continuing value that your team adds to the organization and their return on investment, the CISO must continue to effectively communicate a strong information security posture, and that is accomplished by providing good strong metrics.

PRESENTING FOR SUCCESS

Develop your security "road map" early and provide good metrics to support that story. While the credibility and demeanor of the CISO is important, the presentation of your metrics to senior management will require simplicity and meaningful information that can be translated into cost effective solutions. Using too many bar and pie charts may not communicate your story effectively, especially to non-technology managers. It has to be simple, but effective. Senior management will undoubtedly ask hard and challenging questions, so be prepared to support your metrics. Periodically, your metrics are going to tell a negative story, and while that will be understood, also be prepared to provide a corrective plan of action.

BUILDING A SECURITY ORGANIZATION

Third Party Networks

Customers, business partners and outsourcers are beginning to require companies to provide information concerning their security posture (security questionnaires) as a prerequisite before conducting business with them. Much of this activity is driven by Sarbanes-Oxley legislation and SEC disclosures. As you build your security organization you will be required to factor customers, business partners and outsourcers into your security equation. A company is only as secure as its weakest link, and when you extend your network to a third party, you have effectively increased your risk exposures exponentially. Companies planning to conduct business in the next five years will be required to certify to third parties that they are meeting all legal and regulatory requirements, such as Gramm-Leach-Bliley Act (GLBA)

Insider Notes: It is also important to note that metrics are meaningless without action. Identifying the number of viruses hitting the network, successfully deploying data files and fighting the virus is fine, but the question is why hasn't that virus been caught at the gate?

COMPANIES MUST START VIEWING INFORMATION SECURITY AS A CENTRAL ELEMENT OF DOING BUSINESS, AN INTEGRAL PART OF THE DAILY PROCESSES, AND NOT JUST A DRAIN ON THE BUDGET.

and Sarbanes-Oxley. If they are conducting business in Europe, they will have to meet stricter compliance with the European Data Protection Act (EDPA). Information security programs are at the forefront of these work efforts. Design your security model to reach for the highest bar so your organization will be in compliance with all critical laws and regulations.

INFORMATION SECURITY AS A BUSINESS ENABLER

Your security program should find ways to leverage existing or new security solutions with other business units. It is essential that the information security team develops close working relationships with the business units to understand their goals and business problems.

For example: Your security team is trying to develop an encryption standard across the global environment. While developing this encryption standard, the security team must take into consideration all business units if they are going to have an effective enterprise-wide solution. At first it doesn't seem like there is a satisfactory enterprise email encryption solution available. Eventually a member of the team recommends a Public Key Infrastructure (PKI) solution.

During this process the information security team learns that HR is concerned about their staff sending and receiving sensitive employee information through email. Additional research by the security team learns that the merger & acquisition group is also concerned about sending sensitive information through email.

After surveying other business units the team also discovers that this issue is isolated to just HR and the M&A groups. Working with the business units to understand their business needs and making them feel part of the solution becomes essential. The last thing you want to do is purchase an enterprise wide PKI solution to find out that it is not being used and your limited funding is wasted.

After a little work on your part, you find out that you have a small group of users who will require email encryption. Your team can accomplish their mission by deploying PGP to the HR and M&A teams. They will require some education and training to use PGP, but your team has established credibility, because you listened to their requirements and found a viable solution. It's all about being part of the team and offering the business affordable solutions.

Another example: The information security team would like to purchase and implement a SIM solution. After meeting with various IT and business units to discuss this project, the security team finds out that they can leverage this technology to other groups and enhance their ROI. The infrastructure team would like to use the network utilities tools and dashboard that SIM offers. The services division would like to leverage the central logging capabilities that SIM offers.

When a VP of sales or business development offers to partner with your information security team on new initiatives or customer offerings, you will know that information security has been successful. Differentiating your organization and security environment from other competitors will be critical, especially in a global economy.

Keep in mind that any time the information security team creates a security challenge for the business, it is essential that your team works with them until a solution is found, balancing good security practices with good business requirements. Ultimately, information security should not be viewed as the cybercop, but rather as a positive business enabler.

Insider Notes: When senior management sees the value you add to the organization (a return on investment), and that you are producing appropriate metrics, you become a viable business unit, not just a drain on the bottom line.

DATA SNAPSHOT

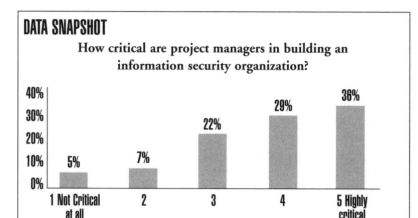

How critical are project managers in building an information security organization?

Based on the metrics, it confirms my belief that as a CISO, you should establish your own security project management office within your organization to ensure success.

Download the complete research study for free at www.blackbooksecurity.com/research
Source: 2005 Larstan / Reed Infosecurity Survey

SECURITY AS A MARKET DIFFERENTIATOR

For many years before 9/11, senior management viewed security as a cost center that did not add to the bottom line. When companies had tight budgets, security was often one of the first line items to be cut. That thinking needs to change, and the CISO is on the front line of that effort. Security departments need to be viewed as viable business units, which make positive contributions to the business. As discussed, metrics are one of the key tools that will help you sell that story.

Information security is beginning to transform itself into a viable business unit and market differentiator. As third parties continue to require good security practices before doing business, CEOs will have to view information security as a central component of its core business plan. A company without good security practices that meets all legal and regulatory requirements will be a big loser in the emerging global marketplace. Sarbanes Oxley has set a minimum security standard in the U.S., but there are other security benchmarks, such as the EDPA. When considering outsourced partners, a company should review their SAS 70 (financial audit for IT controls) for information security controls and compliance matters.

Companies that publicly advertise or certify that they have met generally accepted security standards will be able to use this as a market differentiator. In the long run, it will drive new revenue channels. Companies that have not developed or invested in good security practices will trail the pack.

■ ■ ■

Stephen W. Foster is the Chief Information Security Officer at Avaya. Steve is responsible for ensuring the highest level of protection for Avaya's information assets, including responsibility for information security architecture, design and implementation; corporate network security; Internet and intranet security and access control management. He also provides initial design support to the Business Transformation team for applications and infrastructure security requirements. He helps ensure that Avaya is in compliance with all rules, laws and regulations that affect information security, such as GLBA, Sarbanes-Oxley and SEC regulations.

Steve joined Avaya after a distinguished 20-year career with the Federal Bureau of Investigation. He retired from the FBI in March of 2000. During his career in law enforcement, he managed many international investigations and established the New Jersey FBI "InfraGard" program. The program, which is still in operation today, was established as an Information Security "Outreach" organization, which enhances the sharing of information among all levels of government and industry. He is currently an active member of the Board of Directors for the NJ Chapter.

After leaving the FBI, Steve accepted a position as Director of Information Security for PayTrust Inc, a fast growing financial services company, which relocated to Chicago. Before coming to Avaya, he was the Asst. VP of Information Security for TD Waterhouse Inc., the Brokerage arm of the Toronto Dominion Bank of Toronto, Canada. He can be reached at 908-953-4035 or stephenfoster@avaya.com

[2]
CORPORATE SECURITY AS PART OF YOUR OVERALL RISK MANAGEMENT STRATEGY

You already know that risk management is an inherent part of responsible corporate governance. But does your risk strategy adequately account for security? Here's how to properly meld these two vital and interrelated concepts.

"RISK IS AT THE HEART OF ALL EDUCATION."
- Willi Unsoeld

by GEORGE G. MCBRIDE

Technological complexity breeds risk — a phenomenon popularly known as "Murphy's Law" (if something can go wrong, it will). There's a corollary to Murphy's time-honored pessimism called the "Law of Unintended Consequences", in which systems behave in unexpected and undesirable ways.

Corporate managers are already in the habit of planning for these two facts of postindustrial life. However, corporate security is looming larger as an issue, and it must be calculated into the risk equation. What's more, a new concept of risk management has emerged that managers must understand and embrace.

The fact is, risk should not be regarded with fatalism or defeatism, but with alertness and preparation.

Most businesses are not looking at all the components of risk. This chapter will decompose these components and illustrate a process by which asset stakeholders can decide the levels of risk with which they are comfortable.

People in different positions within a company may have different comfort levels of risk. For example, people involved in certain business functions, such as marketing, may be willing to accept more risk to provide new services to their customers, whereas security and operations personnel may have a lower level of risk tolerance. It's incumbent on risk managers and executive personnel to balance and mediate the variable assessments within an organization to reach a mutually agreeable position of risk tolerance.

Eliminating all risk is operationally impossible, nor is it desirable. Without taking risks, no company or human being can succeed. However, setting limits and expectations are important. After all, the builders of the Titanic never actually declared that the ship was unsinkable — that claim derived from the expectations of her crew and passengers. The doomed ship's fate also illustrates the price of technological hubris.

Additionally, the values of risk and the acceptable level of risk will differ among various members of a business organization. The components of risk will be the same, but the values given to the various components will vary by company position. Currently, very few organizations factor in either likelihood or impact into their application of the risk assessment equation. Moreover, the perception of controls and their effectiveness vary within a company. It is here where a risk management function can work to help sort out and reconcile differing perceptions of component risk and manage the process that provides a corporate-wide overview.

THE NEW THEORY OF RISK MANAGEMENT

Prior to discussing either the new or traditional concepts, the first step is to ensure that "risk" is defined. Risk can be illustrated by the use of an equation that can be measured either quantitatively or qualitatively. The focus and examples throughout the chapter will be qualitative, but apply to any quantitative approach also.

Risk is defined as follows:

$$\text{Risk} = \frac{\text{Threats X Vulnerabilities}}{\text{Controls}} \text{ or } R = (T*V)/C$$

Threats entail two components:

❶ **Likelihood** - What is the probability or chance of the particular threat happening?

❷ **Impact** - How many machines, business units, people, etc. are affected by the threat, how long the system will be down, what cost of a loss associated with a threat will be, etc. In other words, what is the net effect on the business from an operational and security concern if the threat is realized?

There is a second, higher level approach to conceptualizing risk. This approach considers all components of risk, including likelihood and impact, across the entire asset lifecycle and addresses those that can be controlled. Some threats, such as hurricanes and tornadoes, cannot be controlled, but many or most others can be mitigated. Risk generally cannot be driven down to zero, nor is that an optimal goal. But, it can be driven down below an acceptable or tolerable level (a concept addressed later).

RISK MANAGEMENT IS NOT VULNERABILITY MANAGEMENT

It is important to note the difference between risk management and vulnerability management. An organization may proactively review and manage its vulnerabilities, but these reviews generally do not take into account the type of asset, the impact to the organization if it is not available or what threats are poised to strike at it. Vulnerability management generally looks at a particular asset in isolation. It does not factor in external controls, other systems that rely on the system or even the type of data on the

ELIMINATING ALL RISK IS IMPOSSIBLE, NOR IS IT DESIRABLE. WITHOUT TAKING RISKS, NO COMPANY OR HUMAN BEING CAN SUCCEED. HOWEVER, SETTING LIMITS AND EXPECTATIONS ARE IMPORTANT. AFTER ALL, THE BUILDERS OF THE *TITANIC* NEVER ACTUALLY DECLARED THAT THE SHIP WAS UNSINKABLE — THAT CLAIM DERIVED FROM THE EXPECTATIONS OF HER CREW AND PASSENGERS.

system. Risk management can use the data from a vulnerability management program, but within the context of the risk equation to adequately prioritize, address and mitigate risks.

It is necessary for the risk management assessment process to be objective. Therefore, the risk management organization within a company should be a separate function, reporting directly to executive management. It is also recommended that the risk management function be independent of the function that it is assessing. For example, risk management assessment for information technology should report to management outside the information technology department.

Asset function or business process determines who is designated for involvement in the assessment of a particular risk. Risk assessments usually concern assets, but may also be a holistic view of the risk of a function or business process. Assets may also be defined as an individual, a facility, a group of systems or a business process. The nature, qualities and type of asset under review determine who will define the components and acceptable levels of risk.

THREE RISK MANAGEMENT ACTION ITEMS

Take these three actions to embrace the new concepts of risk management:

❶ **Establish a risk management function.** The risk management function should be an organization as independent from the risks that they are assessing as possible. This organization must be chartered to identify all assets across the enterprise, measure the risks of those assets and develop mitigation strategies to reduce those risks. This organization must have a reporting relationship independent of a majority of the assets under consideration to remain autonomous and independent.

❷ **Conduct a complete inventory of assets, or, at minimum, an inventory of critical assets and functions.** This activity is often overlooked and usually relies on work done to support the Business Impact Analysis (BIA) that looks at critical processes in a company. The BIA should be one of many asset inventories, not the only one, since it tends to not be comprehensive.

❸ **Perform a risk assessment of those assets and functions that have been inventoried.** The size of a risk management function should be correlated to the number of assets a company has. Larger companies, by definition, have a larger asset base and generally require more effort in performing an asset inventory and the subsequent risk management.

The salient aspects of the risk management process are as follows:
- Understanding the company's risk tolerance (i.e., what is the acceptable level of risk?)
- Defining and describing the risk tolerance relative to each asset. Such a process should include the perceptions of various departments and individuals within the organization

Risk assessment is the qualitative and quantitative measurement of risk of some asset and process. The new risk assessment model equates risk to (threats x vulnerabilities)/controls. To perform a risk assessment, a company must first complete an asset inventory.

Your company needs to develop an acceptable level of risk for each asset. The level of risk with respect to each asset needs to be compared to a predetermined acceptable level of risk. If the assessed level of risk is at or below the acceptable level of risk, your work is done. Risk level must be assessed again when the environment or circumstances that affect it

Insider Notes: It is necessary for the risk management assessment process to be objective. Therefore, the risk management organization within a company should be a separate function, reporting directly to Executive Management.

DATA SNAPSHOT

One of the most important inputs to a successful Risk Management Program is an understanding of the assets within an organization. With more than half of the reporting organizations indicating that they do not have a complete list of the assets, they cannot adequately identify and prioritize the assets. It is

Do you have a comprehensive asset inventory management program?

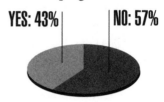

YES: 43%   NO: 57%

important to note that most organizations do not consider assets such as people, buildings or off-site disaster recovery facilities, as "assets", and consequently, are never prepared to address the associated risk.

Download the complete research study for free at www.blackbooksecurity.com/research
Source: 2005 Larstan / Reed Infosecurity Survey

change, or the asset is due for a reevaluation. If the assessed level of risk is above the acceptable level of risk, the company needs to devise and implement improved controls. Alternatively, the corporation may choose to not deploy the system, not employ the asset or somehow reduce the vulnerability, impact or likelihood.

Risk management is a continuous and intensive process that involves a large volume of work. There is a myriad of considerations involved in putting a value to the components of the risk equation for each asset. Risk managers must be fully versed in the characteristics of many different assets and the environmental situations of those assets, to assess and define the level of risk, acceptable levels of risk and mitigating actions if the level of risk exceeds the acceptable level.

Many companies do not have the complete mechanism to measure the components of risk. The complete measurement of risk is a time intensive process, but yields the data required to appropriately mitigate any risks. Companies can choose from any of several different types of risk assessment methodologies that provide a consistent approach to measure the levels of risk within an organization for various assets. Some are open source and publicly available, and others are commercially available. Each of the tools listed below has advantages and disadvantages, and areas where they work best:

- Operationally Critical Threat, Asset, and Vulnerability Evaluation™ (OCTAVE®) and the "Simplified" version OCTAVE-S are two methodologies from Carnegie Mellon University's Software Engineering Institute.
- Consultative, Objective, and Bi-functional Risk Analysis (COBRA) is from C&A Systems Security Ltd.
- SARA (Simple to Apply Risk Analysis) and SPRINT (Simplified Process for Risk Identification) are both from the Information Security Forum.
- The Buddy System is from Countermeasures Corporation.
- The Risk Watch product line is from Risk Watch Inc.
- CCTA (The UK Central Computer and Telecommunications Agency) Risk Analysis and Management Method (CRAMM) is from Insight Consulting

Each of the risk assessment methodologies listed above, as well as others, can serve as the requisite tool to provide the framework to achieve a consistent measure of risk for the assets under review.

THE TRADITIONAL APPROACH TO RISK MANAGEMENT
Now, I will discuss the traditional method of conducting risk management, its inadequacies, and how the new Risk Management Theory differs.

It is important to discuss the "traditional" approaches to information security risk management in any discussion of the "new" approach. Risk management is the identification, prioritization, mitigation and control of risk, and is different from vulnerability management. While risk management takes several parameters into consideration including vulnerabilities, vul-

Insider Notes: If the assessed level of risk is at or below the acceptable level of risk, your work is done. Risk level must be assessed again when the environment or circumstances that affect it change or the asset is due for a reevaluation.

CASE FILES

CASE STUDY: RISKY BUSINESS

The Problem: The firm did not have an inventory that was accurate enough to determine whether published vulnerabilities were applicable to its infrastructure. This cost the firm time and money in reacting to vulnerabilities, sometimes needlessly. It also had no way of obtaining an up-to-date overall risk posture of the enterprise.

DEVELOPING THE RISK MANAGEMENT PROGRAM

Before we initiated any changes to their programs, policies or organization, we spent time on-site, interviewing anybody who had a stake in risk management. These personnel included asset managers, IT and IT security staff and senior leadership. We also reviewed documents and observed the effectiveness of its overall security infrastructure. Also reviewed were vulnerability management, risk management and how controls were implemented and measured for effectiveness.

From this information, a risk management program was crafted. It was critical to develop an implementation plan to allow it to move from where it was today to where it needed to go, with a minimum of business disruptions.

IDENTIFYING AND REVIEWING ASSETS

The firm had to integrate and collate several different asset repositories. Because it was a large bank, it possessed a large number of assets, all managed by several different asset systems. It had an inventory system for the depreciation of capital assets, and a purchasing group that maintained a separate inventory of equipment purchases that included IT-related infrastructure and equipment.

The firm operated other systems that managed software applications that may not have been purchased (homegrown or open source solutions), yet were critical to the success of the company. Other systems were identified through business impact analysis statements or business impact efforts.

We recommended that the company develop a single database for all critical assets. This database required a process to provide growth and to interface with the existing vulnerability database, so that the existing infrastructure could be leveraged. The integration of several different databases into a single database was a significant effort and required a lot of planning to ensure a smooth transition. At this point, the client was advised to begin the design of the database and to ensure that it was flexible enough to manage threats, vulnerabilities and controls affecting those assets that would be further defined during the engagement.

CREATING A RISK MANAGEMENT ORGANIZATION

Based on initial observations regarding the existing roles and responsibilities of the IT security staff, additional staff were hired to support the program plan that was developed. The additional staff included a risk management director charged with running and staffing the risk management organization. Both in-house personnel were reassigned, and outside candidates were then hired as risk analysts. These analysts were cross-trained to make sure that they were equally fluent in both areas of risk management, the selected risk assessment methodology, the threats, vulnerabilities, and controls affecting the company and the company itself.

The risk analysts began the process of reviewing the new asset management database design, the assets, and began to prioritize those assets from a holistic, enterprise-wide approach. While many assets were grouped together to shorten the evaluation period, a lengthy process ensued as the new Risk Management Organization (RMO) worked with the asset stakeholders to prioritize the assets. Care was taken to allot sufficient time to work through any political and business issues when the asset stakeholders and RMO did not initially agree.

PRIORITIZING ASSETS

When the development of an asset database was in a state that was steady enough to allow risk management personnel to review the contents, the prioritization of the assets commenced. Through a holistic view across the assets (some were grouped together by function or business process), the risk analysts prioritized the criticality of the assets based on asset stakeholder input, criticality to the overall corporation, any regulatory or compliance issues and previous efforts such as the Business Impact Analysis.

Through a friendly, yet firm approach, the RMO succeeded in reaching agreement on the prioritization of all of the assets in the database. It should be noted that this project, even with the assets grouped together, could be a lengthy process due to the iterative approach. Additionally, this RMO intended to reach agreement with the asset stakeholders of the prioritization of the assets. Although this is clearly not a required step, it is a significant factor in building up the relationship between the asset stakeholders and the new RMO personnel.

DETERMINING THE ACCEPTABLE LEVEL OF RISK

The financial firm on which this case study is based acts as a holding company for several other companies, each with a significantly different perceived acceptable level of risk. One of the first steps that we took with each of the operating companies was to understand their perceived level of risk and ensure that they were aware of the individual benefits or pitfalls of their particular selection.

Once the baseline was established for the assets across each of the companies, we worked through a number of different assets to determine how the "acceptable" level of risk compared to the preliminary measured level of risk for several of the assets. This process resulted in changes, as the individual companies became aware of the vulnerability of certain assets.

For assets under the control of one of the companies but used by several different companies, we sometimes lowered the acceptable level of risk for a particular asset based on the lowest acceptable level of risk among the sharing companies. This approach ensured that we captured the "criticality" of a particular asset across the entire enterprise and helped us determine how the cost of controls would be determined. For example, in many cases, the division that owned a particular asset would determine an acceptable level of risk for a system as "medium/average," but another division that relied on the system for most of its sales and marketing rated the same system as "low." We recommended that the division that relied on the system for its sales and marketing systems contribute to the cost of the additional controls when necessary, to lower the risk of the system to "low."

It is important to reiterate that there can be several acceptable levels of risk within an organization. This phase requires considerable effort with the company to help it determine the acceptable level and scope of that risk. Will risk tolerance be enterprise-wide or divided by business unit? Perhaps it will be divided among logical (network) locations or perhaps, by country.

After the enterprise-wide accepted level of risk was determined, then acceptable risk levels for each business unit were derived. Several factors must be considered when determining the acceptable level of risk. The most important is the company's reaction, or the published reaction, to previous risk incidents. What happened to the company when it had an incident, how did it impact the company and how long was that impact felt? Was it able to recover? That plays a significant part in setting the risk tolerance level. There is also personal tolerance. Management may be predisposed to a certain tolerance level that affects the organization's tolerance.

SETTING TRIGGER POINTS

The next step was to take a look at all the programs and processes that the company had in place and insert calls to our risk management program to ensure that the risk posture of that asset was in fact measured and addressed at appropriate times. Several programs were reviewed, including configuration management, change management, asset commissioning and decommissioning, inventory, purchasing and business continuity that generally dealt with the assets life cycle.

Our basic premise was that whenever there was a potential change to the network, infrastructure, enterprise, or asset a trigger to the risk management program was initiated so that the risk posture of that asset could be measured prior to whatever change was being proposed. This step included a review of all the program plans and program processes within the organization to identify where in that program a trigger should be placed, so it could be tripped early enough in the process to take action. Trigger points were identified and not enabled, but it allowed us to work with the client to review each of the programs, to make sure that the risk management program was inserted at the proper point and to hypothetically review the program and the triggers.

INITIATING A PILOT PROGRAM WITH A FRIENDLY BUSINESS UNIT

The purpose of the pilot program was to try out all of the various phases of the program, to ferret out problems, and identify areas that needed polishing. With this firm, a couple of additional programs were identified as needing triggers, such as a business unit that didn't have its specific change management program included. Guidance from friendly business units allowed us to further tailor the program prior to rollout. Likewise, it provided the opportunity to "prove out" the asset database and make sure that it had adequately captured all the critical assets for that company, and that all the programs and sub-programs for risk management worked together holistically.

An important problem identified during the pilot program was the excessively rapid development of mediation boards. Consequently, the process was changed to include more negotiation and flexibility, allowing analysts and the risk management organization to resolve problems without alienating asset stakeholders.

ACTIVATING TRIGGER POINTS/ROLLING OUT TO THE ENTERPRISE

The initial configuration management change management, and asset management programs were replaced with the new ones that had triggers in place. This resulted in a flurry of risk management-type triggers, attracting the involvement of risk management analysts. Simultaneously, the risk management program was rolled out to the remaining divisions. The asset database and the risk management database also went live. All of the program plans that are generally outlined in the master program plan, including the risk analysis work, the mediation board and the review boards, were activated and put into place.

During this phase, we worked with the client to perform additional database tweaks of forms and reports based on feedback from the users that were previously brought to the attention of the RMO. We also worked with the RMO to help prioritize the flurry of risk assessment requests. We advised the client that the initial implementation of the risk management program would temporarily increase risk assessment requests. We recommended that instead of hiring additional full-time staff to support increasing requirements, the firm should either bring in contractors or manage the backlog until it subsided.

MAINTAINING AND OPTIMIZING RISK MANAGEMENT

The case study client is currently in this phase, whereby the program is under continual review. We have worked with the client to identify additional areas of optimization, including the definition of factors to assist in prioritization of risk assessment requests, the adjustment of staffing levels and skill sets and the customization of the chosen risk assessment methodology to best fit their infrastructure. The corporation also perfected its metrics, which were used to measure the efficiency of the program. Metrics that provided no insights into the program were dropped.

Once the program is rolled out and smoothly operating, the job is generally done. Metrics and oversight ensure that the program is operating to the best of its ability, or identifying areas that need improvement. It is up to the RMO and the leadership of the corporation to implement the recommended changes and ensure that the program adapts as the business changes.

nerability management is solely concerned with the vulnerabilities or the weaknesses and absence of controls of a particular asset.

For example, a typical vulnerability scanner may identify and rate a particular vulnerability as "high." The risk factor, however, would take into account a number of additional components such as how easy it is to exploit the vulnerability, where the asset is placed on the network and the impact to the organization if the vulnerability is exploited.

Traditional risk management has been implemented in a number of different ways, all of which attempt to manage the risk of an asset and generally reduce it to some negligible amount. Traditional risk management generally revolves around a periodic or cyclical process, usually annually or biannually, where each asset is reviewed. In practice, reviews are far less often

ASSET STAKEHOLDERS WHO ENJOYED A RELATIVELY QUICK REVIEW OF THEIR PARTICULAR ASSETS MAY BE SHOCKED TO SEE THE PROCESS TAKE LONGER AND REQUIRE MORE DOCUMENTATION. HOWEVER, THE ADDITIONAL TIME AND EFFORT WILL BRING A LOWER RISK POSTURE TO THE ORGANIZATION.

since a new assets introduction often interrupts the cycle. In addition, the traditional risk management approach is isolated and lacks a holistic approach that affords an enterprise the ability to view its risk posture from several company perspectives.

Additionally, the asset base that traditional risk management has evaluated has generally been incomplete. One of the most critical success factors of risk management is the assurance that all of the assets of an organization have been identified and prioritized in terms of criticality to support the organization.

THE NEW RISK MANAGEMENT

The new risk management approach recognizes a number of deficiencies and incorporates some additional features to manage an organization's risk posture. If a company were to implement an RMO, that organization would be the primary vehicle to implement the migration from the traditional to new risk management approach.

The organization would be chartered to work with the business units or departments within a company, to understand the assets and help prioritize them on their criticality and sensitivity. From a resource perspective, the risk management organization would have a manager and a number of risk analysts to support the risk evaluations.

The centralized risk management organization should be carefully planned and organized through the execution of a risk management program plan that has executive, and perhaps, board level review and approval. This plan must be developed to comply with regulatory and legal requirements such as Sarbanes-Oxley, Gramm-Leach-Bliley Act, the Health Insurance Portability and Accountability Act (HIPAA) and others. The program plan should also address a number of program issues such as governance, compliance, metrics and maintenance.

The issue of governance is that risk management roles, responsibilities and processes be defined and that they are focused on the important issues. Plan compliance means that appropriate personnel pursue the right functions. The metrics will identify any anomalies in the program and provide the measurement needed for the program to operate at peak efficiency.

A centrally managed, partitioned database is important to a risk management organization. This database could be used to manage all of the assets as well as the known vulnerabilities and the assets that could be impacted by those vulnerabilities. The risk management organization could use the assets and vulnerabilities and map those to particular threats and the controls that are in place. The database could help manage the periodic risk evaluations and interface with other systems, such as the change management database, to initiate a risk evaluation when a change request is processed.

DISADVANTAGES OF NEW RISK MANAGEMENT

The advantages of moving towards the new risk management process are numerous. However, it's not realistic to believe that the new risk management approach is without any disadvantages.

Most significantly, the new risk management approach requires additional effort and usually increased headcount to support the added functionality. It may also increase the workload of the Chief Security Officer (CSO), as

Insider Notes: Risk management is the identification, prioritization, mitigation and control of risk, and is different from vulnerability management. While risk management takes several parameters into consideration including vulnerabilities, vulnerability management is solely concerned with the vulnerabilities or the weaknesses and absence of controls of a particular asset.

AN AVANT-GARDE COMPANY MAY ACCEPT A HIGHER LEVEL OF RISK TO PROVIDE A NEW PRODUCT OR SERVICE. MORE CONSERVATIVE COMPANIES MAY HAVE A LOWER RISK TOLERANCE AND UNDERTAKE NEW VENTURES ONLY WHEN THEY CAN BE APPROPRIATELY MITIGATED AND SECURED.

new tasks are added in support of a risk management function. These tasks will need to be reviewed and understood by companies implementing this strategy.

It may also involve additional costs. If the methodology currently in use by the company can be replaced by a methodology that supports their enterprise more completely, this will involve some additional costs for purchase, tools, and training.

Asset stakeholders who enjoyed a relatively quick review of their particular assets may be shocked to see the process take longer and require more documentation. However, the additional time and effort will bring a lower risk posture to the organization.

KEY CONCEPTS OF NEW RISK MANAGEMENT

The four key concepts of new Risk Management are:
❶ Organizational Structure and Composition
❷ Program Plan and Acceptable Levels of Risk
❸ Trigger Points
❹ Complete and Accurate Asset Inventory

As companies realize the advantages that a new risk management program can provide in terms of increased efficiency and reduced risk, it needs to build an organization to administer it.

At the core of this organization are the risk analysts responsible for performing day-to-day activities such as the risk evaluation of assets. Managing those analysts will be a risk management director. Beyond daily management, the director also will be responsible for generating metrics, conducting performance reviews and prioritizing tasks.

The risk management director must also ensure that the analyst's positions are adequately and properly staffed and trained. Additionally, the director is tasked with preliminary risk mediation efforts, and with being an interface with executive management. The risk management organization should report to an executive with overall corporate oversight responsibility, such as the CSO. There is one school of thought that risk analysts should be placed at the business unit or division level in a decentralized organization, to ensure the leverage of their knowledge of the assets of a particular division or organization. However, placing them at a centralized risk management organization will increase efficiency and ensure a consistent approach. Any ancillary demands or influence from the local business units also will be minimized.

The risk analysts will need to work with the asset stakeholders to understand the business requirements of the asset, the benefits of the asset and the systems and processes it uses and supports. The risk analyst will perform a risk evaluation of the particular asset in the environment that it will be operated in, using the corporate sponsored risk assessment methodology. Each risk analyst should fully understand the risk assessment methodology and have available to them all of the collateral support material.

Methodologies such as the Computer Emergency Response Team's (CERT) Operationally Critical Threat Asset and Vulnerability Evaluation (OCTAVE), RiskWatch, CRAMM and others are all adequate risk assessment methodologies. While it is important that the organization choose the best-suited risk assessment methodology, it is more important to ensure that the methodology is consistently and uniformly deployed and available across the company.

Insider Notes: A complete vulnerability management program should include "trigger points" to ensure that a risk evaluation of an asset is initiated when a vulnerability that may affect that asset is announced.

DATA SNAPSHOT

Less than half of the respondents have a Risk Management Program in place. In order to be completely effective, the risk management program should have a governance component, be integrated with other programs in the organization with risk management triggers, have

Do you have a formal risk management program?

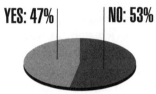

YES: 47% | | NO: 53%

a fully functioning threat, vulnerability, asset and risk database; and the database should be continuously updated. If your organization is part of the half that doesn't have a risk management program in place, you don't have a thorough and complete understanding of those components, and aren't using risk management as a business enabler.

Download the complete research study for free at www.blackbooksecurity.com/research
Source: 2005 Larstan / Reed Infosecurity Survey

Several committees/boards should monitor this organization. One of the most important of these will be the risk arbitration, or mediation, board. When risk analysts measure the level of risk for some asset and find that it exceeds the acceptable level of risk, additional or improved mitigating controls will need to be implemented. If the asset stakeholders disagree with the risk management finding, or cannot implement the controls due to funding or time constraints, arbitration may be required. The risk management arbitration board generally includes an individual outside of the risk management organization such as the CSO or CIO. This individual has the responsibility and final authority to determine the disposition of the asset under review.

In addition to the risk arbitration (or mediation) board, there will likely be a risk management review board that consists of the risk analysts and the risk management director. This board would be the governing entity responsible for managing the daily risk analysis efforts. A risk maintenance board may be composed of a number of analysts who also have the responsibility of ensuring that the threats, acceptable level of risk (described next) and available controls are updated and complete.

PROGRAM PLAN: AN ACCEPTABLE LEVEL OF RISK

There are essentially two different ways for a risk analyst to determine if the assessed level of risk of an asset is optimal. One method is, if the risk level of an asset is "high" or "medium", implementation of additional or improved controls.

The preferred method, and the method discussed in this chapter, is to compare the measured level of risk of the asset with the acceptable level of risk for the asset. This granular approach allows an organization to focus on assets where the measured level of risk is higher that the acceptable level of risk. For example, consider two different assets: a printer and a customer facing web-portal, both with a high level or risk. In the traditional risk management program, the emphasis on mitigating the risks may innappropriately be placed on the printer because it is easier to fix, easier to access, or that nobody will notice it is not available while being fixed. This chapter stresses mitigating the risks of the web portal as the measured level of risk is high while the acceptable level of risk is likely quite low.

In implementing this method, an analyst will measure the level of risk of an asset and then compare it to some acceptable level of risk. The acceptable level is derived from several inputs. To start, there is an inherent level of risk that a company is willing to live with. An avant-garde company may accept a higher level of risk to provide a new product or service. More conservative companies may have a lower risk tolerance and undertake new ventures only when they can be appropriately mitigated and secured.

THE FOUR LEVELS OF COMFORT

There are inherent comfort factors in any attempt to define an acceptable level of risk. Four important conditions affect comfort levels:

❶ **The physical placement of the asset.** Will the asset be out on the Internet where a company generally cannot live with too much risk, as

Insider Notes: Acceptable level of risk will be affected by several factors, including reaction to previous incidents, regulatory and legal issues, industry tolerance, corporate philosophy and the tolerance of the individuals evaluating the asset.

opposed to safely sitting in a secure lab network with test data?

❷ **The type of data that will run on that asset.** Is it customer sensitive information? Is it personally identifiable health care information? Or is it just public information, brochures and marketing boilerplate that don't need protection?

❸ **The number of people who will have access to it.**

❹ **The business processes, calculations or processing that the system performs.**

After the analyst measures the risk posture of an asset, it will need to be compared to the acceptable level of risk that the organization is willing to entertain for that asset. For example, if the level of risk for a particular asset is "medium", a company might find this acceptable if it is willing to take a higher level of risk to make sure that it gets customer facing applications out before its competitors. By contrast, a company with a lower acceptable level of risk may decide that this same asset with a medium risk level can't be deployed out on the network.

TRIGGER POINTS

Trigger points are the ideal supplement to regular or periodic risk reviews. They will help to ensure that a consistent risk evaluation process exists as business, operations and asset conditions change. An assessment and decomposition of each asset can identify a number of factors that, when changed, will affect the risk posture.

The "risk equation" states that likelihood, impact, threats, vulnerabilities and controls contribute to the risk posture of an asset. If any of those values change, the value of risk changes and hence, the risk posture requires a reevaluation. To identify this, a trigger point is inserted into other programs, processes and procedures to ensure that when a change occurs, a formal risk evaluation is initiated.

For example, the likelihood of a threat being exercised would change when new exploit tools are developed and made available by the hacker community, or when additional uncertainty of a program's resilience to buffer-overflow attacks increases. Likewise, the impact value may change when additional organizations within a company begin using a particular asset, or the customer base of an externally facing application increases. Trigger points for events such as these may be inserted into vulnerability management programs, asset lifecycle and maintenance programs or a commissioning and decommissioning program.

Microsoft, CERT, Bugtraq, NTBugtraq, Symantec and numerous other vendors and organizations regularly release information regarding vulnerabilities that are discovered in operating systems, software and hardware. A complete vulnerability management program should include "trigger points" to ensure that a risk evaluation of an asset is initiated when a vulnerability that may affect that asset is announced.

Threats, such as "wardialers" (systematically probing for modems that respond), searching for unsecured wireless access points, or perhaps hackers targeting a particular industry sector that a company is in, should force a risk reevaluation of a particular asset that may be impacted by that class of threat. For example, a newly announced wireless threat should trigger a risk evaluation of a corporation's wireless inventory system, but perhaps not of the data center which doesn't use wireless. A database of threats that may impact a particular type of asset would be extremely beneficial to the corporation over time as the threatscape changes.

Finally, the controls that are used to mitigate the value of risk and lower an asset's risk posture may change. New controls may be put into place such as software or hardware firewalls, routers with access control lists, a more secure architecture or perhaps a new piece of software that has additional security features. As network architectures, applications and systems grow in complexity, a security "benefit" of a particular asset may negatively affect the overall system security. As such, whenever the control changes, a risk evaluation of the asset should be completed.

Insider Notes: Acquisitions, mergers, change control, configuration management and new equipment acquisition are some of the programs that must be reviewed to determine how and where trigger points are inserted.

A number of trigger points can be incorporated into formal programs to ensure that the risk evaluation of an asset is initiated at appropriate points in an asset lifecycle. As mentioned above, some of these programs may include:

- Threat and Vulnerability Management
- Risk Management
- Business Continuity
- Disaster Recovery
- Change Control
- Configuration Management
- Commissioning and Decommissioning
- Mergers and Acquisitions

Alternatively, a number of "triggers" may not naturally fall into a predefined or preexisting program, and may need to be integrated into an alternative program or require the development of a new program.

ASSET INVENTORY

With trigger points, assets will "force" their way into an asset database as required by changing conditions. In addition, there is a base of assets that may not reflect any change activity for quite some time. There are a number of methods that an organization can use to help identify, categorize and prioritize these assets.

Purchasing and accounting records (for asset de-amortization) and traditional inventory may identify overlooked systems. A number of other processes may exist in the organization and can be utilized in the Risk Management program. For example, the Business Continuity and Disaster Recovery function may conduct Business Impact Analysis (BIA) studies on critical business processes to ensure that appropriate steps are taken to secure those systems. From those critical processes, a number of critical assets that are used to support those processes will be identified. Assets can also be identified through change control programs, configuration management programs, merger and acquisition records, network inventory applications and asset commissioning and decommissioning programs.

It is critical that all of the assets be captured into a single database entity to help facilitate the risk management program. This database should be the central location for assets within the organization. If the asset database is contained within the risk management database, software code could be used to manage the frequency of risk evaluations for each asset and alert the analyst when a particular asset is due for review.

TEN STEPS TO IMPLEMENTING NEW RISK MANAGEMENT

Here are the essential steps required to implement a "new risk management" strategy:

❶ **Development of a risk management program plan.** The creation and acceptance of a Risk Management Program Plan is a critical success factor for the entire program. This plan must ensure that the risk management needs of the entire company are properly addressed. It will need approval by senior management to ensure the support and cooperation of the entire company. The plan should detail a number of important factors such as the staff needed to support the plan and their specific roles, the metrics, governance, compliance and reporting responsibilities and the mediation process. Finally, the plan should define the risk management organization and its structure.

❷ **Asset review and identification.** One of the most critical steps taken by a company to start a risk management program is the identification of its assets. No matter how this information is collected or how it is currently stored, it must be combined to a single entity to provide one complete and holistic inventory of company assets.

Some companies maintain several different systems to manage their assets. However, these tend to be hardware assets only, excluding applications, architectures and infrastructures that comprise a company's total asset inventory. For example, a company may have an inventory system used to track computer systems such as workstations and servers,

Insider Notes: Armed with an intimate knowledge of the business and awareness of industry best practices, an audit group provides objective feedback required to maintain a world class risk program.

DATA SNAPSHOT

It is great to see almost half of the responding organizations maintaining a database of threats and vulnerabilities in their organization. However, it is critical that the database be integrated with a complete and accurate asset database to identify the threats and vulnerabilities of par-

Do you use a database to manage and monitor threats, vulnerabilities and risks within your organization?

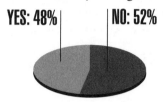

YES: 48%   NO: 52%

ticular assets, and to be able to measure the risk of those assets. The implementation, maintenance and data management issues should be addressed in a risk management program.

Download the complete research study for free at www.blackbooksecurity.com/research
Source: 2005 Larstan / Reed Infosecurity Survey

but it may not capture the critical software assets that run on those systems. These inventory systems are typically used to support the asset's depreciation for tax and reporting purposes.

Companies may also have a Business Continuity and Disaster Recovery Program in place to help ensure continued operation during and after a disaster. As part of this program, a Business Impact Analysis study is often done to identify critical assets and those processes that must be restored to recover full operations. This program also identifies key assets.

It is important to determine the level by which assets will be identified. For example, will all routers and switches be considered, or only the larger infrastructure that supports these items?

❸ **Risk management organization creation and staffing.** The risk management organization defined within the plan will need to be staffed. This can be either with new hires, or by assigning additional responsibilities to existing staff. However, it is essential this staff have sufficient time to perform their new duties. It is also critical that the individuals filling the various roles and responsibilities have the requisite training and knowledge to perform their roles as defined in the Risk Management Program plan.

This step can be taken in tandem with the asset identification step, but is clearly a prerequisite of the asset prioritization step because this staff will likely be tasked with reviewing and adjusting the criticality of the identified assets.

❹ **Asset prioritization.** Once the assets have been identified and entered into a single database, they need to be categorized in terms of their criticality and sensitivity in supporting important business operations.

Assets can be prioritized in relation to each other, or independently on an empirical scale that provides a one to ten, or a "low" to "high", rating. In an organization where several business units may perform the prioritization, it is more efficient to use the "low" to "high" approach to minimize the debates over the more granular numerical scale. Of utmost importance is that all organizations within a company use the same rating schema to prioritize its assets.

An assets prioritization may need to be reviewed and "normalized" if several people from different business units have performed the rating. This will ensure that assets from one business unit are not categorized disproportionately to those in other units.

❺ **Acceptable level of risk determination and review.** Once the assets have been identified and prioritized, the organization will need to determine its acceptable level of risk. Acceptable level of risk will be affected by several factors, including reaction to previous incidents, regulatory and legal issues, industry tolerance, corporate philosophy and the tolerance of the individuals evaluating the asset.

This step should take place after the normalization and adjustment of the identified risks. The company will then be able to gauge the acceptable level of risk and determine whether it has a single acceptable level or whether this level varies by business unit, the logical location of the asset (such as in a DMZ), by function or business process or some other factor. Already determining asset prioritization allows the company to compare the acceptable level of risk to the risk level derived for each asset.

❻ Creation of trigger points. Trigger points are risk management program calls that are inserted into other operations and programs to ensure that any changes are considered as part of any program that impacts assets. Trigger points are inserted anywhere that the risk posture of an asset may change. It is through these trigger points that risk is measured, evaluated and addressed prior to making changes to the disposition of an asset and incurring large costs or needless resource usage when the asset cannot be implemented due to security issues.

Acquisitions, mergers, change control, configuration management and new equipment acquisition are some of the programs that must be reviewed to determine how and where trigger points are inserted.

At this stage, the trigger points should be identified and the process to have the calls to the risk management program inserted. This may be a lengthy process depending on the programs in which they are being inserted. The activation of these trigger points will come later.

❼ Pilot program with "friendly" business unit or division. You must test and prove all aspects of the risk management program, including organization structure, trigger points and the roles and responsibilities of the program's staff. One of the best methods to accomplish this is to initiate actual risk evaluations through a trigger point alert.

Using a "friendly" business unit, a number of concurrent risk evaluations should be completed to ensure that the program plan adequately addresses all of the required areas. Included should be a "forced" risk remediation or arbitration process to test that key aspect of the program.

This activity will provide a real-life scenario that may uncover issues not anticipated during the program development cycle. It also gives business units an opportunity to provide input and feedback to the process and identifies any program deficiencies. Depending on this initial response, the Risk Management Organization may implement program modifications prior to rolling the program out to additional business units.

❽ **Activation of trigger points.** The risk management organization should now activate the trigger points that were previously developed and inserted into the various operational and security programs. The number of triggers developed and deployed, and the number of risk analysts that support the program, should dictate how rapidly this activation process proceeds. Gradual activation has the advantage of allowing the company to manage and gauge resources and minimize any problems that were not uncovered during the trial phase.

The rapid activation of triggers should be well planned, since it may introduce a high likelihood of failure. An organization needs to balance the activation of trigger points with the introduction of metrics and monitors to ensure business operations are not unnecessarily impeded.

❾ **Complete rollout of risk management program.** This phase includes completing the deployment and rollout of the risk management program throughout the company. In addition to the trigger points that were previously activated, a regular periodically scheduled risk assessment process should also be initiated. The remainder of the program, including the development of program metrics, oversight, governance and verification of compliance, should all be rolled out and fully functional.

❿ **Risk management program maintenance and optimization.** The final step of the risk management program includes the maintenance and optimization of the program throughout the asset's lifecycle. The program's metrics and a continual review process that streamlines applicable processes and makes adjustments should keep the program optimized.

Additionally, as part of the program lifecycle, a regular review should be conducted to ensure that it continues to adapt to changing business, operations and security conditions. The "Risk Management Organization" will regularly look inward to review the program and its processes. However, an external perspective, such as that provided by an internal audit group, would also benefit both the program and the company. Armed with an intimate knowledge of the business and awareness of industry best practices, an audit group provides objective feedback required to maintain a world class risk program.

When should a company adopt a new risk management program? When incidents that adversely affect the organization become excessive or fall into a pattern. For example, if a company's computer system repeatedly experiences viral infections through file-shares, its existing risk management program may not be sufficient. Without a complete and accurate inventory of assets and a good handle on internal controls, a company makes itself unduly susceptible to the myriad threats that lurk everywhere.

■ ■ ■

George G. McBride is a Managing Principle in Lucent Worldwide Services, the consulting organization of Lucent Technologies. George's primary duties include the development of client's security organizations and programs as well as leading and conducting penetration tests and risk assessments. Previously, George managed the internal Lucent Global Risk Assessment group where he helped business units globally measure and mitigate risks and ensured that Lucent's policies evolved to address evolving threats and technologies.

George also served as Chief Investigator of internal and external network abuses, and identified and implemented new hardware and software technologies to reduce costs and downtime. Prior to joining Lucent, George was a Senior Network Security Engineer with Global Integrity, and has worked as a Software Engineer as well as a Civilian Electronics Engineer for the U.S. Army. He can be reached at 732-949-3408 or at gmcbride@lucent.com.

[3]

INTEGRATING SECURITY INTO THE EXTENDED ENTERPRISE

As your organization conquers new markets and forges new alliances, you need to create computer defenses along the extended outreaches of your corporate empire.

> ## "THE EMPIRES OF THE FUTURE ARE EMPIRES OF THE MIND."
> - Winston Churchill

by MEHRZAD MAHDAVI & COLIN ELLIOTT

Companies are increasingly defined by the proper combination of 1s and 0s, not bricks and mortar. True wealth exists not as paper money, but as megabytes in cyberspace. This transformation has spawned "the extended enterprise," and with it a fertile breeding ground for attacks on IT systems.

The extended enterprise is a relatively new phenomenon. The

evolution of information technologies, especially communications technologies and the Internet, has enabled the inter-company sharing of data and information, and spawned this new economic entity — the extended enterprise, or virtual company.

This new entity focuses directly on its core competencies and outsources most other functions. Functions outsourced often include human resources, financial administration, and IT operations and support. In addition, these entities also have close-knit relationships with suppliers and large customers that allow them to receive, and then provide the just-in-time delivery of products and services required to remain competitive.

Extended collaboration has enabled firms to focus on what they do best, but it has also created a myriad of interfaces into their systems as they manage all of these supply and outsourcing arrangements. The upshot? A security nightmare.

Before the development of extended enterprises, a company's relationships with its partners were at arm's length with only the most immediate information exchanged manually, or via an overly secure EDI connection, and that almost begrudgingly. Advanced computer networking technologies and capabilities have provided the communications environment required for a successful extended enterprise, with its reliance on many different relationships to provide it with non-core products and services.

The information chains associated with these products and services have become the arteries for success and also the source of growing vulnerability. While at one time a company could "see" where its systems started and ended and provide security accordingly, today, the need for security extends way beyond a company's own "borders."

EXTENDED ENTERPRISE SECURITY

How secure are extended enterprises today? The short answer is, not very. Security has often focused on the tactical, providing a degree of safety for internal systems. However, inter-enterprise information systems require a strategic approach, a technology that is still immature. Much growth in this field of strategic security needs to occur in light of the explosive evolution of extended enterprises and their dependence on secure information systems.

Strategic security differs greatly from tactical security. Most extended enterprise organizations do not have a coherent strategy that addresses the security susceptibility of all of the communication chains that comprise the information system of the virtual or extended enterprise business model.

The tactical behavior of most companies to date has been to purchase and install point solutions, or more accurately, point technologies in the form of worm, virus and intrusion detection systems. Tactical security applications are often applied in a piecemeal and patchwork manner, and are usually specific to a particular software application, such as email virus protection or web filtering software.

They function often as a matter of faith. That is, the user does not understand how they work and what types of security breaches they are identifying. Companies often have bits and pieces of security software not connected together and not working together. Such systems are capable of sounding a plethora of alarms, but often these alarms are not understood for what they are since nobody knows what to do about them. When a security violation is noted by the system, users often do not know if they are real or not. So, like a car alarm blaring in the night, the users wait until the alarm is shut off. Similar to automobile alarms, companies have unplugged the security applications or simply ignore them.

MAJOR AREAS OF VULNERABILITY

The major vulnerability of security systems in general, and in particular for an extended enterprise, is enforcement. Security systems are in place, but their users do not adequately understand how they work. Without this understanding of what the security system does and what types of problems it can identify or solve, customers fail to employ it optimally. A simple analogy is to that of a seat belt that is not used. A good deal of learning is still required for companies to understand and properly utilize the software security systems they already have.

Insider Notes: Extended collaboration has enabled firms to focus on what they do best, but it has also created a myriad of interfaces into their systems as they manage all of these supply and outsourcing arrangements. The upshot? A security nightmare.

DATA SNAPSHOT

Note how a significant number of respondents reported that outsourcing is a standard part of how they do business. This trend will continue as companies focus on their core competencies.

Download the complete research study for free at www.blackbooksecurity.com/research
Source: 2005 Larstan / Reed Infosecurity Survey

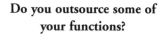

Do you outsource some of your functions?

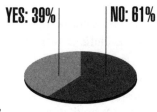

YES: 39%   NO: 61%

Another major area of vulnerability to the extended enterprise is that many small companies (e.g., parts suppliers) cannot afford elaborate security systems, nor do they understand why they need to be deployed. This can be an issue as the security and successful operation of an extended enterprise information system is only as good as its weakest link. As supply chains extend deeper throughout the economy, the smallest company can unwittingly provide hackers with access to systems of a large company several times removed from its own customer base.

An ounce of prevention is worth a pound of cure. Extended enterprise organizations must employ a strategic approach to information security that offers this "ounce of prevention." To do this, they must first understand and identify what they are trying to secure. They must look at the business holistically and identify the key business processes, the associated information technologies, points of security vulnerabilities, security software systems in place and, most importantly, how these security systems will be enforced.

Chief information officers, information security directors and the associated staff of extended enterprises must understand the extended business unit as a cohesive, interrelated organization, and the function of each business and information system within it. They must understand the nature and details of the virtual business to identify what needs to be protected.

For example, automobile manufacturers today produce very few of the component parts of their finished product. They have thousands of suppliers in integrated supply, marketing, sales and perhaps, even finance chains. Information security specialists must understand the nature of these relationships, the content and processes of the information being shared and the security vulnerabilities inherent in the web of interrelated information, and data and information/data sharing systems.

Collaborators in virtual enterprises need to be concerned with the integrity of information and data systems, and develop a common set of standards. Channels and protocols for exchanging information must be established, and a process for enforcing and ensuring such channels and protocols developed and deployed.

One best practice is to develop a minimum set of security standards and communications protocols for all the different entities involved in the extended enterprise. This will require not only a great deal of planning, collaboration and cooperation among the key entities, but also an extensive audit function to ensure that all included firms meet the security standards. It is prudent to start with a minimal workable set of standards. Over time, these can be tightened and enhanced into the optimal standards to be employed and enforced. Set a minimum, and then "raise the bar," as companies in the extended enterprise become more comfortable and adept with the security measures.

A critical concern is small suppliers having the ability to meet and afford the standards of the extended enterprise. Such ability becomes a concern when considering business and information collaboration with a supplier of parts or services. As noted before, the weakest link with respect to information security in the virtual company provides the most acute security vulnerability.

For industries to comply with the information system security standards, it is most wise for the individual entities to collaborate to set those standards.

 Insider Notes: As supply chains extend deeper throughout the economy, the smallest company can unwittingly provide hackers with access to systems of a large company several times removed from its own customer base.

THE TERM "EXTENDED ENTERPRISE" REFERS TO THE CONCEPT THAT A BUSINESS ORGANIZATION IS COMPRISED OF MORE THAN THE BOARD OF DIRECTORS, EXECUTIVES AND EMPLOYEES. THE EXTENDED ENTERPRISE INTEGRATES BUSINESS PARTNERS, CONTRACTORS, SUPPLIERS AND CUSTOMERS INTO WHAT BECOMES A VIRTUAL ORGANIZATION.

With the complexities of today's business arrangements, it is not only necessary to develop and enforce standards within a defined industry, but also across associated collaborating industries.

Whereas larger companies such as General Motors and Exxon/Mobil may be in a position to dictate security standards and information protocols to their suppliers, in most industries, no one company has such clout. It is desirable that the development and enforcement processes relative to such standards and protocols be a collaborative effort with all major companies involved.

In the past, a chief information officer and systems security personnel would be primarily or exclusively involved with internal data and information security concerns. They could build or install security solutions around their internal operations and applications. With the evolution of the extended enterprise and its shared information systems, it has become necessary for such information security professionals to think outwardly towards the inclusion of collaborators. Extended enterprises must allow others into the security structure. Security systems planners for the virtual company must be more strategic and holistic in their approach to information systems security.

EXTENDED ENTERPRISE SECURITY ACTION ITEMS

The main prescription with respect to successful security systems in an extended enterprise information system is the adoption of a strategic planning approach to building such a system. Then, follow these two general steps:

❶ Successfully define and understand the mission, structure and operations of the extended enterprise and its associated information systems.

❷ Create a collaborative planning and administrative process that develops, sets, implements, and enforces standards and protocols with respect to information interchange within the extended enterprise.

You should create standing working committees for developing, implementing, and enforcing security standards and information and data protocol with representatives from all the participating entities. This is an idea whose time has come.

When developing these standards, we recommend that a relatively minimal set of standards that are not too costly or difficult for all cooperators be implemented. The planning process should attend to the future introduction over time of more strict standards of compliance in a process of continuous improvement.

THE ECONOMIC BENEFITS OF EXTENDED ENTERPRISES

The fact is, extended enterprises are important in today's economy. Extended enterprises have become a well established trend in business organizations in recent years. The global competitive aspects of most industries, and the evolution of information technologies and processes have created the need and fashioned the methodology of its emergence. The term "extended enterprise" refers to the concept that a business organization is comprised of more than the board of directors, executives and employees. The extended enterprise integrates business partners, contractors, suppliers and customers into what becomes a virtual organization.

Information systems of the extended enterprise include a network of relationships among a company, its employees, business partners, IT contractors, suppliers, customers and markets. The most common exam-

Insider Notes: Collaborators in virtual enterprises need to be concerned with the integrity of information and data systems, and develop a common set of standards. Channels and protocols for exchanging information must be established, and a process for enforcing and ensuring such channels and protocols developed and deployed.

THE ONION MODEL: AN ILLUSTRATIVE SCENARIO

All organizations are different and reflect varying levels of maturity with regard to information security. This scenario will cover a highly evolved form of security that uses multiple entities, known as the onion model.

Multiple entities are necessary for many reasons, but one in particular is the fact that security is still the new kid on the block for many organizations. Networks have gone through multiple stages of maturity, arriving at the situation today where they tend to work as they are supposed to with no attention from, or even knowledge by, the end users. In addition, the organizations will be from the oil and gas sector, but the lessons learned and the concepts are ubiquitous across all sectors.

In oil and gas, the companies are segmented into a few broad categories: the national oil companies (such as Saudi Aramco), the majors (ExxonMobil being the largest) and the independents. Each of these categories has specific security needs, but, at a broad level, they all have information that they do not want others to have; information that is their intellectual property and gives them competitive advantage.

The onion model for security, as discussed earlier, has multiple layers of security. Those layers are: people, policy & procedure, physical and, finally, logical. Most companies, when regarding information security, tend to be thinking at the logical layer. They forget that their security is only as strong as the weakest link. This only gets worse as organizations become more and more extended enterprises.

The first scenario involves a security assessment. Security assessments should be based on standards such as the BS7799/ISO17799, and, while they are complete in their scope, they do not provide a solid method that provides a clear assessment of security practices with recommendations. In that regard, Schlumberger has developed a patent-pending best practice Security Maturity Assessment.

At the basic level, a security assessment is a piece of work commissioned by an enterprise to look at how well the security layers are working. Due to the differences in concerns and implementation of the security layers, the assessments will differ immensely depending on the customer's needs. While the scope of the assessment will be tailored to meet expectations, the first rule for all security activities is to establish and maintain good lines of communication. This can be done in many ways, but face-to-face discussions are critical.

Once the communication lines have been established, validation of the scope of the engagement can be performed. This ensures that all parties have a complete understanding of what will, and more importantly, what will not be done. As a final activity before anything else is done, the assessor must obtain a signed document stating that the company has agreed to the activities he or she will perform and that it has been sanctioned by the hiring organization.

We advise that this document be prepared by legal council, because the document will be binding in the event that something goes wrong with the activities and the company wants to pursue legal action against any activities that were performed. While this document is critical, the assessor should also maintain accurate accounts of the actions performed during the assessment and times things were done.

A national oil company asked Schlumberger to perform a security assessment. A security assessment performed properly, by people who intimately understand the specific industry concerns, is worth its weight in gold. However, due care must be made by both organizations to ensure that both are protected during and after the assessment; documentation of actions is critical for both parties.

In the oil and gas industry, physical assets and their value to the company are well known, and this company had a very good handle on the physical security. So, as part of the security assessment, we attempted to remove a hammer from one of the plants, but were stopped by security guards at the gates who thoroughly check every vehicle entering and exiting that location. Part of the reason for the intense scrutiny was the fact that ships entered and left the country from their docks and immigration agents screen everyone going to, or returning from, the rigs. So, in this case, the physical security for entering and exiting the site appeared, at first glance, to be handled well.

However, when we asked to see the policies for physical security and employment practices, including background checks for employees, the policies and procedures were non-existent. In addition, a CD, which had confidential information on it, was sitting next to the hammer, but it was not taken.

When the security guard was asked why the hammer was taken and not the CD, the answer indicated that the contents of the CD were not understood to have significant value to the organization. When we asked to see the policies and procedures, there was a pause and they dug around and found a document that had been written a few years before, but had not been updated since then. Assessors found fault with this as it demonstrates the documents are not kept up-to-date and the relative value people place in the information security policy. This assessment also identified a number of concerns in the areas of physical and logical security including network, operating system and administration issues. These concerns are being dealt with first by policy and procedures and, in some cases, by using other mechanisms.

On another recent assessment, the example of user IDs and passwords written on Post-It notes on the monitor or keyboard was observed, but less frequently than before, a testament to education and communication. However, many people still had user IDs and passwords documented and left relatively unsecured (hidden in drawers and in documents with names like password.txt). In addition, we found some more disturbing real-life security concerns, such as entire departments using the same user ID and password to access some applications. This meant that a crucial department and application had literally no accountability since everyone shared the same logon information. It was no surprise to find that people in other departments also knew the ID and password.

This situation of shared IDs and passwords leads to another security solution and case study. Schlumberger provides identity and access management solutions to the oil and gas industry. Strategy, policies and procedures reduce the potential of hiring hackers and other at-risk employees, but do not protect it against those who are unwilling or unable to follow policy.

For example, most of our customers subject people to background checks prior to hire, and during orientation they are given many policies (including one on security) to read and acknowledge their understanding of by signing off on it. In addition, most of the majors, and increasingly, the national oil companies and some of the larger independents, issue employee badges. Traditionally, badges were used for physical access and as a corporate badge. However, problems arose where employees would need to carry multiple badges to access each site. Schlumberger, as an organization, decided to reduce the number of physical access systems by creating a standard and issuing smart cards to their employees.

This scenario has been replicated by many of our clients. One of the major oil companies, for which we implemented smart card technology, reduced its physical access costs by over $8 million in the first year and nearly $3 million annually. The major reduced the number of people needed to manage the different technologies, the number of physical access maintenance contracts and other ancillary costs. Another benefit to these companies was the added security and the ability to expand on their initial investment.

Solutions for each company differ, but in Schlumberger, the smart cards contain a second chip, which can provide even more value for logical security. Digital credentials are stored on the chip and accessed by the PC or one-time password device. This digital information can be used to create VPN tunnels, log onto PCs, and be used to digitally sign email, encrypt files or act as an electronic wallet for purchasing meals in some of our cafeterias.

Identity and access management (IAM) is a critical aspect of the extended enterprise. They determine who an individual is (federated IDs) and what that person is able to access. Great strides have been made in IAM, but the architecture is not fully mature. The scope is very large, so it should be handled separately.

HAVE EXECUTIVES PUT MUCH THOUGHT INTO EFFECTIVELY SECURING THESE EXTENDED ENTERPRISES? THE ANSWER TO THIS QUESTION TENDS TO BE NO.

ple of an extended enterprise is the supply chain. For example, a manufacturer may want to be able to determine, in real time, a supplier's stock condition of particular parts. While we tend to think of extended enterprises in terms of their supply chains, there are many other manifestations of the extended enterprise.

For example, administrative functions such as payroll and health benefits are often outsourced. While separate companies administer them, they still fall under the security purview of the company for which they are being administered, and the exchange of data and information among these entities is necessary and desirable.

Organizations are becoming virtualized in many such capacities. Businesses are outsourcing functions that are not core to their operations, so that they can concentrate on their core business or businesses. There is an integrated need for the flow of secure information to and from these outsourced business segments.

With more people and organizations using the Internet as a network, the whole enterprise has become segmented. Pieces of related information are in different divisions, different enterprises, different locations and different employees. There is a need for data and information flow out of, and back to, the various pieces of the segmented organization. It becomes necessary to secure those individuals and organizations, both small and large, connected to the network.

The pharmaceutical industry is an example of a highly collaborative, supply chain-driven extended enterprise. It is easy to see the importance of accurate data and information in an industry like this, that deals with life and death.

In the oil and gas industry today, mergers and acquisitions are the norm. Companies are being bought or buying other companies every day, and staffs are being mixed and merged. More and more, companies are co-developing oil fields. In the past, Exxon and Shell had no access to each other's data and information. It is different now. The focus is on information flow. External people are viewed as internal for the flow of information and data, but are still viewed as external from an information security point of view.

As part of the evolution of extended enterprises, large consulting and service firms such as Atos Origin, CSC, EDS and IBM Global Services now offer services where they supply the entire, or a very large part of, the data processing and information systems operations and management functions for client firms.

For example, EDS recently signed a contract with Bank of America to manage its data and voice networks. Outsourcing has become a valuable tool for companies that have a plethora of proprietary information and data. In addition, global outsourcing firms will have thousands of other clients, ranging from small to large companies, that allow them to leverage knowledge. Individual employees of IBM will undoubtedly be working on more than one account at a time. Some clients may be in direct competition with other clients.

Information technology has become such a complex undertaking that the specialization provided by IBM Global Services, EDS, CSC, Atos Origin and similar firms leads to the efficiency and effectiveness of outsourcing to these firms, as long as the scope and Security Management Assessments are well defined and enforced. It is a classic "make or buy" decision; as outsourcing services become more available and more effective, more and more firms are choosing to purchase such services. It is important to think about the security and business needs of the extended enterprise while making these decisions.

Insider Notes: Extended enterprises must allow others into the security structure. Security systems planners for the virtual company must be more strategic and holistic in their approach to information systems security.

IMPLEMENTATION OF THE LATEST WONDER TECHNOLOGY DOESN'T ACTUALLY MEAN THAT THE COMPANY WILL BE MORE SECURE.

MANAGEMENT COMPLACENCY

Have executives put much thought into effectively securing these extended enterprises? The answer to this question tends to be no.

Chief executives have tended to push their organizations into extended enterprise arrangements, driven by the pressures of competition, without giving much thought to the security of the resultant data and information flows.

The Information Technology executive tries to secure the enterprise, but the virtualization (nature of the extended enterprise) of the organization makes this task very difficult. When dealing with security issues related to the extended enterprise information systems, there is a trade-off between security and the ability to share information. The first priority of IT personnel has been to make sure that systems work as they should and that people can communicate in an effective and timely manner. Security, thus far, has been a secondary concern.

Developing and implementing security processes and technologies often involves rewriting the information infrastructure. This can be very expensive. Thus, it is highly advisable to develop and implement security measures at the earliest possible date. The more information systems evolve and grow, the more expensive implementing a comprehensive security program overhaul will become.

AREAS OF VULNERABILITY

The three main areas of vulnerability are the processes themselves, the governance model and enforcement, and technology implementation and management issues. The latter is the one that receives the most press (e.g., viruses, worms, etc.). However, an extended enterprise is made more vulnerable by a poorly designed process and poorly run procedures. The technology issues are crucial, but without a full understanding of the business needs, security resources spent may not be in line with the risk tolerance.

The process vulnerabilities are related to the lack of existence of holistic security architecture. Information networks often have many point solutions, or technologies (e.g., IDS). However, these point solutions are not integrated and can often lead to a false sense of security. Very few companies are strategic in their approach to information security. The recognition of this weakness, however, is now widespread, and companies have begun to approach security issues in a more holistic, strategic manner.

Most network vulnerabilities stem from being virtualized. The advent of the extended enterprise has wrought an increasingly larger number of external partners. With this evolution comes the need for the right people to have the right access to the right information in a timely fashion. There is a tradeoff between security and access, which means that tougher security can have a negative effect on access and thus business productivity.

The culture of extended enterprise systems has favored access and productivity over security. While we do not suggest that this not be the goal, we want to stress that it is important to ensure that security is an integral part of the extended enterprise. One area that needs to be reviewed is the need for the classification of the information. Information technology professionals need to establish channels, so that access to necessary and pertinent productive information is not sacrificed for the security of proprietary information, and vice versa.

Coordination with other entities involved with the extended enterprise is essential. The virtual organization is only as secure as its weakest links. Companies need to set standards for participation in information shar-

Insider Notes: It is a classic "make or buy" decision; as outsourcing services become more available and more effective, more and more firms are choosing to purchase such services. It is important to think about the security and business needs of the extended enterprise while making these decisions.

THREE MAIN SECURITY PRINCIPLES

There are three main principles involved in the security of the extended organization:

❶ Implement and manage information security in a holistic manner
❷ View IT as one aspect of risk management
❸ Secure the business process, not just the IT systems

ing; requiring that collaborators maintain and pass a security audit may be in order.

SECURING EXTENDED, AS OPPOSED TO CONVENTIONAL, ENTERPRISES

There is a clear difference. The traditional method involves point technology solutions and putting boundaries around the organization. In virtual organizations, this is no longer enough. IT security personnel need to provide a more holistic approach to the security environment. They have to provide specific security clearance for each individual with access to the network and supply application specific access.

The approach that we are suggesting is that IT managers be able to translate between the business owners and IT. They must understand the core business processes of the virtual organization. They need to secure such processes, understand the data and information flow, and secure access to all components of data and information flows. Corporations that are currently secure and those moving in the direction of secure operations, understand this concept.

We emphasize the integration of security concerns and programs with business partners in the extended enterprise. Information security is no longer a secondary concern, and in more advanced enterprises, it is viewed as one part of your risk management and an enabler of the business process, because it is integrated into the business process.

The questions surrounding information security traditionally have been, "What needs to be secured?" or "Where are we vulnerable?" Now the questions become focused on improving the business by securing and enhancing the flow of data and information. It is the realization of the competitive advantage of providing secure, but effective and efficient access to data and information, rather than viewing security as just a cost of doing business.

IMPLEMENTING A SECURE EXTENDED ENTERPRISE

The Initial Phases

The first phase in implementing a secure extended enterprise is to understand the overall business strategy. This strategy needs to be understood and have buy-in from all levels of the organization. It must also identify where the organization is going and be communicated to, and win acceptance by, the entire organization.

Then, you must develop a clear definition of how the organization plans to achieve its goals and what its contingencies are for unexpected problems. This will help minimize the impact of mistakes and changes in business conditions. With these operational plans in place, the company then needs to define what is core to the business, what is ancillary and what can be outsourced. It is important that all departments are on the same page with this asset positioning. This leads to a mapping of business processes that detail both how business is done, and also where a company's key interaction points with the extended enterprise are.

Once a company has completed these phases, it has an understanding of what it is currently doing, and it has a strategy as to where it is going. Now, it needs to develop the policies and the standards to support this plan. The most important consideration with policies and standards is that they are living documents and should not sit on the shelf. It is not enough just to set policies and standards; a company also must make sure that they are reviewed regularly and employees are held accountable to them.

Insider Notes: Most network vulnerabilities stem from being virtualized. The advent of the extended enterprise has wrought an increasingly larger number of external partners. With this evolution comes the need for the right people to have the right access to the right information in a timely fashion.

DATA SNAPSHOT

A telling graph that shows the importance of security for the majority of businesses. Five years ago, security was not as important as making things work. Security has become much more important as companies have matured in their extended business dealings and as regulations have proliferated.

Is security more important now than it was five years ago for your business?

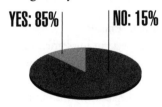

YES: 85%   NO: 15%

Download the complete research study for free at www.blackbooksecurity.com/research
Source: 2005 Larstan / Reed Infosecurity Survey

The overall management cycle of all of these steps is crucial. They are not one-off activities. Hopefully, the business strategy will not change on a regular basis. However, some companies need to change strategy more often. They may have a three-month business plan, execute it, and then decide what to do next. That's fine, as long as everybody understands how that works and is moving in the right direction. So again, it is the overall management of this that is crucial.

REVIEW AND VALIDATION

Concurrently, or after a company has set its strategy, mapped its business processes, and set its policies and standards, it may then review what currently exists in terms of architecture, to ensure that it is securing and protecting the most important assets, whatever they may be. It's crucial that this is not only considered from a technology standpoint, but also from the policies, procedures and standards viewpoint. It is important to verify and validate that what you're trying to do as a business is actually being addressed by the architecture.

The next step is to validate whether the current architecture is meeting the needs of the business. If it's not, a company may decide to plan a new architecture because it is not secure enough. Validation is the key to planning the new architecture and progressing through its implementation. Implement the architecture, then validate that it is still meeting the initial expectations from the beginning. Therefore, it is important to have metrics in place that will measure success or failure of this process.

SYSTEM OPTIMIZATION AND EFFICIENCY

After validating the system against its goals, the company needs to determine if it is operating in an optimized manner. One major concern is that a company may start implementing new technologies without understanding the effectiveness of its current technologies. The problem is that if a company doesn't know how efficient it is running, then how will it know that a change is going to make it better or worse?

If the IT department was running effectively, a company may actually be better off not changing the fundamental operations under the guise of security, or, if the company had already identified and adapted key procedures, this may preclude making some massive security investments. Implementation of the latest wonder technology doesn't actually mean that the company will be more secure.

The mantra of people, process and technology is often heard when implementing security, and it applies here. Technology and security people tend to be focused on the best technology as the way to address a security issue. However, it may or may not end up fixing the overall problem.

The company needs to step back and look at it from a global context. This may possibly be done internally, but it is often easier for consultants to be brought in to provide an unbiased assessment, thus avoiding any political concerns. They need to consider what the future mode of operation should be, and this begins with a company knowing what it has. If it does not know what it currently has, it's impossible to secure it. Once a company knows what it has, then it can move forward. But until then, it's difficult to create a good strategy without knowing the starting point. From

Insider Notes: The most important consideration with policies and standards is that they are living documents and should not sit on the shelf. It is not enough just to set policies and standards; a company also must make sure that they are reviewed regularly and employees are held accountable to them.

there, a company has to manage objectives. It has to have goals as to what it wants to achieve. If it wants to be a billion-dollar company, it needs to plan how it will get there, and what is needed in terms of infrastructure and support.

The crucial steps for your company to follow:
- know what it has
- review and revise its strategy
- map the business processes
- set policies and standards
- review the current architecture (see if it runs properly)
- validate whether the architecture is adequate before and after this new architecture plan
- perform the implementation
- validate that strategic needs are being met
- optimize it

Putting in an IPS system may be something that a company considers crucial, but it is not put in with default settings. It takes time to effectively scale these systems and set them to meet company needs.

CRITICAL SUCCESS FACTOR CHECKLIST

Critical success factors have to be communicated and agreed upon. Having a good change control process and good project management activities throughout all of this process is central to success. A good project manager can save a poor plan.

In medicine, they have an interesting review for major cases called a multidisciplinary review. In this review, everybody involved with the treatment gets in one room to discuss it prior to implementation. That is similar to what is required here. All of the stakeholders need to get together and agree on how to proceed.

The critical success factors are:
- **Communication.** The necessary first part of all of these steps is communication with all stakeholders. This includes everyone in the organization and the extended enterprise. Excellent communication

on every aspect of the project is really what's going to make it successful. Communicating with all parties involved is the critical factor, not just internally, but also throughout the extended enterprise, and making sure that everybody has bought into this idea.

■ **Efficient current operations.** Before changing anything, a company needs to ensure that it is currently operating efficiently. It makes little sense to make huge changes if current activities could meet the needs simply by running more efficiently and effectively.

■ **Agreement on action and timeline.** When a company decides to make the changes, a good project management and a good change-control process are crucial. Agreement on specific actions, outcomes and timelines are critical. The communication back and forth and the validation and verification that these changes have been made, and that they work as advertised and really do meet the needs of the users, are crucial.

■ **Getting buy-in from all of the partners.** If the effort does not have buy-in from everybody, the effort is doomed at the start.

PITFALLS TO AVOID

The failings that tend to occur are all communication-related. Sometimes there are hardware problems, sometimes there are software problems, but mostly it's the communication that's failed. Some causes of this are:

■ Inadequate input by all involved parties into strategy development
■ All the appropriate parties were not asked to be part of the planning process
■ There was no clear objective as to what success looked like

How can the process be best managed? At the end of the day, communication and establishing someone in charge that understands what is trying to be accomplished from the beginning to end provide the best process management. One of the problems in security is that it has generally been an after-thought. If security is part of the fabric of the system from the begin-

> **Insider Notes:** Since it is often too expensive to run a true defense in-depth for the entire organization, companies need to review their organization and identify areas that appear be a good target for an outside intrusion.

ning, it is much easier, and much cheaper, to deploy and manage. For security professionals, it is a welcome sight for security to evolve from being an add-on to actually being part of the overall solution.

CHOOSING THE PROPER TECHNOLOGY

This section discusses how various technologies and security tactics can be harnessed to protect extended enterprise operations.

Before technology can be considered, a company has to determine what it is trying to do and what the organization is going to look like in terms of security. Is security to be structured in terms of domains of trust, which are often envisioned as the onion model, or structured traditionally, as a perimeter defense with a hard exterior and a soft, gooey center? Organizations find that as they become extended enterprises, the traditional approach doesn't work.

The next option to consider is defense in-depth. Defense in-depth can take two forms. In the first form, a company establishes islands of trust that protect certain assets. It is analogous to a package of M&Ms. The package must be opened to access the M&Ms. But even with the package opened, a hard candy coated shell must be penetrated before gaining access to the soft, gooey middle. In other words, there are multiple security steps to get through.

The other form of defense in-depth creates several levels of various types of firewalls. For example, if the external firewall is a Cisco PIX, the internal firewalls may be Checkpoint. This provides an additional protection layer so that if one vendor's product has a vulnerability, the other vendor's product will not be vulnerable. The problem with this approach is it turns into a management problem. The cost of managing all these firewalls and all these technologies, including intrusion detection, antivirus, anti-spam, vendor patching, patch management, etc., is certainly not trivial. Vendors are recognizing this problem and responding with combination security products that provide multiple uses.

Since it is often too expensive to run a true defense in-depth for the entire organization, companies need to review their organization and identify areas that appear be a good target for an outside intrusion. Companies may choose to invest in defense in-depth strategies to protect these highly sensitive areas.

A great example in the oil and gas industry is "tight wells." A tight well is a well that is being drilled that the company doesn't want anyone else to know about. Only the partner that is helping to drill it and the company that's putting up the money for it will know about it. These tight wells can sometimes be running on the same rig as another well that is not "tight." This information likely could use defense in-depth security solutions.

A tight well is also an example of a security requirement for the extended enterprise. Not only does the company have the risk of this information getting out, but it also is operating in multiple locations due to the multiple parties involved in drilling it. Drilling wells can be seen as one area where it is truly extending the enterprise.

In this case, the M&Ms can be viewed as being out of the package and sitting in a candy dish. It's no longer within the company perimeter that the information is being protected. It is now going to multiple parties and thus requires extracted security. Also, this model can be used to describe business on the Internet where trust is suspect. If a company doesn't trust people that are on its network segment, what are its options?

First, it should consider introducing different technology solutions. This can be different firewalls, VLAN technologies for switching, intrusion detection or intrusion prevention systems. The latter may be network based or host based, but it is critical to remember that it is the overall information that needs protecting as well as the integrity of the data. The problem with the network-based intrusion detection and intrusion preven-

> **Insider Notes:** When introducing security technology, cost is a critical concern. All security decisions should be risk based. Quantifying the risk to the organization of the information or asset getting compromised, or the risks to the information if the network is in jeopardy, makes it simpler to identify and sell the solutions to management.

DATA SNAPSHOT

Another two telling graphs...
Notice that not only **partners**, but **customers** are becoming increasingly interested in your company's security posture. Security is no longer relegated to the land of IT, but is becoming more central to your core business.

Download the complete research study for free at www.blackbooksecurity.com/research
Source: 2005 Larstan / Reed Infosecurity Survey

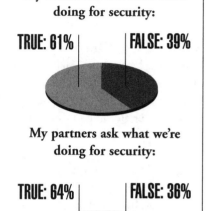

My customers ask what we're doing for security:

TRUE: 61% FALSE: 39%

My partners ask what we're doing for security:

TRUE: 64% FALSE: 36%

tion is that the information flowing across the wire is often encrypted, thus rendering the systems blind. All that is visible by the IDS is intrusion traffic that's flowing in and out. It doesn't know how to respond because it is not the target. Hence, the protection must sit on the intended device.

From a communications viewpoint, a company may have encrypted channels to reduce the risk of sniffing attacks and the risk of someone successfully changing the integrity of the data as it moves through this channel. Once channel security is addressed, the information itself must be considered. Obviously, not all information requires encryption. But tight wells-type of information does. If this information is being sent through a clear channel, then the information itself needs to have some sort of protection.

This protection can be encryption using an ID and password, a PKI with certificate digital signature or some of the latest techniques such as quantum cryptography. While there are many options, it is important to remember that all technologies have cost and management issues. It is important not to go to management with a request for security technology, but with a need to secure an asset that the company must protect.

When introducing security technology, cost is a critical concern. All security decisions should be risk based. Quantifying the risk to the organization of the information or asset getting compromised, or the risks to the information if the network is in jeopardy, makes it simpler to identify and sell the solutions to management.

The next thing to introduce is the firewalls, because a company has to implement something like a firewall, along with some sort of antivirus system, an IDS system, patch management and intrusion protection. The problem here is that a company may not have a way to manage and make sense of all the generated alerts. This is critical.

When a new piece of additional security technology is introduced, the amount of information generated increases geometrically, increasing the difficulty in correlating it and determining the problem. The problem with all of the available technologies is that they are not plug-and-play. A company needs to test them in lab conditions, understand the information it provides and determine what is to be done with this information.

SECURING THE USERS

Traditionally, most enterprises have implemented some sort of user ID and password to protect assets, be they computers, applications or databases. The simplest of these is the single user ID and password that is used by everyone. The problem with this is that you are unable to identify who is doing anything, and, if somebody's done something wrong, it is impossible to determine who should be sanctioned.

The next level is individual IDs and passwords for everyone. Unfortunately, this solution is only marginally better. The problem with this is that although there is one for every user, it doesn't preclude somebody from copying or sharing their password or ID.

Insider Notes: Ensuring that internal security is in place is critical as you push for greater security among your business partners. Be the model for all to follow. Security relies on the network, so it is critical that the network run smoothly.

There are also issues with the password. To begin with, are they simple (e.g., "123") or strong passwords (e.g., "A3cf*rHwh")? The next level would be to use multi-factor authentication. In the first two examples, the one factor for authentication is something that you know. As you introduce multi-factor authentication, users would be given something that they have to have in order to access some asset, application or computer.

Examples of technologies that supply this are PKI certificates that can be either hard drive or token-based. Token-based certificates tend to be more secure and are portable, because employees can take the token with the certificate with them.

Another factor that is currently being put into use is biometrics. These technologies allow the user to prove who they are by allowing the users to present something that they are. Examples here are fingerprint and iris scanners, speech recognition and, potentially, DNA sampling. All of these technologies have many concerns with respect to data privacy that need to be addressed prior to their implementation.

An emerging research area for multi-factor authentication provides answers to the question, "Where is the user?" Going back to the tight well example, an individual might be able to access the information on this rig, be authorized to see it, and have all the appropriate security in place, but not be in a trusted location. Security level is dependent on where the person is when making the inquiry. This already occurs in multinational organizations that operate in countries that do not allow them to export data. The data for drilling and production activities for assets owned by the country have to be held in a data center that exists in that country. The information is a national secret, and as such, it can't go anywhere else in the world.

In addition, access to the data that exists within databases is being segregated. For example, Schlumberger may partner with ChevronTexaco and ExxonMobil to perform test drilling in a particular region. So, for a particular test well that Schlumberger drills, it may be necessary to provide information on certain depths of a well to ChevronTexaco but not to ExxonMobil, and vice versa. Not only are we forced to segregate and restrict access to a particular well, but now we also need to restrict access to a particular section of the well. There is more granularity in what information extended enterprises are allowed to see.

WHERE TO START

First, review company strategy and understand what it is the company is trying to protect. The onion model is generally accepted as a security model to follow and has been implemented in many organizations globally. The levels are people, process, and procedures, both physical and logical. Once security has addressed the people issues, it can move to procedures. If these are secure enough, it can look at securing how physical access to technology and knowledge stores are gained.

From there, the company needs to consider the logical aspect. This is where the company considers firewalls, IDS systems, antivirus and anti-spam for email. Then, users are considered; implement IDs and passwords or PKI certificates with tokens to hold those credentials. A company then can jump to biometrics devices, or location-based authentication mechanisms.

Putting in the technology and making it work is one thing; managing it is another. Typically, enterprises underestimate this cost, especially in small to midsized companies. Understanding the true cost of these technologies is critical to their successful implementation.

As we mentioned before, the security of the extended enterprise is only as good as the weakest link. Ensuring that internal security is in place is critical as you push for greater security among your business partners. Be the model for all to follow. Security relies on the network, so it is critical that the network run smoothly.

Ask yourself: does the network meet the company's needs? Make sure that the network is robust enough not to be impacted when new security technologies are attached. Security cannot operate in a vacuum. Security generates its own load on the network; sa properly functioning network is your first and foremost concern.

If there is no security in place today, start by putting in a perimeter defense that will not impact internal operations. Then, the internal processes have to be put in order. With that done, the company can begin to address the next layers and extend the enterprise. It is also important that the policies are in place that push vendors to raise their security bar to a level that is acceptable for the organization to use them. External partners and external customers are just as large a part of the security infrastructure as anything else.

For example, Sarbanes-Oxley states that outsource functions must have the same controls in place for people, procedures and logical controls as the company itself. Therefore, a company that uses Telecheck now has Telecheck as part of its organization, and this can cause the company not to be SOX complaint if those controls are not in place. A company that has any functions outsourced, and is publicly traded or a partner to a publicly traded company, is affected, regardless of size.

The growing reliance on outsourcing is the perfect example of how the old distinctions, corporate or national, are now gray, at best. Cyberspace is a world without well-defined borders, redefining how we conduct business. Our economy has migrated from smokestacks to cybercash, and your security solutions must reflect this new reality.

■ ■ ■

Mehrzad Mahdavi is Vice President, Enterprise Security Services at Schlumberger. Dr. Mahdavi oversees global consulting and security services for enterprise clients in the energy industry. Previously, he was Vice President of Global Strategy and Consulting, providing strategic direction and M&A for all business units of Schlumberger Network and Infrastructure Solutions. He currently heads the global consulting services group, offering end-to-end network and security solutions.

Colin Elliott is the Global Practice Leader in the Enterprise Security practice at Schlumberger. His focus spans all areas, including physical and logical security considerations, ISO17799 assessments, and PKI design, and implementation and integration using smart cards for the oil and gas industry.

Mehrzad Mahdavi can be reached at 832-646-0648 or madavi@slb.com; Colin Elliott can be reached at 713-513-1112 or CElliot1@slb.com.

[4]

BLENDING CORPORATE GOVERNANCE WITH INFORMATION SECURITY

Securing your IT infrastructure should not be a one-time, ad hoc effort; it must be embedded within your daily operations. For too many companies, security is a knee-jerk reaction to an attack. Here's how to make data security an inherent, proactive and continual aspect of governance.

"CHARACTER IS MUCH EASIER KEPT THAN RECOVERED."
- Thomas Paine

by RON MORITZ

Top corporate managers pride themselves on being responsible leaders, but most have been remiss in at least one important sense: techno-introspection. They dutifully scrutinize cash flow and quarterly profits, but they tend to give scant thought to the security of their information systems.

CULTURAL POLITICS CONTINUE TO LIMIT THE ORGANIZATION'S ABILITY TO BRING VARIOUS INTERESTS TOGETHER TO EMBRACE INFORMATION SECURITY, TO ENSURE GOOD CORPORATE GOVERNANCE.

If you ask a typical manager, "Where does information security reside in your enterprise?", he or she might answer by jerking an indifferent thumb at the IT center. No CFO lists the value of "data" on a balance sheet, yet without data, a company ceases to function. Perhaps it's time for corporate leaders to rethink their priorities.

Back in the Nineties, managers believed that the IT center was where computer security started and ended, because that was where the appropriate professionals kept an eye on information assets and kept those assets under control. Cybersecurity was buried in the periphery of the organization, relegated to a strange little group of people who no one else really understood, charged with defending, at all costs, the information assets of the enterprise.

In those days, if the information security professionals were consulted at all about business strategies, it was well after those strategies were developed and articulated. They were unpopular because it was their job to come in and say "no." No, we can't add more services to that project. No, we can't grant more people access to systems and applications; we can't add bandwidth; we can't deploy this powerful new solution.

They stood their ground, claiming that such actions open up holes and make us more vulnerable. Sure, the projects and plans may also open up new worlds of profitability for the organization, but that wasn't the concern. Information security acted much like the corporate lawyers — overly conservative and risk averse, coming in at the end of a project to list all the dangers associated with the course of action proposed, and, in effect, vetoing plans that could lead to business growth.

If that business model was ever viable, it certainly is not today. Yet, in enterprises both public and private, it stubbornly persists. Cultural politics continue to limit the organization's ability to bring various interests together to embrace information security, to ensure good corporate governance.

CORPORATE GOVERNANCE DEFINED

Today, it is understood that information security is something with touch points up-and-down the enterprise, and that every end-user must be given the tools to participate and engage in information security on their own. Information security is a personal decision, and everyone has an information security responsibility. Moreover, information security cannot be accomplished via remote control from a single point.

Information security must begin at the top, with the Board of Directors, the CEO and the executive management team. Something as important as the information assets of the enterprise, many of which are digital, cannot be cared for by individuals who have accountability, but not authority. Frequently, we find corporate asset protection departments charged with safeguarding the enterprise's physical infrastructure, buildings, plants and facilities, when the real assets reside on technology systems and move through electronic networks. What used to be delegated, relegated, and in a sense hidden away is now something that every corporate governor, every executive decision-maker and every business unit executive must be engaged in and be a part of for the enterprise to move forward and achieve its business objectives.

At its heart, executive management is about taking risks, while at the same time understanding and managing those risks at a level acceptable to the enterprise, its customers, partners and employees. Corporate governance is about understanding and evaluating risk against the upside potential of the proposed action; that is, balancing risk with growth.

Insider Notes: Every first-year business student learns about organizations that have gotten in trouble, even failed, when they took their eyes off the cash flow. Today's CEOs and boards put their organizations at risk when they take their eyes off the information flow. That's why information security must be integrated with the business at the highest levels, and not treated as a separate entity.

DATA SNAPSHOT

As we can see by the survey results, ISG is a relatively new topic. Cybersecurity experts are often too far in the trenches to see that information security has reached the boardroom and is a matter of compliance. Moreover, the results confirm that executives and others thinking about corporate governance are not yet thinking about how the security of their information systems impacts their systems of internal controls.

Do you have a knowledge of information security goverance?

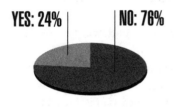

YES: 24%   NO: 76%

Download the complete research study for free at www.blackbooksecurity.com/research
Source: 2005 Larstan / Reed Infosecurity Survey

The flow of information can be as vital to business survivability as the flow of cash. Every first-year business student learns about organizations that have gotten in trouble, even failed, when they took their eyes off the cash flow. Today's CEOs and boards put their organizations at risk when they take their eyes off the information flow. That's why information security must be integrated with the business at the highest levels, and not treated as a separate entity.

In fact, information security is not that different than financial reporting. What CFO or COO can make appropriate business decisions without a solid understanding of the business? And when that business is dependent upon information technology, as most are today, what CEO can guide his organization and have confidence in executive decisions without understanding the risk to his or her IT infrastructure?

Corporate governors are intimately involved with the financial performance of the enterprise; they ensure that the CFOs and COOs are involved in the executive decision making. Clearly, today's successful corporate governors must understand the value of information technology to the company, frequently becoming intimately involved not only with financial applications, but with systems of control around those applications. So, too, must these governors become intimate with the information security infrastructure and ensure that the executive management team is involved in the information security (risk management) decision making.

For executive management and corporate boards to have such insight, security management must be integrated into the business like other management operations. To date, this has not been the case. Information security expertise must be called in early and participate in business development strategies from the ground up. For example, if a company is planning to build physical infrastructure in a developing nation, it must factor in risks right from the beginning.

Well understood risks may include regime changes or foreign currency exchange and fluctuations. Less understood but still addressed are the security risks of people, both to people and to physical property. Too often, however, information or cybersecurity is not considered until other plans have already been laid and execution of business goals begun, if not completed. Information security governance suggests that information security plans must be taken into consideration before and during the design of corporate plans and strategies. Information security risk must be considered with all the other data involved in executive decision making. If it is not, there is no responsibility, nor accountability, and a failure in corporate governance.

To simplify the point, consider playground risk management. For decades, the official strategy for managing playground injuries was to wait until they occurred and then to send the child to the nurse's office — or worse. Obviously, that's no strategy at all. Today, safety is built into the playground through rubberized ground, wood chips, rounded edges and whatever else the child safety experts can imagine might be worth developing. This seems obvious now, but how much damage was done before this

Insider Notes: Information security expertise must be called in early and participate in business development strategies from the ground up. For example, if a company is planning to build physical infrastructure in a developing nation, it must factor in risks right from the beginning.

change in playground risk management occurred, before someone realized that it was being done incorrectly? In the same way, light is being shed on the information security aspects of corporate governance, and it is clear that there is much room for improvement.

Through a new awareness, information security management, which has often been illogical, is evolving toward the logical. Companies building end-to-end applications are now considering end-to-end security. At every stage, the business value of the information assets are being assessed, vulnerabilities associated with those assets are being determined, protection mechanisms are being tailored and, based on real world requirements, risk to the enterprise is being reduced to an acceptable level aligned with business objectives. Obviously, this is not just a technology issue; it's a people and process issue as well.

IMPLICATIONS: A VIEW FROM THE TOP AND FROM THE BOTTOM

At the end of the day, information security governance is a rather simple concept: The CEO and other business heads that don't understand or recognize the importance of their information systems and technologies and do not invest in the security of these systems will fail. And by fail, we are not suggesting that business performance merely suffer. More and more, board members and CEOs are being called on to attest to the state of their operations from a legal and regulatory standpoint and, while they need to put trust in their CIOs, they cannot afford to internalize information security concepts.

As stated earlier, information security is no different than systems of control over financial accounting. As they've done for many years by personally attesting to the financial health of the business, so too must modern executives be prepared to attest to the health of their cyber-assets and be held accountable for their safety.

Although it must be overseen and directed from the top, the need for information security is as widely distributed as the information itself. There is no place in the organization that is left untouched, and no employee of the organization who does not have a responsibility in this regard. This, too, is a significant shift from the way organizations have traditionally viewed information security. Adding to the challenge, the responsibility does not end at the boundaries of the organization; it extends well into the enterprise's ecosystem. Customers, suppliers, partners, contractors, consultants and regulators are as accountable for cybersecurity as the many internal users of the organization's information assets.

If an aircraft manufacturer extends confidential engine data to maintenance engineers at an airline — information that is vital to share — both parties must recognize that this information has competitive value and must be protected to the same extent as any sensitive information. To take it a step further, it is not an overstatement to say that an organization's cybersecurity decisions can have even more far-reaching impact. It was Adam Smith, in *The Wealth of Nations,* who first pointed out that by working toward their own gain and in their own interests, individuals unintentionally provided benefits that improved the society in which they lived, as if by an "invisible hand." He was talking about 18th century laissez-faire economics, but he might as well have been talking about 21st century information security.

With the degree of interconnection in our critical infrastructure, about 85% of which is in private hands, the corporate governance actions taken to forward a company's own interests and protect its information assets also serve to safeguard national security. Unfortunately, the corollary also holds true — actions not taken not only denigrate the enterprise, but also denigrate national security.

This line of reasoning brings up the unpleasant specter of ultimate government intervention into private sector data security, under a banner of homeland security. This phenomenon offers, perhaps, greater incentive for each enterprise to take the initiative and integrate information security fully into its operations, and align it with corporate governance activities.

Insider Notes: Adding to the challenge, the responsibility does not end at the boundaries of the organization; it extends well into the enterprise's ecosystem. Customers, suppliers, partners, contractors, consultants and regulators are as accountable for cyber security as the many internal users of the organization's information assets.

A NEW GROUP OF I.T. SECURITY STAKEHOLDERS

The new face of corporate governance shines on a group of previously uninvolved information security stakeholders. These include The Board of Directors, the executive management team, the Legal Department, the Audit Department, Business Unit Leaders, operations chiefs and eventually every employee. In addition, every customer, supplier, partner and contractor in the company's greater networked ecosystem also has an interest. All are stakeholders who need to be aligned and attuned with the information security challenges that are faced by the enterprise. The overriding challenge for all is not only to assure the confidentiality, integrity and availability (CIA) of the organization's information assets, but also to be able to manage, measure and communicate that assurance whenever and wherever necessary.

For senior managers there are now a number of validation requests that greatly expand their roles, responsibilities and oversight: information security presentations need to be created and delivered across the organization; responses to auditors prepared; compliance letters drafted; and Sarbanes-Oxley documents signed. All of these activities are required periodically or on regular cycles.

While there is greater involvement and more controls associated with more traditional types of business functions, such as budget requests, there is a higher degree of scrutiny applied to each decision and greater understanding required when handling them. Senior managers are finding that they need to draft responses regarding systems of control to multiple sources on a regular basis. What used to take place once a year in response to audit report findings is now happening on a continuum, with daily, weekly, monthly and quarterly reviews of information security conditions.

Make no mistake, this is an enormous challenge. Not only is this vying for time that could be spent on other matters, but it is also a real expense to retrofit business systems to support new information security requirements. At some point, a complete and coherent snapshot of the information security environment will be available in usable form on the push of a button. For now, of course, there are inconsistent results arriving from different systems with no standardization in reporting or measurement.

Increasing threats to IT systems require top managers to incorporate information security within the corporate governance frame. Information security must be strategically integrated into a holistic corporate governance model, one that truly supports the organization's business objectives. Executives who think of information security as a "project" or a "new initiative" will not succeed. Information security needs to be truly built in, layer by layer, and must be embraced as a business enabling capability and a viable component of healthy enterprise infrastructure management. Anything else is simply "band-aiding" security after the fact, and in today's world that is not acceptable.

TRADITIONAL CORPORATE GOVERNANCE

In the traditional model of corporate governance, information security has rarely been a top-of-mind consideration. While many components of the IT function have long been thought of as tools for supporting revenue goals and business objectives, information security was mainly relegated to the bowels of the organization: a technical discipline pushed down onto technologists. Today, information security is no less than a tool for business survivability and, therefore, it must be top of mind for business unit leaders.

In some progressive organizations, traditional or physical security and information security are being merged as executives come to understand that both fall under the umbrella of corporate governance. A department called corporate asset protection, responsible for the physical security of plant and infrastructure as well as executive protection, may be mislabeled and incomplete in a financial services or software company, where the primary assets live in electronic form.

Insider Notes: Increasing threats to IT systems require top managers to incorporate information security within the corporate governance frame. Information security must be strategically integrated into a holistic corporate governance model, one that truly supports the organization's business objectives. Executives who think of information security as a "project" or a "new initiative" will not succeed.

Today, physical security infrastructure such as closed-circuit television cameras are, in effect, cybersecurity tools because they leverage the data network in performing their mission: Security cameras transmit their data over the same data networks we use for email and accessing electronic transactions. Even popular media have embraced the obvious vulnerabilities convergence introduces, with movie plots portraying hackers redirecting or replacing streaming security video for their own ends. The Tom Cruise movie, *Mission: Impossible,* demonstrated how easy it is to inject and alter the video stream that was being transmitted over the existing computer network. Such physical control systems built in isolation from the IT network must be reworked to seamlessly leverage the fact that they run on top of the network infrastructure.

For example, it's easy to see that if you've placed cybersecurity in one part of your organization and physical security in the other, each may have its own continuity programs, but they may be disconnected if they are not joined by the common thread of corporate governance.

THE NEW CHALLENGE

To highlight how far behind we really are, we need only wonder why most systems fail to secure the link between physical and information security. It is remarkable that asset management technology, long considered a non-security technology used for operations and financial management, is only recently being considered a key component of cybersecurity. After all, how can you secure what you don't know? In addition, people, processes and technology are interconnected and can no longer be considered separate from one another, either from a business operations perspective or from a security perspective.

Solutions aren't just from one category or the other. For example, a company cannot simply put a technology in place in response to some issue. The problem must be viewed in a broader sense — who is involved, what are they doing, why are they doing it, what processes and what tools are they using? In that manner, the security issues become intertwined as well. While the people who have access to the network are presumably trusted employees, all the traditional security concerns still apply — theft, fraud, vandalism, misuse, or abuse of facilities and so forth. Companies need to clearly understand and articulate how people might interact with various systems and processes, including any potential malicious or fraudulent activities that may come into play.

It is not yet apparent how information security under corporate governance will be leveraged. However, it can be assumed that enterprises will naturally take a more practical, risk-based, business-based approach to information security, enabling the function to rise from the technical hinterlands to the operational environment inhabited by the executive management team and the Board of Directors. This is beneficial, of course, since those with the oversight responsibility are the ones ultimately responsible for compliance and reporting. Emphasis will be on ensuring there is not interference with information and transaction flows, as opposed to the more esoteric technical goals that have been guiding the art of information security: security for security's sake.

Bringing information security, or all security, into the realm of corporate governance will also support the continuing maturity of the science. Policies will extend beyond a single division, business unit or other entity and be considered at the enterprise level for consistency. Mature policies can help ensure that whatever division is involved, whether the company is using in-house staff or outsourcers in Virginia or Bangalore, the integrity of the information systems will remain as anticipated and as required to manage risk.

A NEW HOME FOR I.T. SECURITY?

There are many organizations today that would not recognize this model and still consider information security an "IT governance" responsibility owned exclusively by the CIO. They consider the IT group to be an

> **Insider Notes:** The Tom Cruise movie, *Mission: Impossible,* demonstrated how easy it is to inject and alter the video stream that was being transmitted over the existing computer network. Such physical control systems built in isolation from the IT network must be reworked to seamlessly leverage the fact that they run on top of the network infrastructure.

THE RISK FOR EXECUTIVES IN NOT UNDERSTANDING THEIR CHANGING ROLE IS VERY GREAT: THE SURVIVABILITY OF BOTH THE BUSINESS AND THEIR CAREER ARE AT STAKE IF THE NEW MODEL IS NOT ADOPTED.

internal services administrative department and, as such, do not give it the authority needed to run information security as an integral part of the business and not simply as a technical support function. Consequently, information security may not always be aligned with business objectives. In fact, the discussion is very similar to the one that took place between Internal Audit and the CFO over many years. The placement of the Internal Audit group, charged with reviewing internal controls, underneath the CFO, who owned those controls, was eventually understood to be a conflict of interest. It makes sense that placing the information security function underneath the CIO diminishes the authority of that function.

As long as the information security group remains inside the IT organization, their perspective will remain technology-driven and will not always encompass as strongly the goals embraced by the business divisions. As a consequence of the current thinking, information security and business unit staff clash frequently and the information security side is not viewed as partners and enablers, but as "no-men" and inhibitors to progress.

The IT department was probably never the right place for information security to live. Even when a potential security failure was viewed as simply resulting in a degradation of service or worse, the failure to achieve some business goals, this level of priority within the context of the business was probably not sufficient. With the knowledge that information security is a business survivability issue, it is clearly too important to be relegated that far outside the executive suite to someone with a title such as "IT Manager" or "Information Security Manager."

Of course, as the distinct approaches to security come together and as disciplines and mindsets merge, there can be cultural dysfunction along the way. Balance must be established. Which protocols are too onerous and a business (growth) burden, and which are inadequate and unaligned with the business risk objective? It can be imagined that when IT or security professionals relinquish control to the business units, the business leaders might step in and blindly violate a security or technical protocol. Obviously, organizations must mesh and align, else a dysfunctional structure emerges.

There is a valid school of thought that executive compensation and bonuses should be tied to security compliance results. One can imagine a day when a successful information security audit results in a bonus, while failure results in unattained personal financial goals. Again, taking a holistic approach, building the converged security organization from the ground up rather than reorganizing existing functions, linking compliance to a bonus point system or placing new objectives within existing organizations might be the keys to avoiding many missteps.

THE IMPLICATIONS OF NOT INTEGRATING SECURITY INTO GOVERNANCE

CEOs who do not understand the role of information systems in this current environment and who don't take the proper steps to ensure the survivability of their systems will fail, personally and professionally. The implications are severe and multifaceted. Nobody will have a job at the end of the day and the impact will be devastating, not only to employees and colleagues, but also shareholders, suppliers, customers and others in the greater corporate ecosystem. Further, there may very well be regulations violated, and there may be criminal, in addition to civil implications.

The risk for executives in not understanding their changing role is very great: the survivability of both the business and their career are at stake if the new model is not adopted. As we've highlighted, information security is no longer merely a technical discipline that can be relegated to a "techie" at some remote end of the organization; it is not simply about switching on an appliance or enabling software.

Insider Notes: There is a valid school of thought that executive compensation and bonuses should be tied to security compliance results. One can imagine a day when a successful information security audit results in a bonus, while failure results in unattained personal financial goals.

DATA SNAPSHOT

Do you think that information security governance must be embedded in the overall corporate governance structure in order to be effective?

The difference here is about the same as the results of the 2004 presidential elections, nearly a draw. The likely factor here is that the Sarbanes-Oxley legislation does not specifically highlight information systems in Section 404. Those answering the survey who understand that systems of control are based on information systems would have likely concluded that information security governance must be linked to corporate governance. However, those who do not understand how information systems are linked to internal control infrastructure likely concluded "no."

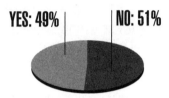

YES: 49%   NO: 51%

Download the complete research study for free at www.blackbooksecurity.com/research
Source: 2005 Larstan / Reed Infosecurity Survey

Information security is about an understanding that information systems and technology and data communication are tied into the survivability of the business or, perhaps more importantly, the potential failure of the business. And, unlike some other types of business issues of this magnitude, it's not a matter of simply making significant investments and enjoying automatic success. The implication to executive management is that if you don't take personal responsibility for information security, if you don't personally understand the issues, if you don't report on a regular basis, there is a real possibility you will fail. And that will affect everyone up and down the organization. Information security, therefore, is a corporate governance issue in the most literal and personal sense.

THE FIVE CORE PRINCIPALS OF CORPORATE GOVERNANCE

Information security is a process that requires the active engagement of senior management. For many public companies, the deadline for implementing Section 404 of the Sarbanes-Oxley Act of 2002 arrived on November 15, 2004. Along with this deadline arrived an increased focus on the effectiveness of internal control systems, which for the most part, are information systems that must be secured.

In trying to understand how corporate governance intersects with cyber-security policy and framework, it is vital to keep in mind that solutions must take into account not only technology, but also people and process. Each will have their place as the organization develops a truly business-based approach to security.

The business-based approach to information security understands that this is not just another technology. Rather, cybersecurity must be considered in connection with business goals. Information security is an important part of the overall business risk and the external business environment that must be intimately understood by the stewards of the business. In establishing this approach, there are five principles that will help guide executive thinking.

❶ CEO Involvement

The first principle is that the CEO must get involved in the understanding of the security program, the measurement of that program and the relation that program has to business operations. The CEO must take the lead in requiring regular reporting, evaluation and review of information security strategies and execution. He or she must engage with management teams throughout the enterprise to discuss what the security results look like, how security might impact the business, and how risk might be created or alleviated. He must then provide an overall assessment of the organization's security performance, including what is being done well, and what is being done to correct previously identified deficiencies. This assessment must be communicated to the board as well as to shareholders, stakeholders and employees.

Insider Notes: The business-based approach to information security understands that this is not just another technology. Rather, cybersecurity must be considered in connection with business goals. Information security is an important part of the overall business risk and the external business environment that must be intimately understood by the stewards of the business.

A good example is what is traditionally done around accounting systems in order to meet regulatory and shareholder responsibilities. Risk assessments today, when they are being done at all, are too often relegated to technicians isolated in the hinterlands of the organization. This process needs to be brought upwards to the executive management suite, translated into real world business terms, and handled formally at the highest levels.

❷ Organizational Understanding of Information Assets

The second principle is that the organization itself has to understand that information assets must be thought of as being as measurable and as tangible as buildings and plants and other valuable business infrastructure. Day-to-day policies and procedures need to reflect the fact that it is up to the organization to protect these assets in the same way.

The policies and the procedures that the company creates have to be well thought out, so the culture is built with the understanding that there is some level of risk involved with the normal day-to-day business use of information assets. These assets need to be cared for and protected accordingly. Appropriate individuals within a security management infrastructure must be given both authority and accountability; one without the other is not sufficient.

Today, the majority of information security officers are often given authority without accountability. For corporate security to be a serious endeavor, these managers must be empowered. Moreover, organizational cultural politics must be overcome so that the newly empowered security executives can engage with business leaders. The IT group can't fix information security alone; modeling risk enterprise requires a broad mandate and cooperation between groups inside the organization who may not have traditionally worked together.

Policies and procedures must make it plain that everyone who has any interaction with the corporate data assets has specific responsibilities, as well as the authority and the authorization, to proceed to protect those assets and to manage the risk inherent in using them. If you are an information security manager in New York and you can't physically manage a particular cybersecurity function in Chicago, you must assign the authority and the accountability to one of your local reports, as you'd do with any vital local business or operational issue.

❸ Integrating Data Storage with the System Lifecycle

Data that is stored on physical systems must not be distinct or separate from the system lifecycle. People would traditionally say, "That's the financial management system", or "That's the HR system", and then create lifecycle management around those applications without necessarily thinking about the individual data assets that reside on that system. We must begin to follow the information and not the system. If this were better understood, the process of information security would likely be different.

For example, consider the financial services sector, where the Gramm-Leach-Bliley Act (GLBA) controls what institutions can do with customer data. Customers receive notices that say that if they don't want the institution to share the data with third parties, they have the opportunity to inform the institution of this desire and the institution will comply. But the way that the systems have been developed and designed, there is merely a field or data element within the data store that says "allow" or "do not allow." The decision is simply another bit set in another field stored with the customer record. There is still no control around the use of individual fields or data elements associated with the customer record. The information, some of it more sensitive than others, is there and visible to certain individuals.

Questions left open include whether these individuals are trained to understand their responsibilities, vis-à-vis this data. Can the restricted information be accidentally released? How do we know that we're complying with the customer's request? Can we validate our compliance? What would the damage be to the customer, and to the organization if data that we were supposed to safeguard were released accidentally? Would the organization be open to lawsuit, damage to reputation

Insider Notes: Appropriate individuals within a security management infrastructure must be given both authority and accountability; one without the other is not sufficient.

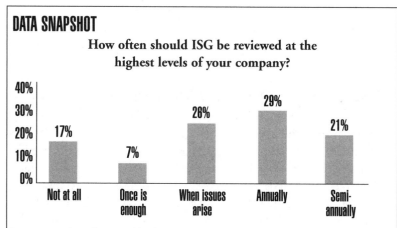

DATA SNAPSHOT

How often should ISG be reviewed at the highest levels of your company?

It appears that there might be a correlation between those who answer annually or semi-annually and those who concluded that ISG and Corporate Governance (previous question) are linked. This makes sense given that those who see a link between ISG and CG would also conclude that the board and executive management team need regular (annual, semi-annual) updates while those who do not see a link (answered "no" to the previous survey question) would not see a need to brief the highest levels on issues of ISG.

Download the complete research study for free at www.blackbooksecurity.com/research
Source: 2005 Larstan / Reed Infosecurity Survey

or regulatory action? Information management and information security must become better aligned and integrated into the way the organization develops, installs, deploys, uses, maintains, monitors and validates the systems that house them.

❹ Systems Must Be Tested

These security systems must be exercised. For example, a traditional accounts payable system dealing with employee reimbursements for travel and entertainment is probably one of the most reviewed systems within a company. There are a series of clerks who reconcile the data that is input against the receipts that are submitted, and then they do follow-ups to validate the information.

This is a well established and understood system of control that is well tested. As we look at the testing around our traditional information systems, there really hasn't been external oversight over the security systems and testing to ensure that these systems are, in fact, functioning. Moreover, many of these systems and applications, along with the information security "band-aids", were never designed to be tested and reviewed from the outside.

The concept of governance demands that we evaluate the information security services that have been implemented and find a way to validate that they are working. Testing needs to be done periodically and, as a formal way of responding to defects — breaches and violations — needs to be established. There also needs to be a way to evaluate and correct deficiencies, as well as a mechanism to communicate the fact that re-mediation has taken place. Just as you cannot secure what you don't know, you can't establish confidence that information security services are functioning without testing and reporting.

Also important is the speed in which a deficiency is remediated and effectively addressed. Information security governance suggests that the company must have a security knowledge management capability not only to understand IT risk, but also to be able to test readiness. Security knowledge management is the ability to transform raw data into information, and information to knowledge.

Think of a central command center in a field of battle. A field commander is presented with an overwhelming amount of information and is required to make decisions based on the knowledge developed from that information. The quality of the information varies yet he must make a command or executive decision based on knowledge derived from that information.

Insider Notes: There are instances where companies have leveraged information security advantages to become leaders in a particular area, inflicting such pain that competitors actually outsourced capability from the leader or innovator. This idea of leveraging information security as a competitive advantage is a valid strategy for some companies.

The commander may be looking at his supply chain, troop location, existing offensive and defensive capabilities, along with peripheral information like weather and topography, intelligence on enemy positions and tactics, and more. And he also needs to understand the relative reliability of each piece of information: some will be assumed highly accurate, others of dubious quality. The commander mixes all of this information in the central command "mixing pot" in order to develop knowledge through which appropriate action can be initiated.

Similarly, information security governance suggests that organizations must establish an incident response capability to deal with crisis. This crisis center operates in a continuous mode just like the commander's central command center in a field of battle. Once this knowledge is obtained, then it is possible to translate that into remedial action to deal with the deficiencies and the information security challenges. Then, just like a field commander who might continually exercise troop readiness, company executives can continuously evaluate enterprise response capability by launching exercises to validate information security readiness.

❺ Comparative Analysis

The fifth principle, every bit as important as the others, is that it is vital for organizations to analyze where they stand in their information security governance efforts compared to others in their industry. The financial services industry is a very good example where most organizations want to be in the middle of the herd, neither desiring to lead or follow. They fear being perceived as either overly conservative or overly aggressive, hence the desire to remain more safely and invisibly in the middle of the herd. Many banks today, in response to the new threat of phishing, simply hope to be less visible to the bad guys than another bank, a short-sighted strategy not unlike the idea of using "The Club" around an automobile steering column to make a vehicle less desirable to a thief. In this regard, resist the herd mentality, which can lead you right off a cliff.

Perhaps a better strategy is to have the ability to make informed, strategic decisions as to the company's place in the pack by knowing what others in the industry and the marketplace are doing with respect to securing their information and by studying standards and "best guidance." This enables the organization to decide what its investment and commitment to information security should be, above and beyond any established mandatory minimums, based on a risk-analysis. One might look at maximums instead, choosing to be ahead of the pack and using information security governance superiority as a competitive advantage.

There are instances where companies have leveraged information security advantages to become leaders in a particular area, inflicting such pain that competitors actually outsourced capability from the leader or innovator. This idea of leveraging information security as a competitive advantage is a valid strategy for some companies. Alternatively, the company might make an informed decision to be a laggard in this area, establishing the bare minimum and using the capital instead to seek competitive advantage in other areas. That company will accept and manage its added exposure, but will have made an informed business decision that investment in other areas is more valuable. This, too, is a valid business decision.

One caveat: companies must be sure that this conclusion is reached by choice and not by ignorance. A bonus is that this type of analysis, using real world external guideposts, will not only help establish a strategic position in the marketplace, it will also provide valuable insights into internal company operations.

FRAMING A SUCCESSFUL INFORMATION ACCESS SECURITY PLAN

A successful security plan to control and manage access to corporate information is comprehensive in scope and assures an enterprise, its suppliers and its customers that the business will continue its operations during a disaster. It ensures that the right transactions will be aligned with the right consumers of data and information.

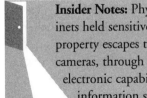

Insider Notes: Physical security used to be king. Locked file cabinets held sensitive corporate information. Today, intellectual property escapes through the USB port or SD cards on digital cameras, through email, instant messaging, and several other electronic capabilities. Consequently, leadership for information security governance must come from the top.

However, that's just the baseline. Any successful security plan will also identify risks to a business and how an enterprise would respond in each risk scenario to protect sensitive information, as well as to ensure that information needed to continue business operations gets to the right place. Such a plan would also identify the responsibilities of all key players, from the board and CEO at the top, to employees on the front line.

A well conceived plan meets two tests:

❶ The plan is described after it has been drafted and tested with the participation of board members, the executive leadership, line managers, employees and those outside the enterprise who would be directly impacted.

❷ It produces reports that describe in detail how the plan performs when tested.

As part of the information security governance framework, the plan must describe how it will actually provide security for networks, for systems, for applications and for individual members of the company's ecosystem, in addition to company employees. The ecosystem includes suppliers, business partners and customers. There are a number of reference models that are commonly used, such as ISO 17799, and Control Objectives for Information and Related Technology (COBIT) and the Generally Accepted Information Security Principals.

Practices vary, but they have one thing in common: they help enterprises assess risk within the structure of a reference standard. It's important to consider policies and procedures that address the security risk, including evaluation of life cycles. The plan should also describe the awareness and training that are being offered employees, suppliers, contractors and customers.

TESTING THE PLAN

Periodic testing is critical, especially of those actions that will be taken by operations staff. These tests must be monitored. When it comes to testing cybersecurity, procedures need to be more rigorous than the fire drills that are commonly practiced in the realm of physical security. A company needs to:

- Include remedial action taken as the result of test results
- Be alert to how response procedures can affect daily operations

■ Take into account the need to amend the business continuity plan to reflect changes in the information security, including information access, that result from testing

The results of these tests must be reported. Effective reports must meet several criteria:

■ Their findings can be independently verified
■ They accurately convey that risk levels attained during tests are within the acceptable limits defined in the written plan
■ The mechanisms of the tested procedures are open, capable of being audited and reportable

THE FIVE AREAS OF RESPONSIBILITY

An organization that will be successful in implementing an information security governance program needs to divide the work across five areas:

❶ **The Board of Directors.** The program must be very clear about the board's responsibilities. It will assign strategic oversight to the board, and ensure that the strategic oversight is aligned with the actions taken by the executive management team.

❷ **The CEO.** CEO responsibilities will be clearly defined in regard to accountability and authority. The CEO is the top executive and the only one in a position to oversee compliance. It is the CEO's role to assign the responsibility to make sure that accountability and authority are in place. The CEO is also there to set the tone and drive the culture of information security.

❸ **Executive Committee.** The executive committee will be responsible for ensuring that the security programs being put in place are actually aligned with operational and business goal risks. Not too much, and not too little. They must make certain that money is not being wasted on unneeded security and that security is not placing an undue bur-

Insider Notes: Instead of viewing continuity of operations as a "silo" concept, approach it as a quality that must be embedded into all corporate functions. Integrate security and continuity procedures throughout the enterprise, to make them a part of daily operational reality. Hackers and terrorists plan ahead; so should you.

DATA SNAPSHOT

Since 9/11, even the federal government has recognized that we cannot protect the critical infrastructure, from physical attack without considering the cyber infrastructure since the two are intimately related. Beyond considering both physical and cybersecurity, it is clear from the results of this question that

Should recovery and business continuity plans be a part of the ISG?

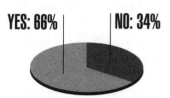

YES: 66% | NO: 34%

business continuity planners must also contribute to our overall enterprise security. At the end of the day it is about our responsibility as caretakers of data and information. Without this data and information, we will not be able to complete transactions. Consequently, BCP is in fact part of the ISG program.

Download the complete research study for free at www.blackbooksecurity.com/research
Source: 2005 Larstan / Reed Infosecurity Survey

den on the organization and adversely affecting operations and business objectives.

❹ **Senior Managers.** Senior management will have responsibility for day-to-day monitoring of risks within their area of responsibility. They're accountable for the mechanisms implementing the policies coming out of the security program and for ensuring that operations are secure.

❺ **Employees.** Each individual employee must be aware of the challenges of information security. Ultimately, security is a very personal matter, so each member of the enterprise should have an understanding of information security and why it's important. They should know their individual roles, so they can report accurately through channels. Just as we are trained to ask an un-badged person we see walking through our building, so too should we, as individuals, be taught to challenge information security deficiencies that we encounter.

BUILDING A PLAN FROM THE GROUND UP

Information risk programs should be designed by cross-functional teams. This will ensure that stakeholders across the enterprise, as well as up and down the business hierarchy, are aware of current risk objectives, as well as the baseline acceptable level of risk that will determine how an enterprise will respond to attacks including natural disasters. The ecosystem in which the enterprise is operating should also be included, if possible. Every entity has an ecosystem; even a government agency has a contingency it serves.

A good starting point is to realize that when a business is enabled, information technology is aligned with business practices and business goals. Extending that concept, the value of information is greatest when it is allowed to flow out of the enterprise to customers and to business partners. That's where the security maturity model referred to in part one comes into play: the security of inclusion, exclusion and accountability.

The security of exclusion battens down the hatches and closes off information. That is the baseline, or foundation. Next is a goal to sustain the flow of information that supports critical business needs. The flow addresses support for the most important internal business plans, like growth, as well as providing information to external groups that are key to a company's success.

The security of inclusion is the second step. In this step, business leaders who are responsible for third-party relationships must be engaged in the planning, design, prototyping and implementation of an access management system that allows an enterprise to manage its relationships with third-parties. For example, corporate channel managers need to move information to and from the third-parties when important information from third-parties is received; it needs to get delivered to the appropriate parties so it can be factored into the goods and services that keep the enterprise in business.

Information security governance means that management has a way to control this information flow and report on its performance. This is not a completely new way of thinking. But to do it in the context of a structured plan that evaluates information integrity, confidentiality and availability, applying these assessments against risk management, as related to the new business "enablement" capability, is a new way of perceiving the classic processes of access management.

INFORMATION RISK PROGRAMS SHOULD BE DESIGNED BY CROSS FUNCTIONAL TEAMS.

THE NEED FOR ACCESS CONTROL — AND BEYOND

A second best practice within the framework of governance is the need for a broader capability around access authorization control. Clearly, there is a need for a third-party access management system. But beyond that, there's also a need to define relationships and support operations that enable it to provide services to link the business information logically with resources, access controls and various risk profiles that are associated with the different risk scenarios. In other words, it's not simply about information security in isolation.

Several years ago a movement began to bring cyber and physical security together. Physical security classically is the gates, guards, and guns that control entry to a facility. Prior to 9/11, the two types of security were not considered together. Post 9/11, we attempted to bring two cultures together: Cybersecurity folks who were, for the most part, self-taught, while physical security folks came from disciplined professions such as law enforcement. The people interested in information security were engineers at heart, and the two security cultures did not mesh. There was no cooperation. There was no enterprise authorization mechanism or process that controlled access to both plant and network and that included both the cyber and physical components.

Physical security used to be king. Locked file cabinets held sensitive corporate information. Today, intellectual property escapes through the USB port or SD cards on digital cameras, through email, instant messaging and several other electronic capabilities. Consequently, leadership for information security governance must come from the top. Fortunately, most executives understand that corporate asset protection extends well beyond access to paper and file cabinets. As such, it is important to understand that these two mechanisms, authorization and access controls, go hand in hand.

DEFINING RISK FOR GLOBAL OPERATIONS

Risk profiles have to support control models that are aligned with business strategies and new business capabilities and services. For example, a company may look to expand into a geographical market that is not familiar with western business principals and ethics.

In those emerging nations, the manufacturing plants of today leverage information technology to support just-in-time inventory management and enterprise resource planning. No enterprise would envision building a plant in a remote market if it couldn't leverage the competitive advantages developed in the home market, which includes competitive advantages derived from investments in information systems and technology.

Therefore, it is necessary to think through how the enterprise authorization control systems work together to design the right control models that match the business goals for expansion. A manufacturing company building business plans for growth in Asia, for example, must build information security into those new business capabilities in the same way it builds a foundation for the physical plant.

It is not glamorous, but it is the base on which the business is built and managed. You must look at the overall access control framework and then logically link business information and resource access scenarios with risk profiles. In that way, control models will match the business, and be aligned with the new business models, capabilities, and services.

IDENTITY MANAGEMENT

Another best practice is the issue of identity management. Companies have developed islands of identity. There are multiple identities the enterprise assigns customers and suppliers, as well as employees. The enterprise must now consider the idea of entitlements and the strategies involved for planning a common security infrastructure that can be leveraged across all business units and all the relationships with suppliers, customers and employees. Information security governance requires an understanding of federation that will enable the construction of a universal identity or entitlement infrastructure that can be shared with others.

BUSINESS CONTINUITY PLANNING

In many instances, an unstructured attack impacts business operations, but does not necessarily impact the survivability of the business. Business continuity anticipates how different attacks will impact the enterprise and includes plans to address the various disaster scenarios, both natural and manmade. It's important to differentiate between disaster recovery, which is singular, and business continuity, which is an ongoing activity.

Disaster recovery basically deals with the issue of capability not being available and the need to switch over to an auxiliary capability. Ultimately, this is the ability to differentiate between structured attacks that may impact business survivability and unstructured attacks, which may only degrade capability or services, possibly only temporarily.

Instead of viewing continuity of operations as a "silo" concept, approach it as a quality that must be embedded into all corporate functions. Integrate security and continuity procedures throughout the enterprise, to make them a part of daily operational reality. Hackers and terrorists plan ahead; so should you.

SECURITY EXPERIENCE MANAGEMENT

We are experiencing a convergence of the need for reliability, privacy and accountability. Commerce and IT are interconnected in ways that could not have been envisioned a generation ago. Data security and privacy concerns are pervasive, while threats include situations that are simultaneously intentional and difficult to quantify and anticipate. The only logical response to the requirement to maintain financial integrity, investor confidence and sustainable operations, is a program with a comprehensive approach to corporate governance as it relates to information management, security and availability. Security experience management is one method that allows us to begin to manage security from a business perspective.

As Thomas Paine wrote, "Character is much easier kept than recovered." Character comes from strong leadership. Leaders with integrity and respect naturally motivate an organization toward compliance. Such leaders establish a culture of compliance. Some even recognize the opportunity to differentiate their firms, even creating competitive advantage in the marketplace, through a strong corporate DNA around governance.

As we enter the second half of the first decade of the 21st century, across the board we find that restoring investor confidence requires a strong character. Boards recognize that it is not possible to regulate integrity. Rather, integrity is a key quality they now seek when searching for a CEO. To restore investor confidence they seek a chief executive who can restore integrity in the market. Such an executive understands that restoring confidence requires personal engagement and active risk management. This executive must be aware of all weaknesses associated with systems of internal controls. As such, if he is not tuned into the idea that his internal controls are dependent upon information systems and technologies, he will fail in his mission of creating a culture of compliance.

Managing compliance is a cross-departmental effort, and, at the end of the day, the CEO is responsible and personally accountable. The CIO can be indicted if control breakdowns are not reported. Responsibility and accountability continue to evolve, and enterprises will find themselves reacting through policies and processes that achieve the required results, an expensive way to run a business. One opportunity that lies ahead for executives is driving down not only the risk, but also the costs of compliance by standardizing on a particular set of platforms and tools. Leveraging partnerships with information systems and technology solution providers to establish out-of-the-box usage enables organizations to maximize compliance-oriented services and applications.

Finally, a word of caution: Compliance for compliance sake is not a sustainable venture. This is not a temporary phenomenon like Y2K. While many have suggested that we simply need Y2K-like leadership and focus to address issues of cyber-security, system auditability and compliance, it is unlikely that such a program, a onetime initiative, will yield prolonged results. It turns out that cyber security is more like quality assurance, a process of continuous improvement.

As Orson Swindle, commissioner of the Federal Trade Commission, has pointed out, there is no single technological bullet to solve the challenge we face in strengthening the information security that supports our nation's physical security and supports global commerce. As such, information security is not a technical issue, but rather a corporate governance

INSTEAD OF VIEWING CONTINUITY OF OPERATIONS AS A "SILO" CONCEPT, APPROACH IT AS A QUALITY THAT MUST BE EMBEDDED INTO ALL CORPORATE FUNCTIONS.

responsibility that involves risk management, reporting on controls, testing, training and executive accountability.

Without the active engagement of business unit leaders, executive management teams and boards of directors, a sustainable information security program cannot exist. This is no longer a technical problem relegated to the bowels of the enterprise. This is a challenge that requires a coherent information security management framework that aligns with the set of policies and internal controls used by enterprises to establish a culture of compliance and that will support the implementation of information security programs across all industries.

When we work with people on the betterment of the business, systems and network — managing the people, processes and technology from a business perspective — we end up with smart end-users who are engaged in the business. When we engage leaders of strong character who protect the business and the quality of the business, then we will have more secure systems as a natural end product. The goal is to create safer operating conditions across the critical infrastructure, which taken together, will also help to protect our national security interests. Without forward progress, possible only through executive attention, we can expect only more regulation.

The time to embrace information security governance is now. Integration of information security into the core of enterprise management and governance must come about. And, focusing on security experience management will allow us to begin to manage security from a business perspective.

■ ■ ■

Ron Moritz is Senior Vice President and Chief Security Strategist at Computer Associates. He is responsible for maintaining CA's technical lead in world-class information security software by shaping the strategic direction of CA's eTrust™ security solutions brand. Ron joined CA after founding Moritz Technology Corporation, a management advisory firm serving emerging security technology companies and the venture capital community. Earlier, he served as Senior Vice President and CTO of Symantec Corporation and as CTO of Finjan Software. As an internationally recognized cybersecurity expert, Ron is a spokesperson to the business community on security issues, solutions, and strategies.

He serves as co-chair of the U.S. Department of Homeland Security National Cyber Security Summit Task Force on Security across the Software Development Lifecycle. He also is a member of the U.S. Chamber of Commerce Homeland Security Policy Committee and co-chair of the subcommittee on Security and Privacy. Previously, he served as a member of the U.S. delegation to the G8 meetings on international cybercrime and cyberterrorism. Ron can be reached at 631-342-6213 or ron.moritz@ca.com.

[5]
IDENTITY-AWARE BUSINESS SERVICE MANAGEMENT: AN INTEGRATED APPROACH TO SECURITY AND BUSINESS PERFORMANCE

The implementation of Business Service Management (BSM) brings a comprehensive change in how a company views its IT infrastructure and assets. Notably, it allows a company to deduce the most critical components of its IT systems based on a business metric.

"THE MOST VALUABLE COMMODITY I KNOW OF IS INFORMATION."
- Gordon Gekko, in the movie *Wall Street*

by SOMESH SINGH AND RAMI ELRON

With each passing day, the world becomes driven more and more by information. Proprietary information is our chief competitive asset, and our livelihood depends on our ability to protect it.

THE IMPLEMENTATION OF BSM REQUIRES A COMPREHENSIVE CHANGE IN HOW A COMPANY VIEWS ITS INFORMATION TECHNOLOGY INFRASTRUCTURE AND INFORMATION TECHNOLOGY ASSETS.

And yet, too many companies don't take a holistic approach to data management and security. That's where Business Service Management (BSM) comes into the picture.

BSM is an "identity-aware" approach that enables companies to realize significant security and business performance benefits. In this chapter, we'll explain BSM, review the advantages of implementing it and discuss the procedures companies should consider for an effective implementation.

We'll also examine Identity Management (IdM) and its key attributes, as well as its value proposition when combined with BSM. Identity-aware BSM offers many advantages, and Identity Management is critical in addressing key BSM requirements of security, as well as connecting people to processes.

In addition, we'll explain how IdM completes a BSM solution and offers best practice recommendations. We'll also outline key business cost alleviation and revenue enhancement issues and use case studies to illustrate BSM implementation.

BUSINESS SERVICE MANAGEMENT: WHAT IS IT?

BSM is a method for assessing the impact of IT asset availability and performance on a company's business objectives, by correlating between a company's services and IT assets (hardware, software, networking, etc.) upon which it depends. With BSM, each company service (e.g., a financial services firm developing a quarterly investment performance report for customers) is mapped to the systems and applications required for support of its creation, management and termination.

This differs from the traditional view of technology management which examines and assesses each component of an IT infrastructure as a separate, independent element. Each system component is evaluated according to its reliability and availability, which in turn results in an "uptime" metric that's utilized as a measure of effectiveness.

Consider measurement of availability of a storage array in an enterprise. The fact that, in the last 12 months a storage array has been "up" 99.9% of the time, in itself, has no reference back to the mission of the company or the services that the company provides to its customers. This is especially true if the 0.1% of downtime had negatively affected a critical company operation. Still, this IT-centric view prevails and drives companies to invest increasing amounts of money in technology that may provide greater speed, more storage or higher throughput, but might not appropriately address its critical business needs.

The implementation of BSM requires a comprehensive change in how a company views its IT infrastructure and IT assets. A company begins the process by identifying and recording a comprehensive set of services that it provides to customers and prioritizing these services according to its corporate mission or other metric.

Each of these services is then mapped to the systems and applications that are needed to deliver them. The combination of these two steps — mapping of services to IT systems components and prioritization of these services — allows a company to deduce the most critical components of its IT systems based on key business metrics. For example, it is more important to understand the impact of a system or application's availability to the corporate mission or on a business objective, rather than on an IT metric.

Deployment of such metrics assists the company in determining which system component failures call for immediate action, and in determining how to prioritize remediation in the face of multiple failures competing for attention. This ultimately provides a clear view of IT importance to business line management.

 Insider Notes: Linking the identity of people and their roles in delivering business services is a critical aspect of an effective BSM solution.

CASE STUDY: GHOSTS IN THE MACHINE

Key problems: high labor costs, proliferation of "ghost-IDs," non-compliance with industry standards.

The challenge: a telecommunications company with employees deployed in 39 countries needed to deliver language specific support to its growing customer base. The company also was adding employees who needed proper access rights to applications, servers and data.

How the company originally dealt with the challenge: The company needed to establish and enforce appropriate access policies to its information assets, to give appropriate employees access to the right information in a timely manner. To accomplish this goal, the company assigned a large number of people to manage user access for specific applications and files. This incurred a high overhead cost to the company and also resulted in effort duplication that negatively impacted the company's effort to meet its Service Level Agreements (SLAs).

How Identity-Aware BSM helped address the challenge: The company decided to implement an IdM solution built around its business services. This system was installed to: (1) standardize levels of control for administrators; (2) minimize manual efforts for users to manage their IDs and passwords, and (3) protect corporate assets through comprehensive management of access.

With this approach, this company was able to:
- Reduce the number of people required to complete SLA around identity provisioning requests
- Institute self-service management of passwords and IDs
- Automate the de-provisioning process to eliminate "ghost" accounts

BSM, as described above, enables a company to map IT performance to each corporate service. However, there remains one additional asset consideration: the company's personnel. Linking the identity of people and their roles in delivering business services is a critical aspect of an effective BSM solution. With this additional knowledge, numerous processes are enhanced, including analysis of system failure impact, determination of priorities, as well as improving the delivery of business services to internal and external customers. Identities and the management of identity-related tasks are therefore key aspects of any comprehensive BSM solution. Consequently, no BSM initiative is complete without IdM.

IdM is a discipline that converges processes and technologies to create efficiencies in the organization, mitigate risk to the corporation's intellectual property and create fundamental compliance and audit capabilities. To begin implementing IdM, people and responsibilities are efficiently aligned with systems and applications. The next step is to assess the criticality of these assignments to the successful delivery of an identified business service — essentially mapping resources to services through people. This process ensures that people are granted access rights to required systems components in accordance with business service objectives, and are thus able to create appropriate value in the delivery of an important business service. Additionally, management of appropriate access rights according to predefined policies protects organizations from internal security breaches and allows forensic investigation of suspect activity.

WHY ARE IDM AND BSM IMPORTANT?

A company is characterized by the services and products it delivers, not by the systems that enable it to do so. Therefore, a company's focus on IT as an end to itself is misplaced. BSM provides a systematic approach to tying internal IT systems to corporate deliverables.

When IdM is implemented within a BSM environment, IT resources and corporate deliverables can be correlated with personnel, enabling a richer and more precise impact analysis, along with better support and maintenance practices. The ability to map the existing impact relationships among

Insider Notes: Ponder this: An uptime of "99.9%" might be considered by a company to be an acceptable availability target for many system components. However, if the downtime had an adverse impact on one or more critical business services, is the 0.1% downtime still acceptable?

AS PROCESSES BECOME MORE COMPLEX AND THE NEED FOR MORE INFORMATION TECHNOLOGY INFRASTRUCTURE COMPONENTS AND APPLICATIONS RISES, THE NEED TO PERCEIVE AND EVALUATE I.T. AS ASSETS INTEGRAL TO THE CORPORATE MISSION INCREASES.

IT systems, business services and user identities offer notable benefits:

- **Better system utilization.** An employee's interaction with an IT system component is prioritized according to the business services that are affected. This will more closely tie all IT utilization to the primary goals of the company.
- **Better internal communications.** When a system fails, the individuals affected by the failure are quickly identified. This will help prioritize problem resolution and reduce employee frustration, because they will be notified quickly when a key IT component or service that effects them goes down.
- **Better risk management.** By incorporating IdM tools, a BSM solution treats personnel as an additional resource type, whose availability greatly affects business services. Such a system identifies, for example, how the absence of a key person might impact the delivery of an important service.
- **Better security compliance.** If the IdM system is violated, the company determines which services can be operated within tolerances.

These impact relationships provide management visibility into how IT operations and their failures directly affect the company's bottom line. They also provide a higher level of IT security by mapping and prioritizing employee access to specific IT components.

IMPLEMENTATION CHECKLIST

The implementation of IdM in a BSM environment provides the insight that many companies need to assess IT investment in terms of business value and, more importantly, to control and understand who has access to key systems. Here's a checklist of questions that all companies need to consider for effective implementation:

- Can your company provide a comprehensive list of its goals and services and prioritize them according to a corporate mission?
- Is IT in your company a goal unto itself? Is the need for bigger, faster and more capacity related directly to a business mission or simply to IT performance? Can you define each IT system in terms of its effect on the company's bottom line?
- Who has access to your systems? Can you quickly identify who can use specific system components or applications and quantify their access?
- If your system experiences multiple failures, how do you prioritize remediation? Is it by IT preference or by service impact? Can you identify the personnel affected by an IT infrastructure component failure? Does this information work into your prioritization decision?
- Do you know who has access to your key intellectual property, and can you quantify the level of risk you are assuming?
- In case of interruption in a service delivery or breech of security without an impact on IT element performance, are you able to conduct a forensic investigation to pinpoint the source of the breech?
- Are you able to audit and comply under various regulatory requirements, such as Sarbanes-Oxley, HIPAA, Basel II and others?

As processes become more complex and the need for more IT infrastructure components and applications rises, the need to perceive and evaluate IT as assets integral to the corporate mission increases. BSM provides this capability. With IT assets becoming more strategic, the need to manage access grows. IdM provides the visibility into IT asset usage necessary to manage both security and performance.

A NEW APPROACH

The traditional approach of information technology planning and measurement is focused on the investment needs and performance of individual components. Companies deploy a point solution with all metrics used to monitor system performance referenced to the technology. Each hardware component, software application, and networking/communications device

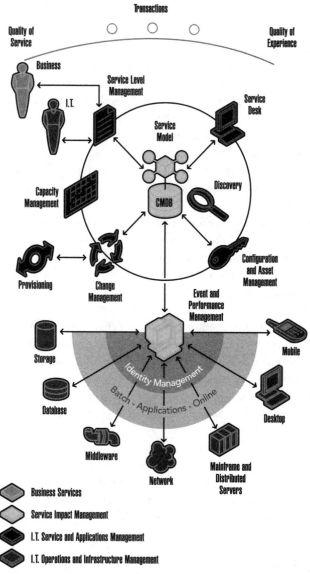

This chart details how identity-aware BSM addresses critical company business requirements, by utilizing identity management. Viewing from the bottom up, identity management is applied to all devices and applications on the network. This information is fed into a configuration management data base, where it is combined with the service model and used as input in both configuration and asset management and change management processes. It is also used to drive service level management and to derive performance metrics.

BSM ENABLES COMPANIES TO FOCUS ON RESOURCE EFFECTIVENESS IN LIEU OF RESOURCE EFFICIENCY, AND ALLOWS THE PRIORITIZATION OF CRITICAL COMPANY PROCESSES AND THE OPTIMIZATION OF THOSE RESOURCES AND SERVICES.

is evaluated as an independent entity and not in reference to how its availability might affect business.

In companies with more mature IT processes, Service Level Agreements (SLA) based around groups of IT elements specify key performance, availability and reliability metrics expected from system components. Hence, when assessing performance, companies are not considering the full range of things that need to be considered and measured. Each system component is assessed according to its own efficiency and effectiveness. An uptime metric is often employed to determine how well a component has performed over a period of time. In other words, the uptime metric indicates the efficiency of a component, and in light of its past or promised performance, this metric is either viewed as acceptable or not acceptable.

Ponder this: An uptime of "99.9%" might be considered by a company to be an acceptable availability target for many system components. However, if the downtime had an adverse impact on one or more critical business services, is the 0.1% downtime still acceptable? And, is this component's efficiency higher than that of another device that may have a 99.9% uptime rating but is always available when needed to perform in a critical business service?

Insider Notes: Companies need to prioritize business services and focus on a handful of key processes first. This will allow their employees to reap initial successes, learn from their experiences, and understand how BSM works.

CASE STUDY: GOVERNMENT IDENTITY CRISIS

Key problem: an inability to enforce security policies.

The challenge: This government agency has thousands of employees who are required to manage information on millions of citizens. This information is highly confidential and the service that the agency is required to provide must meet strict high-level expectations.

In addition, agency security administrators manage a variety of disparate environments and separate sources of information that must be consolidated for overall audit and tracking purposes. The agency ultimately requires a comprehensive view of resource access activity, such as who has access to what and who has accessed what.

A solution that strengthened password policies, kept help-desk calls down and improved the quality of service provided by its employees was an important agency goal.

How the agency originally dealt with the challenge: The agency had never before implemented a comprehensive password policy that could enforce expirations and strengthen the password selection strategy. As a result, regular changes to passwords placed an enormous burden on the administrators and help-desk personnel.

How Identity-Aware BSM helped address the challenge: The agency decided to implement an IdM solution. The solution empowered the agency with the ability to automate identity management-related tasks that have previously demanded allocation of many employees. The solution offered the following additional benefits:
- Reduced number of help-desk calls concerning password reset by up to 80%
- Established real-time synchronization of identity information
- Initiated password expiration and strengthened policy enforcement

BSM enables companies to focus on resource effectiveness in addition to the traditional focus on resource efficiency, thus allowing the prioritization of critical company processes and the optimization of those resources and services. Even better, by employing an identity management approach, BSM maps the most important asset of a company, its people, into the delivery of these services.

INCREASING EFFECTIVENESS WITH IDENTITY-AWARE BSM

Identity management is a discipline that correlates people, processes and technologies to create efficiencies in a company, mitigates risk to the company's intellectual property and creates fundamental compliance and audit capabilities. Specifically, this means IdM is the practice of governing the complete lifecycle of people and resource identities across pertinent company systems.

This practice encompasses all aspects relating to these identities, including their creation and management (suspension/renewal, termination and any other related operation) and the connection to the needs of the business. It enables automated identification of users, automated creation of appropriate, secure relationships between users and resources and the management of such relationships over the full user account lifecycle as the needs of business and the needs of individuals change.

While first-generation IdM solutions generally manifested a technical, central control philosophy catering mostly to administrators, recent IdM solutions adopt a more user-centric philosophy, emphasizing user-friendliness and offering services that are specifically designed to be used by the organization's end-users.

As the Internet continues to play a critical role in global commerce, the need to manage identity-related information securely and efficiently is

Insider Notes: A building block approach is best. A company needs to ensure that its system management and identity management capabilities are in place first. Each element needs to be brought in and made operational in turn, but keeping in mind that full BSM is the ultimate goal.

TIGHTER CORPORATE GOVERNANCE IS THE FUTURE, AND AN IDENTITY MANAGEMENT ENABLED BSM SYSTEM WILL NOT ONLY PROVIDE VISIBILITY INTO THE RELATIONSHIPS AMONG CORPORATE SYSTEMS, PROCESSES AND PERSONNEL, BUT ALSO A WAY TO BETTER MANAGE REGULATORY COMPLIANCE.

accentuated. IdM solutions must offer high performance, scalable, secure and reliable services. However, in order to support the enterprise's business objectives and complement BSM, IdM solutions must be flexible enough to align with the changing requirements of business process management.

An identity-aware approach to BSM enables the extension of BSM's effectiveness by virtue of being an authoritative service point for managing the company's system users, and an optimal means to incorporate the people element within a business impact model. As business objectives are dependent upon business processes involving people, IdM's role within BSM is emphasized. Besides being an organizational resource that should be monitored (similar to other BSM-monitored sources), an IdM solution is also utilized by BSM as a reference point of identity information to correlate between various data sources to better assess business service impact.

Auditing Controls — Who does what, and why

The collapse of Enron and other high profile corporate scandals has created a sense that some companies are out of control. They neither understand their business processes, nor have well-defined policies and procedures or a means in place to identify and react to bad employee behavior. This has resulted in an outcry for more controls, that have been met at both the state and local levels across the industrialized world, by introduction of more regulations. Regulations such as Basel II, HIPAA and Sarbanes-Oxley demand increasing diligence on the part of companies to understand how the business operates. Tighter corporate governance is the future, and an identity management enabled BSM system will not only provide visibility into the relationships among corporate systems, processes and personnel, but also a way to better manage regulatory compliance. This will provide companies with confidence that the corporate mission is being met in the proper manner.

THE FIVE STEPS TO IMPLEMENTING BSM

This section provides a detailed review of the steps companies must take to implement an identity-aware BSM strategy. It presents what they can expect from this implementation and the critical factors associated with a successful implementation, as well as pitfalls to avoid.

There are five important steps to implementing an identity-aware BSM strategy:

❶ Identify the organization's deliverables.

This step entails first listing critical company deliverables to the end customers, and second, identifying key activities that must happen to make such deliverables possible.

❷ Distinguish the criticality of each key activity to the execution of the key deliverable.

This step requires differentiating among the various activities a corporation performs to successfully serve its customers. Some of these activities are more important than others based on their contribution to the business objectives of creating and providing the deliverables identified in step one.

Several metrics should be used to determine the priority of each step. For example, what is the impact on cost or revenue if that activity were to be disrupted? The prioritization process should take into consideration not only easily quantifiable short-term costs and revenue issues, but also more strategic and longer-term (albeit subjective) issues, such as customer satisfaction.

> **Insider Notes:** The business process owner not only needs to be involved, but also needs to lead and steer the process. IdM and BSM projects should not be managed as IT projects; they are business process driven projects and must be managed as such.

AN IDENTITY-AWARE BSM APPROACH PROVIDES A HOLISTIC SOLUTION THAT ENSURES THAT CRITICAL BUSINESS SERVICES ARE SUCCESSFULLY DELIVERED, SERVICE LEVELS ARE CONSISTENTLY MET AND ALL AFFECTED PARTIES RECEIVE CONSISTENT COMMUNICATION.

The result would be a measure of risk assessment and risk management characterized in terms of "pain degree" and "pain tolerance." Pain degree describes the damage caused from any schedule delay in the provision of this deliverable, while pain tolerance denotes how long a company could sustain this deliverable being non-functional without sustaining heavy damage. Combined, they provide a pain scale for any given delay in providing a specific deliverable.

❸ **Identify the company's operational processes pertaining to the key activity identified in Step 2.**
The objective of this step is to identify essential processes that the organizational deliverables rely upon. This would likely be a mixture of manual and automated procedures.

For example, for a manufacturing company, the activity of getting parts and raw materials to the manufacturing plants and getting finished products to the loading dock could employ the entire supply chain process, including inventory management, manufacturing scheduling, resource planning and facilities management.

The activity of order fulfillment processes may include order processing, shipping, billing, accounts receivable and cash collection. The activity of financial reporting may include processes covering inventory management, cash management, accounts receivable, fixed asset management, ledger consolidation and more.

❹ Analyze processes to identify influential factors and critical success factors.

Identify factors that influence the processes identified in Step 3. These factors include the people, applications, databases, and operating systems in the process as well as any other IT resources that are used to enable these processes.

❺ Identify relationships among processes and resources.

Map people and IT resources to the processes, and establish their interdependencies, which in turn are mapped to the key deliverables identified in step one. For a successful implementation, these relationships must be dynamic enough to reflect the reality of business at any given time. In other words, architecture design should include a robust discovery and change management process for all IT and people changes to ensure that an organic and adaptive process is put in place that responds dynamically to changes taking place in the organization.

EXPECTED OUTCOME OF AN IDENTITY-AWARE BSM IMPLEMENTATION

A Business Perspective

An identity-aware BSM approach provides a holistic solution that ensures that critical business services are successfully delivered, service levels are consistently met and all affected parties receive consistent communication. This is accomplished by incorporating IdM capabilities that integrate change management processes. These processes respond not only to the changes in physical IT assets but also people and organizations. This direct line of sight created by BSM improves the quality of decision making and can achieve a significant improvement in customer satisfaction. When events occur, companies will be fully prepared to prioritize them in terms of their impact on the business, and focus their resources accordingly.

Insider Notes: IT must be considered a valuable company asset and a business driver, rather than a cost center or part of the fixed cost. The objectives of IT and the business have definite interdependencies that many companies do not properly recognize.

THE LESS A COMPANY CUSTOMIZES THE APPLICATION, THE EASIER IT WILL BE TO ADOPT ADVANCED TECHNOLOGY.

A Technology Perspective

An identity management driven BSM implementation will directly and positively impact the company's risk assessment and risk management process, along with its event management and problem resolution processes.

CRITICAL FACTORS FOR A SUCCESSFUL IDENTITY-AWARE BSM IMPLEMENTATION

A successful identity-aware BSM implementation depends on the following factors:

From a Business Perspective

- **Active support from senior management.** First and foremost, visible and active support from high-level management is essential for successful BSM implementation. Success relies on a consensus across various process owners. Visible support from executives transcends organizational boundaries and empowers project managers to break down information silos within an organization's departments, enabling consensus.
- **Clearly defined business objectives.** Companies need a good understanding of their objectives before they embark on the implementation of the project. They need to develop and adhere to a very pragmatic project plan and employ tight project management. In some instances, a company's tendency is to try to implement BSM across many or most of its processes all at once. However, for all but the smallest companies, this is a very complicated and high-risk endeavor. Regarding IT governance and regulatory compliance, policies and regulations must be clearly defined and acceptable ranges of compliance must be established. Without this clear articulation, enablement and enforcement of these process steps will be meaningless.

■ **Focus on critical business processes.** Companies need to prioritize business services and focus on a handful of key processes first. This will allow their employees to reap initial successes, learn from their experiences and understand how BSM works. With these first successes under its belt, the organization can expand BSM to other processes.

■ **Careful assessment of the effectiveness of existing processes.** The company should take this opportunity to enhance and simplify existing processes instead of just automating what they have.

From a Technology Perspective

■ **Comprehensive mapping of resource-to-business relationships.** Companies need to fully understand how all its assets (IT and people) are connected to each other and how they are connected to business processes. The discovery and mapping process is critical and not as intuitive as it may appear. Fortunately IT asset management, asset discovery, configuration management and identity management solutions provide companies technological capabilities to address this very important need.

■ **Practical approach to change management — cover all changes.** Change management is a critical issue. Change must be managed carefully and tightly on both the IT side and on the people side. Once again, IT change and configuration management solutions, in combination with identity management solutions, provide a technological way to address the complex task of ongoing change management in corporations.

■ **Well-defined problem resolution process.** Technologically, service-desk or help-desk capabilities are a central part of implementing identity-aware BSM. To create a seamless BSM implementation, data integration and synchronization is critical. Various building blocks of BSM must communicate well to be effective in delivering the value an identity-aware BSM project promises.

Insider Notes: Any business can reap the benefits of an identity-aware BSM deployment. Creating a tangible ROI model is easy for companies that can qualify and, more importantly, quantify the damage resulting from business service disruption.

CASE STUDY: TREATING A SECURITY ILLNESS

Key problem: low accountability concerning access to sensitive information, non-compliance with regulatory requirements and security risks concerning sensitive data.

The challenge: This healthcare organization is a dot.com that provides services to healthcare entities worldwide. The implementation of those services demands that the organization maintain a high level of control over its user's data and its user's access rights to patient information. The organization is paid to provide assistance to all entities involved in the medical service business, and therefore, needs expertise not only in medical issues, but also in coverage plans, claim filing and payment planning.

The infrastructure serving the healthcare administration should enable quick and secure access to information by medical experts when and where they need it. Moreover, it is imperative that patient information is highly secure and accessible only by designated personnel. Additionally, the information being used must pertain only to the relevant patient being treated — erroneous filing is unacceptable.

- **Effective reporting and auditing procedures.** Finally, companies need a way to audit and report on compliance with company policies and requirements from regulatory bodies. Audit and reporting capabilities are key parts of a complete BSM deployment.

PITFALLS TO AVOID

To implement identity-aware BSM successfully, companies need to avoid some well-known pitfalls.

- **Taking on too much, all at once.** Companies need to plan and build the model carefully, and implement deliberately. Patience and prudence are the watchwords.
- **Underestimating technical complexity of deploying too many applications, too soon.** A building block approach is best. A company needs to ensure that its system management and identity management capabilities are in place first. Each element needs to

Establishing the policies governing which doctors, nurses and other personnel have access to which patient data records and when, is complicated by the quantity and variety of pertinent departments, expertise classification and medical referrals. This might result in an excessive number of access requests, updates, modifications and even account terminations. Knowing who made such requests, when they were made and when they were completed is critical for auditing and patient confidentiality.

How Identity-Aware BSM helped address the challenge: Using an identity management solution, the healthcare organization deployed a complete tracking and escalation approval process that was fast, automated and secure. Audit and reporting requirements were built into the solution from the beginning of the implementation.

The solution provided the following benefits:
- It minimized delays in granting access rights through escalation and rerouting of access requests.
- It implemented automated handling of requests, approvals and the granting of access rights to information.
- It created a process to track, manage and report access to patient information.

be brought in and made operational in turn, but keeping in mind that full BSM is the ultimate goal.
- **Underestimating the potentially adverse effects of organizational change on employees.** Be aware of the importance of people in the business service delivery process. All processes start and end with people who often have the most impact on its operation. IdM is critical for the optimal success of BSM.
- **Too much customization, too soon in the process.** Reduce application customization. Companies often purchase standard applications, then implement numerous customizations to fit precise needs. However, each customization makes it more difficult to inte-

Insider Notes: Not surprisingly, building an ROI model for an identity-aware BSM solution requires a good understanding of the impact IT infrastructure has on major business services.

DATA SNAPSHOT

How important is it that senior management demand to understand how IT investments contribute to the attainment of the business objectives?

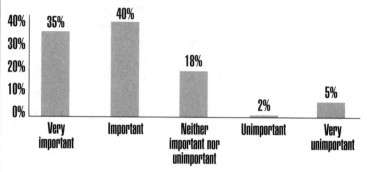

A significant percentage (75%) of the respondents agree with the hypothesis. This evidence corroborates our hypothesis that senior management demands to understand — how IT investments contribute to the attainment of the business objectives, which investments are crucial, and how can investments be optimized. It also verifies that a great majority of companies already acknowledge the value of an effective alignment of IT with business objectives, which is the key objective of BSM. Such alignment results in a more effective, focused IT organization that can better support the business' goals.

Download the complete research study for free at www.blackbooksecurity.com/research
Source: 2005 Larstan / Reed Infosecurity Survey

grate that application with others, causing even more customization. The less a company customizes the application, the easier it will be to adopt advanced technology.

■ **The temptation of automating existing processes.** Companies must review their key processes and simplify them as much as possible. The temptation is to take an IT solution and automate the process exactly as is. However, a simplification will facilitate its inclusion into BSM.

MANAGING THE PROCESS FOR SUCCESS

Key management requirements were highlighted in the critical success factors identified above. Prerequisites of success for an IdM project or an identity centric BSM project are commitment from the senior management team and effective project management skills. Additional elements of success include:

- Getting buy-in from the business process owner at the onset of the process. The business process owner not only needs to be involved, but also needs to lead and steer the process. IdM and BSM projects should not be managed as IT projects; they are business process driven projects and must be managed as such. The business unit owner needs to have examined the project's value proposition and ROI, and should be convinced of the benefits.
- Setting short-term milestones and benefits, as well as long-term milestone and benefits. This allows an organization to maintain consistent effort throughout the project lifecycle.
- Effective training of users and support personnel. These projects are neither easy nor quick to implement; they involve considerable analysis and planning to deploy, monitor and maintain effectively. A comprehensive, yet focused, training program is instrumental to achieve successful implementation.

BUSINESS ISSUES

This section discusses key business, cost alleviation and revenue enhancement issues that can be expected with an identity-aware BSM implementation.

IT must be considered a valuable company asset and a business driver, rather than a cost center or part of the fixed cost. The objectives of IT and the business have definite interdependencies that many companies do not properly recognize. Lacking this recognition, these companies find it diffi-

> **Insider Notes:** BSM will significantly reduce cost of operations by providing the ability to prioritize resource allocation on the IT problems. The increased efficiency in utilization of resources will not only reduce cost but also increase customer satisfaction by automating compliance with internal policies.

CASE STUDY: HOW TO TELL ABOUT A TELLER

The problem: A cumbersome and ineffective access rights management process.

The challenge: This finance company operates in one of the largest cities in the world. They have hundreds of branches in the city and surrounding locations. The company was experiencing problems with teller turnover and teller fraud.

How the company originally dealt with the challenge: In an effort to reduce the risk of teller fraud and manage teller resignations, the company implemented a rotational program. Within this program, a teller was required to change locations on a regular basis. With tellers rotating among the company's branches, the company had a new challenge: to define, manage and enforce proper access rights of these tellers to sensitive information.

A simplistic approach would suggest granting tellers access rights to all accounts. However, this approach would likely expose the company to more risk. Instead, the company decided to implement "business profiles" defining essentially "who has access to what."

cult to justify various IT-requested expenditures, even though the expenditures would assist achievement of business objectives.

Without the means to understand (let alone measure) how IT resource availability impacts business objectives, IT managers resort to employing a technical approach for gauging system efficiency. This ultimately results in a quest to attain the highest technical efficiency possible from a system availability standpoint, rather than trying to achieve high effectiveness from a business standpoint. For that reason, measurement and monitoring of impressive looking system specifications that warrant high expenditures do not always result in a better attainment of business objectives.

In contrast to that approach, BSM focuses on assuring business service delivery, rather than focusing on IT infrastructure availability alone.

This approach demanded that whenever a teller moved to another branch, the pertinent access rights would be adjusted correspondingly. However, as the company's processes were manual, they took a long time to implement these changes, which essentially resulted in a procedure that turned out to be ineffective and cumbersome.

How Identity-Aware BSM helped address the challenge: The company's business objectives demanded a solution that integrated well with existing procedures and systems while remaining focused on customer service and fast execution

Using an automated and business IdM solution, this company was able to both automate the process of reassigning its tellers and effectively manage their access rights assignments, thus maintaining a proper access policy procedure regarding customer information. The company was able to implement this program and improve teller retention without sacrificing customer privacy while protecting revenue streams.

The solution offered the following additional benefits:
- Ability to align management requirements with business objectives
- Integration of solution with existing procedures

This offers the means to accomplish three important goals:
1. Correlation of company resources (including people) with business objectives
2. Definition of pertinent interdependencies
3. Quantification of how low-resource availability affects business services and, ultimately, business objectives

Identity-aware BSM augments this proposition further by facilitating qualification and quantification of a service disruption impact on users, as well as qualification and quantification of the impact's "pain" based on the

Insider Notes: A BSM solution that has integrated IdM capabilities shines a bright light on all resources allocated, physical as well as people, in the problem resolution process.

CASE STUDY: QUICK IDENTITIES

The problem: The provisioning of identities took weeks, and identities and system passwords were being shared among employees.

The challenge: This retail company delivers services in one of the largest markets in the world. The organization experiences tens of thousands of new hires and terminations each month. The current service level agreement for establishing new identities and passwords is over three weeks long. Given an employee model where a new hire's employment expectancy might be only months long, this length of time to establish a password was deemed unacceptable.

How the company originally dealt with the challenge: To accelerate the aforementioned process, local managers decided not to wait for the ID/password creation process to be completed; new hires were instead given the usage of other employee's identities and passwords (including managers), thus essentially granting them pertinent access rights. This put the company at significant risk for corruption and misuse of access, as well as the potential for information theft.

identity of users that were affected. Identity-aware BSM enables the IT organization to better prioritize the resources and expenditures that are allocated to resolving problems. An inability to do so can badly allocate key resources, perhaps toward lower-priority problems.

For example, the failure of a given server indicates a disruption of a certain business service function, but this may not provide in itself enough information to conclude that the business service was in practice impeded, and if it was impeded, to what extent. Identity-aware BSM indicates that even though a given server failed, the pertinent business service was not severely impacted, because other servers hosting similar services still allow the personnel responsible for the business service to continue working at an acceptable performance level. BSM thus facilitates the creation of an optimized IT budget and better IT management practices. This allows SLAs

How Identity-Aware BSM helped address the challenge: After analyzing its policies and operational procedures and identifying its workflow bottlenecks, the retail company was able to pinpoint the source of the delays. By implementing an IdM automated process for approval of access right requests across all local and remote systems that were connected to the change request system, the retail company was able to significantly reduce the time required to create identities from weeks to hours and, eventually, to minutes.

In addition, the automated approval process provided auditing functionality, including an audit trail of approvals and user access, which enabled proper and effective de-provisioning of resources after an employee terminated his employment.

The solution offered the following benefits:
- Streamlined approval and creation procedures for identity and password setup
- The ability to perform comprehensive auditing of request approvals, access rights operations and more
- An effective and efficient de-provisioning

oriented toward attaining business objectives to be better monitored, measured and delivered.

THE SIX BUSINESS DRIVERS

There are six major business drivers that influence a company's decision to implement an identity-aware BSM solution:

❶ **Business efficiency.** Shortening and optimizing the process of creating, modifying and terminating accounts in response to business account lifecycle requirements and in accordance with company policies. Also, the optimization of help-desk support and quality of service, via increased self-service and automated-service options.

❷ **Business agility.** Greater responsiveness to resource availability changes, with the objective to ultimately adopt a proactive approach, rather than a reactive one.

❸ **Business security.** Enforcing policies, implementing security best practices and mitigating risks concerning excessive user rights, orphan

---

DATA SNAPSHOT

As 39% of the respondents maintained that their respective IT management is more concerned with IT component availability than with business process availability, this evidence supports our hypothesis that *'Many IT organizations are more concerned with the availability and performance of IT components, than with the availability and performance of business processes'.*

My IT management is more concerned with the availability and performance of IT components than with the availability and performance of business processes.

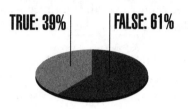

TRUE: 39% | **FALSE: 61%**

Download the complete research study for free at www.blackbooksecurity.com/research
Source: 2005 Larstan / Reed Infosecurity Survey

---

accounts and unmanaged accounts.

❹ **Business productivity.** Providing an effective solution to resource allocation and enabling the business to experience higher resource availability, and exploiting this to maximize the productivity of employees and the business as a whole.

❺ **Business costs reduction.** Optimally utilizing internal resources, reducing service support requests and reducing both system and user downtime, resulting in higher business service availability with lower costs.

❻ **Business compliance with regulations.** Addressing auditing and identity management requirements implied by both federal and state government regulations.

Those six issues will compel companies to implement IdM capabilities. Meanwhile, there are three key issues that challenge the deployment of an identity-aware BSM solution:

❶ **Scalability.** The ability of the solution to continue providing acceptable performance when supporting and managing a high and ever-increasing number of identities;

❷ **Interoperability.** The ability to not only segregate access to the information in accordance to internal and external policies and regulations but also the ability to seamlessly work with other systems influencing service management decisions.

❸ **Consistency.** The ability to create and keep roles, responsibilities and process relationship data consistent across the enterprise on a continual basis.

An examination of these issues tells us that an IdM solution should incorporate auditing and regulation compliance capabilities and offer a central point of management. A better understanding of how information is scattered across the enterprise is necessary to optimize some of the processes needed for the company to obtain its business objectives.

No two businesses are exactly alike. Each company demonstrates a different business model that reflects the special characteristics of the business environment and objectives, warranting special critical success factors for a relevant BSM implementation.

Previous sections explained how the implementation of an identity-aware BSM solution could provide considerable benefits for businesses, including support optimization, business agility and quick responsiveness to change, focused expenditures, minimization of service disruption and high quality of service.

Any business can reap the benefits of an identity-aware BSM deployment. Creating a tangible ROI model is easy for companies that can qualify and, more importantly, quantify the damage resulting from business service disruption. Such companies may be subject to quantifiable penalties, fines or other financial damages as a result of missing the service delivery requirements set in Service Level Agreements. For example:

■ **Companies that are required to comply with regulation directives; companies that require high and manageable quality of service.**

Insider Notes: A company without an IdM enabled BSM system is operating in a fog that will often lead to sub-optimal decisions and, ultimately, higher costs — all for less security.

Inability of a company to comply with regulation requirements might result in severe damage, including financial loss, reduction of business opportunities and penalties. An identity-aware BSM deployment enables IT to easily identify potential sources of problems that might impact crucial business services and risk regulation compliance. More importantly, an identity-aware BSM deployment enables IT to exercise a policy-based approach to react faster to problems that impede critical services and provide IdM audit capabilities that address many regulatory compliance requirements.

> ■ **Companies that are an online business and employ services that require high-availability to external customers; companies that are constantly required to meet business deadlines.**

Examples of "highly-availability" services include billing, inventory, ticket reservations, help-desk and more. Inability to satisfy highly-available service requirements or inability to meet business deadlines (e.g., submission of financial reports) might harm the business considerably.

A lengthy disruption of a service might result in financial damage and might even impact the company's share value. To meet those requirements, it is imperative to both manage operational risk and to employ an effective proactive (and even a predictive) approach to service disruption. As was mentioned previously, identity-aware BSM lends itself well to support these objectives, enabling quick response to events that demand a minimal time-to-service.

Not surprisingly, building an ROI model for an identity-aware BSM solution requires a good understanding of the impact IT infrastructure has on major business services. That said, the actual procedure for creating a BSM business model resembles the practice typically exercised for any project where money is involved, starting with a data collection process which serves to identify a client's pertinent "pain."

The analysis of the data provided by the client during this process leads to the identification and definition of the corresponding project's goals, key success factors, scope and, ultimately, to an appropriate solution proposal.

Creating an effective and serviceable business model for the project typically demands that key client personnel are involved in the data collection phase; furthermore, the business model is ideally crafted jointly by the client and service provider based on the data that was collected.

The following sections elaborate on key cost and revenue issues that should be considered when defining such a business model.

COST ISSUES

BSM will significantly reduce the cost of operations by providing the ability to prioritize resource allocation on the IT problems. The increased efficiency in utilization of resources will not only reduce costs but also increase customer satisfaction by automating compliance with internal policies. An additional benefit of a BSM solution is the ability of the organization to keep a strong regulatory compliance posture.

The most insidious of all cost elements is the misallocation of resources. This cost gets imputed into the infrastructure of a company that disappears from the managers' sight, making it very difficult to quantify. Over a period of time, either managers start believing that they are operating at as efficient a level as possible, or are frustrated that they do not have enough information to be able to put their finger on where to reduce costs. A BSM solution that has integrated IdM capabilities shines a bright light on all resources allocated, physical as well as people, in the problem resolution process.

One of the biggest difficulties IT managers face today is the ability to quantify impact of an event on business in dollar terms. When a problem occurs, IT managers can calculate the cost of the downtime of physical assets, but the cost associated with the people not having access to their desktops, key applications, etc. is not available. Questions, such as, how many people, what organizations, what roles, what disciplines were impacted and for how long are impossible to answer. Lacking this information, IT managers are often forced to rely on guesswork. With an Identity Management capability integrated in the BSM solution, the effects of an event on people is clear and crisply quantifiable.

For a business service to be reliably and consistently delivered, people, technology and processes must be integrated for a common purpose of delivering the stated service. The integration of Identity Management capabilities in a BSM solution provides companies an end-to-end business service management capability. It gives companies the ability to be agile in their response to changes, spanning their IT and organizational environments.

REVENUE ISSUES

BSM also will provide revenue enhancements by improving the service delivered to the company's customers. The prioritization that occurs with BSM will ensure that more resources are applied to high-priority items that go directly to delivering services with high revenue correlation.

A company will accrue benefits and revenue enhancements that will follow improved services, increased customer satisfaction and cost reductions provided by the improved ability to manage and more effectively apply internal resources.

This chapter has presented how a Business Service Management implementation enabled by Identity Management can significantly improve the security posture and overall performance of a company. The correlation of a company's assets (personnel and capital) to its core service deliverable assets, provides management with an unobstructed line of sight from deliverable, to physical assets, to people assets. This enables management to make informed decisions on security and remediation priorities for IT. In addition, it provides insight into personnel requirements.

A company without an IdM enabled BSM system is operating in a fog that will often lead to sub-optimal decisions and, ultimately, higher costs — all for less security. As security issues become more complex, companies with an IdM enabled BSM system will have the insight to protect what is most important and to prioritize remediation according to business goals.

■ ■ ■

Somesh Singh is Vice President and General Manager, and Rami Elron is Senior Architect for BMC Software's Identity Management Business Unit.

Somesh has held several executive positions at BMC Software, including Vice President of Operations for Global Sales and Marketing Organization, Vice President of Corporate Operations, Vice President of R&D and Common Development and his current position as Vice President and General Manager of Identity Management Business Unit. The flagship product of his business unit is CONTROL-SA, the leading identity management solution available in the market today. From 1999 through 2001, Somesh was President and Chief Operating Officer of iVita Corporation, a Houston-based asset management software startup he helped found.

Rami Elron has responsibility for design aspects concerning BMC Software's Identity Management solution, CONTROL-SA and the solution's next generation architecture and features. An industrial engineer, Rami has over 15 years of experience in computing infrastructure and development environments as a developer, project manager and system architect, and has lectured in academia and at prominent computer industry conferences. Rami has extensive background in Windows and Java technologies, application development, UI design, identity and security management technologies and system infrastructure and implementation of frameworks such as MSF. Before joining BMC Software, Rami served as VP Technologies of a large system integration firm. Rami was appointed by Microsoft to be a Microsoft Regional Director for Operating Systems, and received several notable awards, including 'Person of the Year' and a special award for the promotion of Microsoft technologies. Rami is an active member of the OASIS PSTC (Provisioning Services Technical Committee) that created the international SPML standard for provisioning and identity management. Rami co-authored a best selling book on Windows XP and has written numerous articles on Windows, security and identity management technologies.

Somesh can be reached at +01 713-918-3410 or Somesh_singh@bmc.com; Rami can be reached at +011 972-3-766-2434 or rami_elron@bmc.com.

[6]

MULTI-LEVEL SECURITY: YOUR KEY TO DATA SAFETY

Multi-level security, with its capacity for sharing resources across several security compartments, provides more efficient and, ultimately more secure data workflow.

> "HISTORY DOES NOT TEACH THAT BETTER TECHNOLOGY NECESSARILY LEADS TO VICTORY. RATHER, VICTORY GOES TO THE COMMANDER WHO USES TECHNOLOGY BETTER."
> - Office of the Chief of Naval Ops.

by JIM PORELL

During the Cold War, it was called "fail-safe," meaning a multi-level nuclear warfare system structured with enough redundancies to make the probability of failure extremely remote. During this new era of information warfare, think of multi-level security (MLS) as a fail-safe data system.

In the broadest definition, MLS consists of sharing resources across separate security compartments.

A MULTI-LEVEL SECURITY ENVIRONMENT HAS PROTECTION LEVELS BUILT IN TO STOP SOMEONE FROM DECLASSIFYING, MISCLASSIFYING, OR RECLASSIFYING DATA.

These resources might represent data, applications and networks. A security compartment can take different forms, whether as hierarchical levels of security, or as specific company projects. It is also defined by determining who has access to what information. By sharing, a lot of redundancy is eliminated in an MLS, as compared to the commonly deployed alternative, the multiple security levels (MSL).

In an MSL environment, each department only has whatever it needs to function. It may have its own network, its own applications and its own data. These multiple departments, or multiple communities, each with its own computing infrastructure, get quite costly, especially when data and applications have to be replicated.

By contrast, the concept behind MLS is to share data and, ultimately, applications to reduce operational complexity. In addition, the timeliness of data is ensured since the time lag required to replicate data and sanitize it for different departments is eliminated. The policies to backup, protect and secure the data are also consistently applied in this shared environment.

As I will explain, MLS results in data operations that are streamlined, consolidated, more efficient, less costly and considerably more secure.

COMPARING MLS TO MSL

In an MSL environment, an analyst has a PC on their desktop. This person will have a distinct network that's identified only to run data that is specific for that PC or for the project that the person is working on. This network is then connected into a server, which may have access to data defined for that department. This same analyst might work across three separate departments, and might have three separate computers in their office, with three separate networks all going to three independent servers, with each of those servers having its own specific data. There is no mechanism to share. That analyst can't copy, paste or move data from one computer to another.

MLS is about finding opportunities for sharing. In the last example, some data that comes in on a project might be relevant to each of the three areas identified, as well as other areas. It may arrive initially for one area, but then could be shared with another. To make this information accessible to them, it can be copied, or the analyst can be granted access to this other area. However, the data's classification needs to be protected. If it came in secret, it can't be declassified. A multi-level security environment has protection levels built-in to stop someone from declassifying, misclassifying or reclassifying data.

MULTI-LEVEL SECURITY ACCESS ELEMENTS
Two security elements are central to a multi-level security environment:
- Discretionary access control (DAC), under which an employee is a member of a group, and that group has access to resources. In turn, the employees get access to the resources.
- Mandatory access control (MAC), under which an employee has to be explicitly defined to have access to those resources. It implies certain process rules and functions as an enforcement mechanism. It dictates who is allowed to see this data, who is allowed to reclassify this data and, in some cases, who is allowed to know this data exists.

An example of MAC: an individual is in the insurance department of a company that does banking, as well. It would be good for that individual to know how much is in a customer's account, so insurance policies could be tailored to them. If a customer has $1 million in the bank, the insurance policy would differ from someone with $10,000 in his account. In some cases, that sharing of personally identifiable information is against the law. Federal regulations governing information use, such as the Health Insurance Portability and Accountability Act (HIPAA) and Sarbanes-Oxley, say this information should not be shared. The insurance depart-

Insider Notes: A major opportunity for an MLS commercial deployment is in the privacy area to enforce regulations like Sarbanes-Oxley, HIPAA and the California Privacy Acts. The compartmentalizing of business processes that require mandatory access control will become more prevalent.

MLS RECOGNIZES THAT CORPORATE INFORMATION IS JUST ALL ONE GIANT WORKFLOW THAT CAN BE MANAGED BY SHARING DATA, APPLICATIONS AND OPERATIONS.

ment cannot see any of the personally identifiable information from the banking department. Enforcing access to that kind of information is one of the commercial applications of multi-level security.

THE COMPONENTS OF MLS

The initial impetus for MLS has been in the government sector, in particular the intelligence community. However, there is a growing need and desire to leverage this same capability in the commercial space.

Three system components that should be optimized for an MLS system:
- the database server
- the applications server
- the presentation device

Each component can have elements of multi-level security applied to IT. The state-of-the-art is that there are several existing database servers that can provide a level of compartmentalization. There are currently no general-purpose, off-the-shelf application servers with this capability commercially available. Some specific ones are built to government specifications. There are some efforts now being undertaken to build thin client terminals that will have a level of compartmentalization in them. The focus for the industry today is in the database server itself. Other than customized specific applications, there are no credible end-to-end MLS solutions in the marketplace today.

COMMERCIALIZING MLS

There's definitely a desire to develop this MLS capability for the commercial marketplace, but some developmental work on hardware is still required. The presentation server is the next component being developed and optimized for MLS. Application servers are also in development, but it will be several years before any robust MLS-aware application servers come to market.

The storage capability required for MLS is already deployed, since a database server is dependent on its storage device. Therefore, tape devices and some of the Redundant Array of Independent Drives (RAID) storage devices can run as compartmentalized data stores. MLS capabilities, such as erase-on-scratch, were added to the hardware devices, since it is no longer acceptable to just remove a file from a directory on a storage device. It must be ensured that nobody can take that storage device offline and find residual data. Business processes also need to be in place to look at removable media and online media and determine its life span, so that nobody can go off and pick up the remnants of some data because it has been partially written over.

A major opportunity for an MLS commercial deployment is in the privacy area to enforce regulations like Sarbanes-Oxley, HIPAA and the California Privacy Acts. The compartmentalizing of business processes that require mandatory access control will become more prevalent. The world is a distributed computing environment, and no one computer can meet all of a businesses' needs. The mainframe can't do it because it's blind and deaf. It does not own the human computer interface, so data has to be moved to a device with that capability.

A large mainframe might have all of a company's transaction files in one place. However, these files are accessed and replicated to run in a business intelligence application on UNIX servers. Each time this data is replicated, the preservation of policies protecting that data, like privacy, security levels, or access control, are put in jeopardy. It's very easy to copy data; it's extremely difficult to copy the policy and to have the same policy being implemented on a completely different type of server. A critical success factor to facilitate the sharing of data is to have consistent policies that manage resources, and, more importantly, that can be utilized for audit, compliance and risk assessment against these resources.

 Insider Notes: A critical success factor to facilitate the sharing of data is to have consistent policies that manage resources, and, more importantly, that can be utilized for audit, compliance and risk assessment against these resources.

This is a fundamental point where companies need to start changing their whole perception about how they do computing. Currently, many companies opt to use the cheapest and smallest computers, so they copy, cluster and replicate. This process makes the data accessible to a broad range of servers. However, the key issue is whether the company is consistent in maintaining privacy and management policies with each replicated instance of that data. Companies had an audited server in the first instance where the data was generated, but did they have a similar audit on each subsequent instance of that data?

When companies start looking at the new government mandates and realize that they are very complex and require new software and new workflows to facilitate policy management, they will question why these policy decisions are all independent and why they are not incorporated as part of the corporate workflow.

MLS also means getting away from the stovepipe mentality that dictates separate and distinct computers for customer relationship management applications, for human resource applications and for point of sale transactions. MLS recognizes that corporate information is just all one giant workflow that can be managed by sharing data, applications and operations. By doing this, costs can be reduced dramatically, along with risk exposure and the need for continual, complex compliance analysis.

Companies are initially handling these newly mandated security regulations as a matter of just going through the old audit checklist. In reality, compliance can be automated if the volume of replications is minimized. MLS is one method to minimize replications and to consolidate servers. It also starts to incorporate and simplify policy management along with server consolidation.

Forty years ago, someone would flowchart an application to determine which tasks it was supposed to accomplish. But now, with business process integration, data is moving all over the enterprise through these silos of computing. This is the new business workflow. The question is whether this movement is orchestrated or simply being passed to the next decision-making unit — from the point of sale application to the customer relationship management to target marketing, or web-based management. If

DATA SNAPSHOT

This isolated approach towards managing userids separately can lead to errors in attempting to correlate security across multiple systems.

Download the complete research study for free at www.blackbooksecurity.com/research Source: 2005 Larstan / Reed Infosecurity Survey

Are user IDs managed at an enterprise level (across servers) or against each individual server?

ENTERPRISE LEVEL: 40% **INDIVIDUAL SERVER: 60%**

this entire workflow is considered, perhaps the better decision is to move some of the application, not the data. Flowcharting the data can be a tremendous exercise in reducing complexity. Eliminating data movement can save time, which saves money. When looked at from the policy perspective and the cost of managing policy against the data, there are even more opportunities for tremendous operational savings.

MLS takes what might have been operational issues that the security administrator does and goes back to the fundamentals of business architecture and business workflows, and ultimately makes the business organization more efficient.

Below, I define the traditional security paradigm and discuss its inadequacies, and then present how MLS differs from the traditional approach. I discuss the opportunity for MLS, how it would work and its implications for executive, IT and security management.

THE TRADITIONAL SECURITY PARADIGM

The traditional data security paradigm is based on the three As: authentication, authorization and access control. Audit capabilities may also be included. This paradigm focuses on a discrete user or group of users and defines

Insider Notes: The traditional data security paradigm is based on the three As: authentication, authorization and access control.

MLS IS JUST BECOMING GENERALLY AVAILABLE. IT PROVIDES COMPANIES WITH FLEXIBILITY AND PRESENTS A CHANCE TO CHANGE SECURITY MANAGEMENT POLICY. IT SIMPLIFIES OPERATIONS.

their access to a fixed resource such as data, a printer or a particular program. However, patterns of use change as the role of the user changes. For example, a systems programmer could have access to some system data set during a test environment to facilitate change management. When you get into a production environment where you have to manage change a lot more tightly, this person may still have authorized access to that data set, but the company does not want to facilitate change management there. That is the evolution of access control.

Access control has existed in the government for some time, but now, because of Sarbanes-Oxley, HIPAA and the like, it is also evolving into the commercial space. How it gets implemented is yet to be determined. This is the opportunity to promote some of the concepts and philosophies of MLS as a way to manage and achieve this evolution.

An example of how MLS works: a person in a banking role may have a particular access to data, but if he is working in the same business in a stock or insurance role, he may not be authorized to that same level of information for that specific task. Part of MLS is to identify what role a user is playing or what compartment they are working within for a particular task environment, and then to enforce the security policies for that role. The user could have access to all kinds of information when looking at all the different roles that they could have in their job. But in a given task, they are restricted access to certain information, either by law, by corporate policy or by customer initiated request, and they are not supposed to make decisions based upon this restricted information. Therefore, that information should not be accessible to them during that function.

The key differences between these paradigms are the roles that people play versus the access control that any single individual might have, and defining more policies based on role and upon the life cycle of the data or application.

How does multi-level security change the way companies address the security paradigm?

MLS is just becoming generally available. It provides companies with flexibility and presents a chance to change security management policy. It simplifies operations. New data security regulations offer another opportunity, since there is no programmatic way to enforce these laws. Compliance becomes a paper exercise, an audit trail, a post-processing exercise, or a lot of activity to set up stovepipes of information. What multi-level security does is present a method to share data and systems and facilitate working together without affecting regulatory restrictions.

THE MULTI-LEVEL SECURITY OPPORTUNITY

Nobody is currently using multi-level security commercially. There are multiple situations for its effective implementation. Multi-level security is focused on roles. In the government intelligence community, it deals with various compartments, considers the task that each individual needs to execute and applies its level of access accordingly.

Commercially, an individual might have access to a broad wealth of data, information and applications within their company. But when they are in a specific role or executing a specific function, then they might (by law, policy or request) only be allowed to do certain tasks.

For example, in the healthcare industry, a claims administrator might have a wealth of knowledge of personally identifiable information about a particular client. This insurance institution might also be selling other forms of insurance or annuities and mutual funds. That personally identifiable information should not be leveraged for the sales of the mutual funds. If they are selling stock, they are not supposed to have all the information

> **Insider Notes:** A MLS implementation requires a combination of hardware and software optimized for this type of sharing. The manner in which a server enforces MLS may be proprietary. However, it is then the role of the network to ensure interoperability between two environments that may implement MLS differently.

OUTSOURCERS ARE EXTREMELY RIPE FOR AN MLS ENVIRONMENT. LEVERAGING MLS, OUTSOURCERS ARE MORE EFFICIENT BECAUSE THEY HOST MULTIPLE CLIENTS IN THE SAME COMPUTING INFRASTRUCTURE AND ENSURE THAT ONE CLIENT CAN'T SEE THE DATA OF ANOTHER CLIENT.

that the claims administrator can access. These businesses will restrict an individual to one task only, be it banking, insurance or selling stock.

With MLS, a person can identify themselves to a task or compartment. If they are executing a stock action, they can only use the information that is legally accessible to them. Policy is being enforced based on the business role versus individual user. That individual may have access to personally identifiable information, but only in the banking role, not the insurance or stock selling role. MLS can facilitate this solution. This may allow some companies to reduce their infrastructure and their operational costs by replacing separate, compartmentalized systems with people who can handle multiple business roles.

THE OPPORTUNITY IN THE EXTENDED ENTERPRISE AND OUTSOURCING

The extended enterprise depends on business-to-business communications. All of these interactions start with sharing data, but at some point, content is being shared, which means sharing the application. This results in a person from one company running on a computer of another company. This is similar for an outsourcer.

Outsourcers are extremely ripe for an MLS environment. Leveraging MLS, outsourcers are more efficient because they host multiple clients in the same computing infrastructure and ensure that one client can't see the data of another client. In turn, the outsourcer is saving dramatically in their operational infrastructure. Instead of having a computer system or a collection of servers for each customer, they are sharing that infrastructure across multiple customers.

In business-to-business communications, lots of data gets transmitted. An example is the local phone companies that actually do all the metering for long distance calls. At the end of the month, they separate, parse and burn a lot of computing time to distribute that information to the long distance line carriers who, in turn, receive it, and process the bills using their own computing infrastructure. If the long distance carriers and the local carriers could share some of this computing infrastructure, each of them would probably save a considerable amount of computer processing time.

In another example, a company in the content management business, such as eBay, may be able to leverage this infrastructure to conduct private auctions only for people who sign up for it. Others would have no knowledge of, or access to, this private auction. However, the database infrastructure could be shared, saving operational expense for the content hosting service.

MULTI-LEVEL SECURITY — GETTING IT TO WORK

MLS implementation requires a combination of hardware and software optimized for this type of sharing. The manner in which a server enforces MLS may be proprietary. However, it is then the role of the network to ensure interoperability between two environments that may implement MLS differently. Part of what MLS does is reduce the heterogeneous nature of a system, but still employs virtual private networks, IP security and data encryption over the wire. Those are the security standards that facilitate interoperability. On the local systems, how MLS may be achieved is an implementation detail, and typically, proprietary to that type of server.

On the operations side, synergy is important. This is where standards will emerge. For example, the radio buttons of a management interface, pushed to develop or implement a MLS environment, ultimately requires some

Insider Notes: The core of how MLS works is in the mapping process. Compartments are defined by correlating privacy statements or sensitive data to the various functional roles that exist within a company. These policies are then made operational by identifying information compartments that are accessible to employees as they assume various roles within their function.

EXECUTIVE MANAGEMENT CAN VIEW MLS AS A METHOD TO BREAK DOWN THE ACCESS STOVEPIPES AND REDUCE COSTS BY ENABLING ONE PERSON TO LEGALLY ASSUME SEVERAL ROLES WITHIN THE COMPANY.

consistency. What's behind that radio button can be anything, as long as the operations are consistent. But that is more of a visionary statement, not an implementation detail, and certainly not what is currently the state-of-the-art. As systems become heterogeneous, more consistency is required in operational models to reduce complexity. Here are the implications and benefits of MLS across the business structure:

- **Executive Management**. Executive management can view MLS as a method to break down the access stovepipes and reduce costs by enabling one person to legally assume several roles within the company. This is accomplished by eliminating or reducing data movement, evolving individual roles and providing the computing infrastructure to facilitate a true business role based management philosophy. This should also save operational costs.

- **IT Management.** MLS will implement the differences in access demanded by a production versus a test environment. Systems programmers in a test role can do anything they want. They can reboot the system and make changes dynamically just to get the product working. Individuals may also have the same responsibilities in the production environment, but not the same freedom or flexibility to do changes. MLS will enforce those roles and that policy.

- **Security Management.** Security management will be responsible for administering these roles. This will demonstrate that security management can have a large impact on the company by developing this business role-based paradigm that will eventually lead to company savings. Therefore, how security management charts this course and helps identify infrastructure changes necessary for an MLS implementation will help to establish a much more resilient, economically feasible and more cost-competitive operational environment.

Now, I'll describe how an MLS system can be implemented.

UNDERSTANDING THE WORKFLOW AND FUNCTIONAL ROLE

The key part of implementation is in understanding the business work-flows within a company and the roles and functions that employees have within it. It is a difficult task to take those business roles and map them into the access control, authentication, authorization and audit policies necessary to define the compartments required by MLS. To accomplish this, a company really needs to focus on the end-to-end workflows of its business processes.

MAPPING LEVEL OF ACCESS

Once these workflows are understood, a company can map out the data and information to be made accessible to those employees functioning within specific business roles. It can then define the level of access control for sensitive data and information that must be maintained and managed when an employee is in that business role. This is how a company maps security policy into the actual workflow of its infrastructure.

For example, if a person is a bank teller, the company needs to understand what their function is in detail and what data and information access they need to have to do their job on a day-to-day basis. This gets more complex when an employee has a position in selling insurance, as well. If part of his function is to handle client requests, he may have access to personally identifiable information.

However, when that same person is handling unsolicited sales requests, then he can't have access to all of this information, while in that role. Within an MLS structure, the role that an employee is performing is critically important in determining how much information is made available to them at that given time. This is where MLS begins to provide compartmentalization.

Insider Notes: A company must identify what personally identifiable information and other sensitive data it needs to protect from general access. It must precisely define when it can use this data to target markets and when it cannot.

PUTTING IT ALL TOGETHER, A COMPANY NEEDS TO DEVELOP A ROAD MAP THAT DEFINES AN ACTION PLAN FOR IMPLEMENTATION. IT THEN NEEDS TO BUILD A MATRIX OF SENSITIVE DATA AND PERSONALLY IDENTIFIABLE INFORMATION DISTINCT TO THAT COMPANY.

Mapping roles to information access is a complex task and may require new tools to get it done right. Often, when a company maps privacy policy and sensitive data access to a corporate function, it finds that it has multiple policies that may affect the same role, or policies that may not let a business role function adequately. This mapping process allows a company to review its security policies in detail and determine how it affects the company's workflow.

The next step is to turn these access control policies into actionable items that can evolve into security compartments. This entails defining the security policies and then mapping specific business roles against them that detail the degree of access to the types of sensitive information that each role should have. This ensures that the rules and responsibilities are clearly understood, and enforced companywide. The goal is to make access control of sensitive information trivial to audit, so compliance with the new regulations are easy to demonstrate and difficult to fault.

The core of how MLS works is in the mapping process. Compartments are defined by correlating privacy statements or sensitive data to the various functional roles that exist within a company. These policies are then made operational by identifying information compartments that are accessible to employees as they assume various roles within their function.

THE ACCESS/COMPANY ROLE MATRIX

Research is now being conducted to utilize employee prose and natural language parsing to identify the various access needs of business roles, such as the needs of a bank teller, a client service representative, a problem management person, an insurance sales person, etc. This automatically

DATA SNAPSHOT

Understanding who has a need-to-know for particular data simplifies the deployment of a multi-level secure environment.

Download the complete research study for free at www.blackbooksecurity.com/research
Source: 2005 Larstan / Reed Infosecurity Survey

Is employee access to data managed on a need-to-know basis?

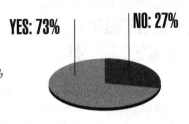

YES: 73%   **NO: 27%**

helps determine the level of access each of these business roles may have to sensitive data.

In addition, a company needs to identify what personally identifiable information and other sensitive data it needs to protect from general access. It must precisely define when it can use this data to target markets and when it cannot. The company also needs to know what its policy is when a customer checks the box saying that the company can use this information for target marketing, as well as the policy when the company said that it would never sell its list.

The result of these decisions can be put into a matrix that models a company's privacy policy and defines what specific business roles can access and can take actionable efforts against this personally identifiable information and sensitive data. The first step is to determine what the personally identifiable information is (or other sensitive information that a company does not want made available to other business roles or another company), and second, determine how the computing infrastructure can enforce that privacy strategy.

Insider Notes: Within an MLS environment, where mandatory access control is being enforced, it can be set up so that an unauthorized user is not even aware that other resources exist. This eliminates the fishing that someone might have to perform to gain access to that data.

SENIOR MANAGEMENT MUST BUY IN COMPLETELY BECAUSE MULTI-LEVEL SECURITY IS A WORKFLOW, NOT A STOVEPIPE DECISION. IT'S NOT A SERVER DISCUSSION OR EVEN AN INFORMATION TECHNOLOGY DISCUSSION; IT'S AN ENTERPRISE DISCUSSION.

To a large extent, MLS and privacy are related because the whole point of this implementation is to hide certain types of information from certain individuals within specific business roles that don't have a need to know. It is basically dealing with some form of need-to-know while also facilitating data and application sharing and reducing operational infrastructure.

THE FINAL STEPS

Putting it all together, a company needs to develop a road map that defines an action plan for implementation. It then needs to build a matrix of sensitive data and personally identifiable information distinct to that company. The company then applies the security policies that define each compartment and details the business roles and information access contained in each, and determines what data and information can be shared, and what cannot be shared. Finally, the company must determine who else may have access. If it is a business partner that has access, than it must be decided what sub-roles within that business partner's company has access to this information, and at what level.

Senior management must buy-in completely because MLS is a workflow, not a stovepipe decision. It's not a server discussion or even an IT discussion; it's an enterprise discussion. It's about how a server implementation of MLS adds value to the enterprise and all the other systems that are connected to it. It's neither a technology nor an individual business unit decision; it's an enterprise-wide decision.

DIFFERENCES WITH NON-MLS ENVIRONMENTS

In a non-MLS environment, discretionary access control, permissions and access control lists are applied against individual users or groups. An employee that is part of a group is allowed to access certain data.

However, in these situations, there is no consideration for networking issues or for network enabled applications. The focus is on a discrete resource or object, like a file or a database. MLS differs in that a company has the opportunity to apply access control to the network and to the applications.

In some respects, mandatory access control is implemented in MLS. Another important difference is that an employee may know that a resource exists under the non-multi-level secure environment, but not know what the content of this particular data field or data-set might be, and he doesn't have access to it. He might then try to gain access by asking someone else to provide him with it. Within an MLS environment, where mandatory access control is being enforced, it can be set up so that an unauthorized user is not even aware that other resources exist. This eliminates the fishing that someone might have to perform to gain access to that data.

If the view of data provided for a business role doesn't have any excess information, a user might be aware that some personally identifiable information exists, but unaware of the depth and breadth of that information. Maybe there are eight pieces of data and the user may be cognizant of only one and not aware that there were seven other major data fields that were hidden. This provides a greater level of security, greater isolation and compartmentalization of tasks on behalf of the company.

SETTING UP MLS - ACCESS CONTROL DECISIONS

Setting up the MLS environment and facilitating mandatory access controls is the first and most difficult step. There are a lot of knobs that need or can be turned to describe access policies. Companies have a tremendous amount of flexibility as to how granular an MLS implementation is required. On one hand, a company could decide that it's just user and key data that they will compartmentalize. They could get down to a field level within a database.

Insider Notes: The problem among the mainframe, UNIX and Windows environments is they are typically separate security domains. To simplify the operations and enforce consistent policies, the security policies should be merged.

CASE STUDY: SECURITY IS A MANY-LAYERED THING

The Problem: A financial services company typically encompasses multiple business units. A small company will often have personal banking, insurance and stock brokerage operations; larger companies may have even more.

A variety of laws prohibit companies from leveraging all the information of one business unit (such as personally identifiable information collected within, and for the banking operation) to target market a consumer for other business units (such as the insurance and stock brokerage units).

To meet the requirements of these regulations, the finance company needs to compartmentalize or isolate the applications and data within each business unit to prevent the emergence of conflicts. This will require the company to install redundant systems and storage capacity to facilitate this isolation. In addition, it adds an entire level of complexity for change management activities and opens additional opportunities for error with the required replication of certain data and the need for accurate information on all systems.

A WORKFLOW FOR THIS FINANCIAL SERVICES COMPANY

A customer enrolls in one of the business units. Information is gathered about that individual to open an account. This enters the customer into the company's Customer Relationship Management (CRM) system. An initial transaction is executed on behalf of that customer, such as depositing money into an account, executing a stock trade or acquiring insurance. This transaction typically occurs on a mainframe system.

Now the other business units within the company are interested in acquiring this consumer's business as well. The operational data store (ODS) for the transaction system will be "mined"; data will be extracted, filtered and sent to a data warehouse or decision support system (DSS). These functions typically reside in a UNIX systems environment.

From there, applications will be run against the "allowable" information in that data warehouse. A target set of "pre-approved" consumers will be defined and a mailing or call will be placed to the consumer in order to interest them in new business elements. Should the consumer accept this new offer, this cycle repeats itself, beginning with updates to the CRM system.

Each time the data moves between these systems, it is important to ensure that the privacy policies are enforced. Audits need to be conducted to ensure that the policies have been enforced and then correlated across each of the systems to ensure there are no irregularities. This postprocessing operation can be complex, cumbersome and error prone, especially if it is not kept properly in synch across each of the application execution environments, which span across somewhat independent business units.

HOW MULTI-LEVEL SECURITY ADDRESSES THIS PROBLEM

Multi-level security can be leveraged to alleviate much of this complexity. The data for each of the business units can be shared in a common database. This will require a cross-company effort to ensure that the proper database schema is identified to capture each business units' unique information. Compartments can then be identified at both the row and field level within these databases.

Categories can be set up to identify collections of customers for each individual business unit or customers with activities in multiple business units. For example, in this company, security labels could be established such as BANK, INSURANCE, STOCK, BANKINS, INSSTOCK, BANKSTOCK, BIS. This will create a hierarchy of labels that would be generated for a consumer within the CRM application. The label would be modified, based on which business units the consumer belongs. From that point on, each businesses' applications could operate against the common ODS, but only operate against their specific customers.

For example, a bank reconciliation application might run with a security label of ALLBANK, which includes BANK, BANKINS, BANKSTOCK and BIS. The ODS running MLS would never access any nonbanking customers resident within the server and would not impact any summary counts or averages. This would help reduce some database programming by avoiding additional "WHERE" clauses that avoid or ignore customers.

In the non-MLS environment, each business unit may have had their own decision support system for targeting new opportunities. In the MLS environment, the same decision support system may be shared across the business units. Leveraging applications that specify a security label with their processing provides a mechanism to ensure that specific consumers, identified by their database row security label or secure views against field level information, do not get targeted inappropriately. More importantly, business unit actions can be audited since system options are available to record both failures and successes against specific data within the ODS or DSS.

An MLS system will enable a company with multiple business units that require separate security postures to use the same database and the same applications without breaching security protocol. This will result in a simplified configuration without redundant systems that will provide fully audit-friendly security for sensitive and regulated information.

A company could also decide that only an internal network will support a certain level of information, and from an open network, such as the Internet, the volume of information made accessible will be reduced for security reasons. It can decide that only specific applications can access the data or that certain data can only be viewed within a specific procedure. It is through an access control program that these rules will be decided. In addition, a company can decide to put flashes on printed output, such as confidential, classified, or privacy-act-like statements that state that this information needs to be protected against copying or further dissemination.

COMPANY DECISIONS

The company first needs to determine its critical information processing infrastructure and the critical assets that it needs to protect. The evolution in applying MLS to this infrastructure is in understanding what are critical assets, what are critical data, the applications that access that data and the network that it gets accessed over. You must determine the level of protection necessary to meet a particular government requirement or to enforce a privacy policy. Critical assets can be on stored media, the database itself and anywhere there are files. It may be a field or a row within a relational database. It can be a removable media, tape devices, optical storage carousels or printed forms. Companies make a privacy commitment to their consumers and they need to put this into practice.

FLOWCHARTING

The simplest method to determine access to critical data is to chart the data flow. From that data flow a company can determine who has access to the various elements of that data all through its lifecycle. This really comes down to a lifecycle management structure. With input, process and output visualizations provided by a flowchart or other lifecycle tooling, a company can look at:

- how the data gets from one point to another
- how that transfer is secured
- who had access to that transfer
- what programs accessed that data at each point
- the persons who can access those programs at each point

These capabilities allow a company to begin to understand where it needs to setup its access control and permission lists. But even more importantly, it helps to identify company groupings so mass customization of security can occur. If a company can reduce the number of data moves and shares of information across applications, then it will reduce the complexity of operations.

Most of this implementation is in execution or just in a normal work-flow. How the company wants to provide an audit, conduct compliance or complete analysis reports, to determine that it has properly protected its assets, will determine the level of granularity and the completeness of the process. If this is done on behalf of a government regulation, it will be more detailed. Companies would apply similar granularity on behalf of customers.

However, for internal use, the implementation may be less detailed as the company may be willing to take more risk. As a company has greater accountability to either a government entity or its own consumers, it will

THE COMPANY FIRST NEEDS TO DETERMINE ITS CRITICAL INFORMATION PROCESSING INFRASTRUCTURE AND THE CRITICAL ASSETS THAT IT NEEDS TO PROTECT.

want to use rigor in how it implements this audit and compliance management process.

RESTRUCTURING THE EXISTING WORKFLOW

The lifecycle of company data probably entails several replicated data moves and several different applications manipulating new images of this same data in what can be termed a stovepipe approach of operation. It might have a mainframe setup for point of sale and ATM type of transaction processing, a UNIX server setup for some type of decision support and data warehouse environments, and a Windows system setup for human resources applications.

Each one of these application environments is independently managed, but the reality is that the same data is flowing through all those elements. Therefore, if they are independently managing and securing them, they will have difficulty in guaranteeing the security and management policies against the data throughout its life cycle. These companies will have to change some of their management approaches to look at those separate application processes as a single, consistent business workflow and manage the security consistently across it.

The problem among the mainframe, UNIX and Windows environments is they are typically separate security domains. To simplify the operations and enforce consistent policies, the security policies should be merged. The first issue is whether the company can merge any of the data. This can reduce the number of data moves to simplify policy management operations. A data merger would mean that the teams that were working independently before on different aspects of this business workflow would now have to work a lot more closely together.

It may also change some of the infrastructure. It is critical for the company to recognize that these systems will have to be peers in terms of working

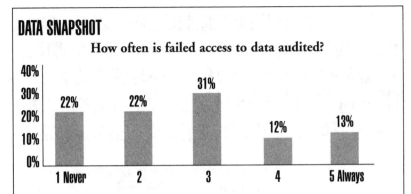

DATA SNAPSHOT

How often is failed access to data audited?

Like searching for shoplifters in the retail industry, if no one ever looks at the videotapes or closed circuit TVs, a business can't stop or inhibit losses. Audit is an important element of preventing and inhibiting security loss.

Download the complete research study for free at www.blackbooksecurity.com/research
Source: 2005 Larstan / Reed Infosecurity Survey

together, because the company's workflow is distributed and will remain so as long as the company has applications servers on Windows and UNIX systems and the data on a mainframe. There might be a hierarchy in terms of how controls are implemented, but they need to have peer services and consistency in management. It might be different implementations based on server specific needs, but applying consistent security concepts across the platform is a critical success factor.

Not only do systems need to be a data server, but they should also be data clients. A system might have data in a UNIX or Windows environment that a mainframe application wants to have access to. Or a system might be pushing data out from the mainframe using a client file protocol to a Windows or UNIX server just to simplify the workflow.

Where the mainframe has direct access to another system, via a file transfer operation, one system will be a data client and the other will be a data server. The systems must communicate, and there has to be some degree of credential sharing between those systems. One thing that the mainframe can do is function as an enterprise authentication server. This will allow a

FORTY YEARS AGO, SOMEONE WOULD FLOWCHART AN APPLICATION TO DETERMINE WHICH TASKS IT WAS SUPPOSED TO ACCOMPLISH. BUT NOW, WITH BUSINESS PROCESS INTEGRATION, DATA IS MOVING ALL OVER THE ENTERPRISE THROUGH THESE SILOS OF COMPUTING. THIS IS THE NEW BUSINESS WORKFLOW.

company to authenticate this business workflow in a single place with a common user identification structure that is then used as the access control mechanism on each independent server. By centralizing user registration enrollment and authentication, the company will start to pull together security controls across the enterprise. That will assist in reducing operational complexity.

HOW TO MAKE THIS WORK?

One of the simplest steps for a company to consider is how it provides registration, identification, and authentication of users, who defines the roles, and how they are defined. Progressing from there, the company starts to consider how to share some of the data within common user credentials. If the business starts looking at centralizing some aspects of authentication across the business workflow, it should find that the sharing of data or facilitating the sharing of data will become operationally simpler. This in turn yields a reduction in storage management operations against that data.

Multi-level security is focused on the sharing of compartmentalized data. It is intended to manage and enforce common security policies against that managed data. It will certainly take some additional effort to understand what resources can be shared across multiple communities. However, once that activity is completed, a single shared instance of data will reduce the total cost of operations against that data, proportionally to the number of communities that share the data.

These savings will be earned by:
- streamlining security operations
- consolidating storage management tasks (such as backup and recall)
- reducing the number of physical server and storage devices
- lessening the complexity of audit and compliance post-processing activities
- shortening the time to make information accessible to additional communities, because now the business will not have to wait for a replication or copy of the data

The fact is, multi-level security facilitates data sharing that can yield significant operational savings to the customer across many fronts.

▪ ▪ ▪

Jim Porell is a Senior Technical Staff Member and Chief Architect for IBM's mainframe software. He chairs the zSeries Software Design council that brings together all IBM technology utilized in the deployment of customer solutions utilizing mainframe technology. Jim led the architecture for IBM's Multi-Level Security technology for z/OS, including the database server, DB2. These became generally available in March 2004, though the base technology dates back to 1987.

Jim focuses on Security and Business Resilient solutions for customers. He has been consulting to government and commercial customers on secure computing infrastructure for 10 years. He has participated in several government efforts ensuring the protection of critical computing infrastructure. He can be reached at 845-435-6593 or jporell@us.ibm.com.

[7]

DEFENDING THE DIGITAL YOU: HOW TO FIGHT ONLINE IDENTITY THEFT

Your very identity as a human being is increasingly intertwined with IT security. Your academic transcripts, driving record, credit history, employment background — they're all stored in easily hacked computers. Here's a look at the growing problem of identity theft, and how to combat it.

> "THE INDIVIDUAL IS THE CENTRAL, RAREST, MOST PRECIOUS CAPITAL RESOURCE OF OUR SOCIETY."
> - Peter Drucker

by TONY ALAGNA & HOWARD SCHMIDT

This book is devoted to bolstering corporate security, but what about defending your identity as an individual? Losing control of the data that defines your life — now that's the ultimate security dilemma.

But don't kid yourself: even if identity theft doesn't specifically happen

THE INTERNET IS THE 21ST CENTURY VERSION OF THE WILD WEST, A LAWLESS DODGE CITY WHERE HACKERS AND CRIMINALS STEAL FROM THE VULNERABLE AND THE UNSUSPECTING. INSTEAD OF NOTORIETY, THEFT IS THE NEW GOAL OF MOST CYBERCROOKS.

to you, everyone has a stake in halting the problem. Its occurrence incurs social costs and affects the corporate bottom line. For example, many companies maintain policies by which they reimburse individuals any money that is stolen from their banking or credit card accounts. These companies either eat the cost, or pass it along to all customers.

Online identity theft is defined as criminals using the Internet as a medium for stealing a user's private identifying credentials, often for the purpose of further theft or fraud. This thievery has been around as long as the Internet, but the nature of the threat has changed dramatically.

In the past, the biggest perceived threat was a precocious teenager taking down a major website like Yahoo, with a "distributed denial of service attack." Viruses were an act of vandalism, like graffiti. Malicious code and hacker attacks were about glory, vandalism and anarchy. They were typically created and deployed by isolated and random individuals.

In his cautionary book about technology, *The Greening of America,* Charles A. Reich wrote: "What we have is technology, organization, and administration out of control, running for their own sake...We have turned over to this system the control and direction of everything — the natural environment, our minds, our lives." When was this book published? In 1970! Imagine what Reich would say now, 35 years later.

Today, we have the Internet, and it's a far scarier place than it was as recently as five years ago. The Internet is the 21st century version of the Wild West, a lawless Dodge City where hackers and criminals steal from the vulnerable and the unsuspecting. Instead of notoriety, theft is the new goal of most cybercrooks. Whether it's stealing intellectual property, corporate assets, money or identity, hacking is about robbing people.

The incidence of cybertheft has risen sharply. Exacerbating the problem is that more and more of these attacks are being perpetrated by organized crime. Many losses have been traced back to gangsters, even directly to the bank accounts of specific crime entities. It is believed that organized crime elements in Russia and Eastern Europe are behind a substantial percentage of Internet stealing. These days, Tony Soprano won't whack you; he'll hack you.

THE THREAT DEFINED

There are two general techniques by which consumers are being exploited. These techniques differ, but the goal of each is the same — to get consumer's usernames, passwords, identifying credentials or sensitive information. These two techniques are malicious code and phishing.

■ **Malicious Code.** Malicious code is the worms, Trojan horses and viruses that often attack computer networks. Many of them are designed to steal. In 2003, about 78% of worms contain a backdoor which is built to listen to keystrokes, capture a screen, see what it is being logged onto, take over the system, and steal what it can. This trend continues to rise in 2004 while worms, Trojan horses, keystroke loggers and eavesdropping software are propagated all throughout the Internet. Many of these backdoors planted by worms over the past few years are still sitting on unsuspecting machines and stealing from its victim.

■ **Phishing.** Worms and viruses are not new to the Internet user, although their ability to do harm and commit theft has increased substantially. Phishing, or spoof sites, are less well known, but no less dangerous. In conducting a phishing expedi-

Insider Notes: Get users to use more secure computing practices, such as not clicking on unknown email, running the latest antivirus software, using a personal firewall, and ensuring that the site is encrypted.

tion, a spammer will send out millions of emails that look like they came from a legitimate source, usually a financial source or an ecommerce entity.

This email contains a misleading link or URL that takes the unsuspecting user to a web page that looks exactly like the login of the consumer's bank. When an unwitting "customer" enters in their username and password and "login" they either go nowhere, or, in more sophisticated scams, they are redirected back to the real site.

The goal of phishing is to trick the user into entering their username and password into a fake site that is being hosted from some random IP address. Mobsters can then capture this data and use it to accomplish several sinister things, such as steal directly, open up credit cards in consumer's names or buy merchandise online.

Unfortunately, forensics on the Internet is sometimes unclear. It is difficult to know what method was used when one specific individual has lost their identity or password, and current security products have limited scope.

IDENTITY THEFT'S IMPACT ON COMPANIES

The same type of attacks are being used against both individuals and companies. The plague of identity theft has impacted companies in two important ways. First, as alluded to above, most banks and financial institutions have what is referred to as a "make-whole" policy. This policy states that if money is stolen out of a customer's bank account, the bank will refund the money, often in full.

Since it is impractical for a bank to investigate every incident of theft, most have established a dollar amount under which it will provide a total refund with no questions asked. Unfortunately, information about these make-whole policies is beginning to become well known. Hacker sites have been found that list banks that have these make-whole policies along with the maximum theft amount that the banks will make good, "no questions asked." The result is that the hackers are enabled to rob banks with impunity.

In addition to these small, but unstoppable losses, phishing attacks have begun to erode confidence in online marketing channels. As more people get burned in these scams, trust in the Internet, as a legitimate channel of commerce, wanes. If people start distrusting their email, or the website that they are on, or, in the extreme sense, the Internet itself, it will create serious problems for companies relying on the Internet.

While this trend will have a critical impact on companies such as Lending Tree, Amazon.com and others that are pure Internet entities, the impact will be broad based since the Internet has proven to be a very cheap way to conduct business, especially within financial services. Banks want people to do business online because of how inexpensive it is to service them. However, this business relies heavily on customer's trust in this channel. Online identity theft impacts companies immediately, by stealing money from them. It also impacts them over time by eroding not only their brand, but the key thing that makes Internet commerce possible, trust in the channel.

THE TRADITIONAL BUSINESS RESPONSE

The traditional business response was to deny everything. This was not a "head-in-the-sand" policy, but one developed from witnessing the experience of others. There was a major "hack attack" against a large U.S. bank that the bank acknowledged. The immediate losses to the bank from the attack were not significant with respect to its size and were all made good. However, the publicity from this attack, whether fairly applied or not, labeled the bank as insecure and vulnerable. Its very largest customers began to leave because of this bad publicity. The policy adopted after that has been to deny and cover-up. In essence treat these attacks as PR problems with a PR solution.

A CHANGE IN RESPONSE

The traditional "head-in-the-sand" policies have begun to change. Some of this is in response to state and federal regulations that are forcing compa-

Insider Notes: Understand the problem and the types of attacks that are infiltrating your environment and plaguing your online customers. Realize their pervasiveness and the real danger that they pose.

ONCE AN IDENTITY IS STOLEN FROM THE I.T. ENVIRONMENT, ALL TYPES OF FRAUD CAN OCCUR, INCLUDING MASSIVE LOSSES IN CORPORATE INTELLECTUAL PROPERTY.

nies to disclose attacks such as these. But even more so, it's in response to the sheer number of attacks occurring. The growth of these attacks has followed an exponential curve over the past 18 months and is reaching epidemic proportions. Consumers are fed up and beginning to lose their enthusiasm for the Internet. Companies have finally begun to take this problem seriously and respond. Their first response has been to admit that there is a problem; their second is to explore new techniques and methodologies such as:

- **Education.** Get users to use more secure computing practices, such as not clicking on unknown email, running the latest antivirus software, using a personal firewall and ensuring that the site is encrypted. These commonly preached computing practices, even when perfectly followed, are only a step in the right direction, not a solution.

- **Organizational cooperation.** Companies, even arch competitors, are uniting in anti-phishing organizations to try to stop phishing and spoof sites. This includes looking out for what appears to be spoof sites and informing each other of their existence.

- **New technologies.** This includes old technologies being implemented in new ways, emerging hot fixes and brand new "shift the trend" technologies. Behavioral technologies are the future.

Another problem is that current best practices using existing security software is not good enough; they are still vulnerable against the new, evolving techniques that bad guys are using to fool people.

This appears, at first blush, to be a problem restricted to individual Internet users. However, the general adoption of advanced communication technologies and mobile computing by corporations has extended corporate networks beyond its perimeter firewall. Hence, the corporate network is no longer a contained LAN that can be defined and protected. Road warriors, telecommuters and contractors can access corporate resources everywhere. This has made the corporate environment susceptible to what used to be user-based attacks. Once an identity is stolen from the IT environment, all types of fraud can occur, including massive losses in corporate Intellectual property.

TWOFOLD ACTION LIST

There are two key points that readers should take from this chapter. Understand the problem and the types of attacks that are infiltrating your environment and plaguing your online customers. Realize their pervasiveness and the real danger that they pose.

Identify what you are currently doing about these problems, and identify what else can be done. Determine how best to address these problems from both a policy and procedural recommendation as well as from a technology recommendation.

DEFINING MALICIOUS CODE

Probably the most important thing to know about malicious code definitions is that there is no clear agreement among experts about how to exactly define, name or categorize malicious code.

Take for example, four of the biggest malicious code outbreaks of 2004: MyDoom, Netsky, Bagel and Sobig. These pieces of "malware" were commonly called "worms," yet they are all mass mailer attacks — meaning they propagate through the email. A worm is classically defined as a type of malicious code that can propagate or infect machines without the user's help or needing the user to do anything. A virus, on the other hand, needed a user to take some type of action, like opening an email, for the virus to continue spread.

Many of the variants of these four big mass mailing outbreaks required the user to take some action, in some cases even opening an attachment. Why are these things called "worms," when they more closely fit the definition of

> **Insider Notes:** Consider an infection by any "malware" tool to be a full invasion, because everything the infected machine does or has stored is sent back to the criminal.

a virus? I suspect a marketing decision somewhere decided "worm" would be the sexier word to describe many different types of malicious code attacks.

There also are conflicting definitions for the words Trojan and spyware. A Trojan is classically defined as malware that comes disguised as something else, which is an incredibly broad definition. Almost all malware comes disguised as something else, meaning that it won't have a name like HeyImavirus.exe. When malicious code experts use the word Trojan, they are generally referring to Remote Access Trojans, which are backdoor programs that give an attacker full access to the infected machine. Trojans are similar to commercial Remote Access utilities and have extreme takeover capabilities — e.g., accessing the file system, gaining full view of everything on the screen, capturing keystrokes, hijacking the mouse, turning on the victim's webcam or microphone and recording what is seen or heard.

Consider an infection by any "malware" tool to be a full invasion, because everything the infected machine does or has stored is sent back to the criminal. Spyware is again a broadly used word that can encompass many genres of malicious code, including adware, Trojans, keyloggers, dialers, browser hijackers, etc. Unfortunately, some vendors in this space like to include even relatively benign privacy violations such as cookies.

Cookies, in rare cases, can be harmful, but you should know that having a small amount of text gathered about a user's surfing habits pales in comparison to utilities such as Trojans that have stolen gigabytes of proprietary source code with disastrous consequences for the victimized corporation.

One more piece of definition confusion: a single piece of malicious code might have multiple names depending on who you talk to. Why would one individual worm have three names; Lovsan, MS Blast or Blaster? The answer is that the separate antivirus firms detect the worm at different times and sometimes in different parts of the world, and do not cooperate fully. Making matters worse, they pick up many more worms than make the headlines, and they cannot tell which handful will be the next big one. If they could, maybe naming for at least some percentage would become more standardized.

In the face of this lack of clarity, maybe it is more important to focus on the capabilities or attributes of the malicious code and how it can negatively affect your computing environment, as opposed to being hung up on a name or category. Attacks are blending many elements of different types of malcious code, and many outbreaks will not fit cleanly into one box or another.

BYPASSING ANTIVIRUS TECHNOLOGY

Bypassing antivirus (AV) is actually trivial for malicious code. Antivirus heuristics are generally ineffective against new types of malicious code. Most experts in the security community do not believe that antivirus has effective heuristics or effective behavioral technology because if it did, it wouldn't constantly need updates. That means, whenever a new worm, a new Trojan or a new piece of malicious code came out, the antivirus would not need an update to be able to detect it or clean it off your machine.

An effective behavioral solution should be able to detect new or modified malware even being years out of date. But antivirus is reactive. A virus breaks out, then, some time later, antivirus will be able to detect it, hopefully before infection gets to your machine.

Antivirus is signature-based technology. If antivirus were using effective behavioral techniques, they wouldn't be able to name the malicious code that they found either. The fact that they call a piece of malicious code "Blaster" means that a human looked at it, analyzed it, created a signature for it and named it. There is no program inside of antivirus that is doing some auto naming that gives it cute names like that.

In addition, if one of the antivirus companies had more effective heuristics or behavioral technology, they would broadcast it widely every time a new piece of malicious code came out. They would say how they protected

> **Insider Notes:** Cookies, in rare cases, can be harmful, but you should know that having a small amount of text gathered about a user's surfing habits pales in comparison to utilities such as Trojans that have stolen gigabytes of proprietary source code with disastrous consequences for the victimized corporation.

their customers without needing an update at zero hour or zero minute or zero day (the first day that a malicious code comes out on the Internet). You do not see those types of press releases because it is not happening.

How does malicious code get around antivirus technologies from a "signature perspective?" Two ways:

❶ **Malicious code propagates faster than the antivirus infrastructure can handle.** The worm " SQLSlammer," for example, spread through the entire Internet and infected 90% of vulnerable systems in eight minutes. That is faster than the antivirus update infrastructure. Even if antivirus already has the signature for it and was trying to distribute that signature at the same exact time as the worm came out, the worm can actually propagate faster than antivirus can update its infrastructure. Worms and other malicious code have gotten too fast. Malicious code can move with more speed than an update because of their small size, exponential spread and push distribution.

❷ **Malicious code writers are well aware of antivirus programs.** Antivirus is everywhere. Up-to-date or not, almost every computer has either current antivirus or some type of remnants of old antivirus on it. So, antivirus is not a secret to malicious code writers who react to it in several ways. If they know that there is a known signature for their malicious code, they do simple modifications of their binary to bypass antivirus. They usually can bypass antivirus by modifying their binary by only a couple of bytes, which creates a variant.

There is a current worm that has 900 variants, because it is trivial to make a variant. Just open up the binary, take a hex editor, modify a few bytes, make sure that the thing still works, and then pop it back out to the "wild" and it's a new variant that antivirus hasn't seen and will not detect. Creating variants will eventually break the back of antivirus companies because they will not be able to forever keep up, as signature lists become impractical.

Another simple method of creating a variant is to use file compression technology. Antivirus firms try to make their signature-based systems accommodate popular file compression utilities, such as Winzip, and still pick up malware obscured by these tools. However, if the malicious code writers use a compression utility that is less common and/or they password protect the compressed file, antivirus will again miss it.

Keep in mind, many types of malicious code are freely available for anyone to download off the Internet. Often, when malware is downloaded, it will state exactly which engines have been modified to bypass and test against. There are tools that even a novice can use to help modify malicious code to bypass antivirus. It is a trivial thing to accomplish, it takes five minutes, and the signature is changed. With access to the source code, it is even easier to change its signature because just adding a few dummy programming loops here and there will result in a different binary and a new variant of malicious code that existing antivirus signatures will not see.

ANTIVIRUS HEURISTICS

Antivirus does have a form of heuristics. What's meant by that is the AV software can look for smaller and smaller signatures. In theory, by signaturizing an entire file, the modification of just one binary byte would break that signature (depending on the brittleness of the signaturization system). To have more flexible signaturization, smaller signatures, dispersed across different parts of the binary, are required. This can potentially make modifying a variant slightly more difficult for the modifier and it may allow antivirus to pick up a variant of malicious code that is built by a kit.

For example, if the antivirus is looking for the string "I love beer" inside a piece of malicious code in the middle of the binary, the next variant that works slightly differently (but still has 'I love beer" in the middle of the binary) might be identified. That's because that key portion of the small signature is unchanged. In this way, a malware creation tool may leave signs

> **Insider Notes:** Keep in mind, many types of malicious code are freely available for anyone to download off the Internet. Often, when malware is downloaded, it will state exactly which engines have been modified to bypass and test against. There are tools that even a novice can use to help modify malicious code to bypass antivirus.

that allow antivirus software to pick up variants that come from the same tool or "family," but only if those smaller signatures remain unchanged.

That is what antivirus means by heuristic. It is hoping that its smaller signatures remain throughout variants of malicious code.

Malicious code writers almost always modify the worm in such a way that it will bypass antivirus. In fact, it is often tested. In the "read me" sections of downloaded malicious code, it will state that it was tested against specific antivirus products with a certain signature database on a specific date and was not detected. If malicious code writers know about it, it is a trivial effort for them to bypass these signature-based antivirus technologies.

ATTACK SCENARIOS — ATTACKING THE LAN

Malicious code writers had to evolve their technologies since the mid-90s because most environments that they enter are now behind network address translations ("nat") or they are "natted" in some way either by a proxy, a router or a firewall. Even home computers often have a LAN and a private IP address. Malicious code writers realized that to communicate with the Internet they had to evolve from an old model that was based on the assumption that each machine had its own IP address on the Internet. In 1996, a machine infected with a piece of malicious code had its own address, so the code could just open up a port and listen, and anyone on the Internet could talk to that machine.

However, when computers were put behind a router or firewall, communication with any non-trusted computer was stopped. A computer behind a router, firewall or proxy has to talk out to a computer on the Internet; it has to initiate the first part of the communication. Therefore, listening is no good in that environment. Malicious code landing on a machine and listening doesn't matter because no machine will be able to talk to it unless they are also trusted behind the same firewall or on the same subnet.

Malicious code writers evolved their technology to be able to communicate within the limitations of this new environment. They developed a number of mechanisms to use to talk within this firewall and/or router environment. One of the most popular is called reverse-connecting malicious code, or inside out connecting malicious code.

There is a piece of malicious code on the Internet called Beast — it is a reverse-connecting remote access Trojan. In some versions of Beast, its first order of business is to look in its registry for any proxy setting that it might have. Proxy settings are there almost always (if the proxy has ever been successfully logged-into at all, then that data will be there). The malicious code grabs these proxy settings, and then injects inside of Internet Explorer where it will initiate its connection sequence outbound, out to the Internet, and it will do it in an encrypted channel.

Through this process, the malicious code is "trusted" by the corporate firewall, the corporate proxy and the corporate routers. It is allowed to talk to whatever machine it wants, because it initiated the connection sequence outbound. The hacker may hard code an IP address or server (often an IRC server) that it wants this malicious code to talk back to as to obscure the originator of the infection.

EMBEDDING MALICIOUS CODE — BEATING THE FIREWALL

Using embedded code is a hacker technique that has existed for some time but has seen an upswing in popularity with recent malware, such as the MyDoom worm. Originally used to provide stealth capability (avoid being listed in Task Manager, for example), embedded code also gives an important advantage to malware: inheriting the credentials of the host (infected) process. This is particularly effective for bypassing personal firewalls. Be

Insider Notes: Using embedded code is a hacker technique that has existed for some time but has seen an upswing in popularity with recent malware, such as the MyDoom worm. Originally used to provide stealth capability (avoid being listed in Task Manager, for example), embedded code also gives an important advantage to malware: inheriting the credentials of the host (infected) process. This is particularly effective for bypassing personal firewalls. Be aware of the fact that Internet Explorer is a popular target host for malware, because it is almost always excluded from restrictions in personal firewalls.

IF EMBEDDING MALICIOUS CODE ATTACKS A SYSTEM WITH A PERSONAL FIREWALL, THE SYSTEM WILL FUNCTION FINE AND THE VICTIM WILL NOT KNOW THAT ANYTHING SUSPICIOUS HAPPENED ON THE MACHINE.

aware of the fact that Internet Explorer is a popular target host for malware, because it is almost always excluded from restrictions in personal firewalls.

In general, "embedded code" refers to an executable component infecting an already running, valid, process. There are numerous techniques for getting this done; some examples are using Windows Hooks (coaxing the OS to do the code injection), using CreateRemoteThread (a more direct approach), and there are also a plethora of spots in the registry listing components where an application should load automatically (legitimately intended for plugins and extensions).

There are also some more covert mechanisms, such as directly allocating memory in another process and stimulating code execution therein. When these techniques are used, the embedded code is part of the host process, rather than being a distinct process of its own. This avoids being visible to the end-user, as mentioned before, but also since credentials (for doing things like accessing the Internet) are done at a process-level, it means the embedded component will now be able to perform actions in the same manner as its host.

As I stated, Explorer is a vulnerable target, because it tends to be excluded from personal firewall restrictions. Ostensibly, this is because the user experience would be damaged by having to approve every network action, since IE is obviously network-intensive.

This carte blanche to use the network is precisely what is desirable. By effectively becoming part of Internet Explorer, almost any action can be done without scrutiny. The user has a disincentive to use aggressive checks with IE because it would render IE unusable. Moreover, how does even the human know which network actions are needed for the normal functioning of IE, versus ones that are possibly malicious in intent?

Internet Explorer has an additional advantage in that it provides numerous extensibility hooks that can be exploited to get malicious code running within it easily. The Windows shell, Explorer, is also popular for the same reasons, but to a lesser extent.

The embedded code technique is particularly effective against personal firewalls, when combined with the reverse-connecting technique. Since restrictions are even more relaxed for outbound connections, this technique is effective against even dedicated (hardware) firewalls in addition to personal (software) firewalls.

It's useful to realize that the embedded code technique does not alter the binary image of the host process, so it is not useful to apply signatures there. Signatures could be used against loaded DLLs, however this is not a general technique, since malware can also embed itself into the host without being a file-based entity at all.

Simply put, personal firewalls prompt the user when an application requires network usage, therefore making it suspicious to the user. Using embedding techniques, malicious code can hide inside an application that has already been approved or trusted by the firewall. When malicious code embeds in these trusted applications, it can perform any network connectivity operation without the user being alerted. If embedding malicious code attacks a system with a personal firewall, the system will function fine and the victim will not know that anything suspicious happened on the machine.

THE ANATOMY OF AN ATTACK

Trojans can be distributed in a myriad of ways: inside a worm that infects one million machines; insertion into a macro of a Word document and emailed out to 2,000 corporate users; insertion into an MP3 that takes advantage of the player vulnerability on a machine; or posted on a Napster

> **Insider Notes:** Trojans can be scripted to do many nefarious things. They can look for credit card numbers, for mother's maiden names, or for specific information, such as a company name, and target that company by tracking all visits to that company's internal websites.

FROM A CORPORATE DEFENSIVE PERSPECTIVE, NO MATTER WHAT TYPE OF "BEST PRACTICE" DEFENSE IS THROWN AT IT, THE MALICIOUS CODE WILL STILL BE ABLE TO COMMUNICATE JUST FINE.

file sharing networks for 50,000 downloads. Wherever or however the endpoint is infected, a Trojan has compromised the system and it is talking back to this central place, which is likely to be an IRC chat server that is already set up. Trojans can be scripted to do many nefarious things. They can look for credit card numbers, for mother's maiden name, or for specific information, such as a company name, and target that company by tracking all visits to that company's internal websites.

The only ways that Trojans can be contained from a defensive point of view are somewhat unrealistic — e.g., not to allow any network connectivity. If users can access www.myfavoritesearchpage.com, they can see the Internet, and so can the malicious code. From a corporate defensive perspective, no matter what type of "best practice" defense is thrown at it, the malicious code will still be able to communicate just fine. It will bypass gateway antivirus, by being a variant; it will bypass desktop antivirus, by being a variant; it will bypass desktop firewalls, by injecting itself or tricking the user; it will bypass a corporate proxy, by grabbing the password settings; it will bypass network based intrusion detection, by using custom protocols and encryption and rendering itself invisible to intrusion detection techniques. It will bypass corporate firewalls and corporate routers by initiating its connection sequence outbound. So it doesn't matter what defensive layers are thrown at these things. Normal readily downloadable off-the-Internet malicious code can bypass every available endpoint protection mechanism as well as every best practice corporate defense mechanisms.

ATTACK SCENARIOS: THE UNMANAGED ENVIRONMENT

There are many different types of remote access solutions for mobile employees. There is SSL VPN, which is a web-based VPN device. There are also different types of webmail as well as Outlook Web Access. Also, some bigger companies like Citrix have secure gateways. Classic IPsec

VPNs, as well as different types of portals and intranets and extranets, can also be used for mobile computing.

The quality that all remote access has in common, regardless of the method used, is that it is an endpoint machine and is as vulnerable as any other system on the Internet. In some cases, they are managed machines — a corporate issued asset that is managed by the corporate IT that has all of the corporate security provisioned security programs.

Corporate resources can now be accessed from anywhere, with most places far from trustworthy. The danger here is extreme, because mobile computing environments plug into random places and in unmanaged systems. Vendors are aware of this security threat, and they're increasingly recommending the deployment of different types of security and scanning technologies. The problem is that most security technologies are not readily deployable. Antivirus is a very large application, so it is not practical to have anyone who is logging-in remotely to download this software and then scan the hard drive for half an hour before they can access email. Antivirus-type technologies in the "unmanaged space" must be behavioral, small, fast and transactional. Some are emerging in the marketplace.

However, the vulnerability in this mobile communication model is obvious. Besides the general threat of malicious code, these machines have no physical access restrictions. Anybody can load whatever they want on it (the risk of a keystroke-logger, regardless of whether it has network connectivity, is huge). A person can walk up five minutes before it was used and five minutes after it was used and capture everything that was done on that machine between those two time points.

> **Insider Notes:** Corporate resources can now be accessed from anywhere, with most places far from trustworthy. The danger here is extreme, because mobile computing environments plug into random places and in unmanaged systems. Vendors are aware of this security threat and they're increasingly recommending the deployment of different types of security and scanning technologies.

The threat of malicious code is even greater in this unmanaged machine space. Sometimes the people using IPsec VPNs feel safe because this technology prevents split-tunneling (the ability for two or more applications to be communicating simultaneously while the VPN connection is going). Preventing split-tunneling only creates an illusion of safety.

A reverse-connecting Trojan functions in the same way in this environment as it does in a corporate environment, by initiating its connection sequence inside out. So, if users can see the Internet, then so can the malicious code. Even without Internet access, malicious code can be scripted to steal or perform actions whenever it comes back online. Malicious code is basically winning in every environment regardless of the situational defenses. All situational defenses can do is minimize the types of attacks; it cannot stop attacks.

STOPPING WORMS — IS PATCHING THE ANSWER?

A general definition of a worm is that it self-propagates. Historically, with viruses, the user had to do something, such as open an attachment, to be infected. Worms just infect and keep propagating without the user's help. Nowadays, worms and viruses are blended — they can share traits. Any way that a file can get on a machine, so can malicious code.

There is a false notion that patch management — compliance techniques — can immunize against malicious code attacks. This is not true. There are many different infection vectors for worms that have nothing to do with vulnerabilities and patches. Malicious code can thrive even in a fully patched environment. Patch management is a "band-aid," not a fix.

A mass mailer worm does not have to use any vulnerability to attack a system. MyDoom was one of the more widespread worms of 2004, yet it required no vulnerabilities. Getting an email with an attachment is not a violation of any vulnerability on the system.

Because of the flexibility of the operating system, many of the things that malicious code does are completely normal and within the range of the rules of the operating system. Trojans, spyware and keyloggers almost never need vulnerabilities to perform their nefarious activities.

In addition, the time between vulnerability identification and the introduction of a worm that takes advantage of that vulnerability is decreasing rapidly. A development period that took 60 days from announcement to worm, now takes nine days. There are also worms that use zero day or unreleased vulnerabilities.

PHISHING

Phishing is the act of using spoofed sites to trick Internet users into thinking they are on a legitimate site so that they provide login, credit card, or other important personal identity items. A spoof or phish site is usually a good copy of a legitimate site.

Users are lead to this site by an email that is often mass mailed to millions of users, which is spam for the purpose of phishing. This email also will resemble a well known company and declare that the users must go to that site for some important reason such as "we need to verify your information." Large financial institutions have been a visible and often hit target because of both their large Internet presence and abundant theft possibilities.

Phishing is a quick-hit scam operation. Some users identify it for what it is and report the site. A spoof site is usually shut down within 12 hours after it is discovered by the victimized corporation, but that is usually sufficient time to collect enough personal data from unwitting users to be profitable. Also, phishing scams can utilize hundreds of sites at once so that its lifecycle is greatly enhanced. These scams often utilize the free web hosting services provided by many ISPs, and they are recently attracted to foreign ISPs. The foreign ISPs are sometimes not as responsive to spoofing complaints and tend to keep the site alive longer and provide less help in efforts to catch the perpetrators.

Insider Notes: There is a false notion that patch management – compliance techniques – can immunize against malicious code attacks. This is not true. There are many different infection vectors for worms that have nothing to do with vulnerabilities and patches. Malicious code can thrive even in a fully patched environment. Patch management is a "band-aid," not a fix.

The lure that Phishers use to trick users is referred to as a "ruse." These ruses fall under two categories; the victim needs to come to the site for something good, or the victim needs to come to the site to prevent something bad. The positive ruses are less common and include messages like "click to register for your prize" and "you have pictures, click to view them." Much more common are the negative ruses that have themes around an urgency to verify account data before the account is closed.

THE PERFECT CRIME?

Tracing the criminals behind these spoof sites is extremely difficult, because there is so little information left behind. The free hosting sites require no identification, nor do the hotmail email addresses. The FBI, which is extremely concerned with this activity, can only follow them by following the dollars. They cannot actually stop the scam itself. The FBI and other federal agencies have not been very effective in tracking these people down; they almost always get away, so there is not a strong deterrent against running this scam. Some of the paths traced from spoofing have pointed to Russian organized crime.

CAN SPAM FILTERS HELP?

People who feel that they are protected because they have a spam filter are grossly mistaken. There are a number of techniques used by phishing scams to get around and through spam filters. Some of these include: encoding, encrypting, dynamic frames and redirection. In redirection, the phisher creates an empty page with a link to the phish page. All of this is transparent to the end-user.

Another popular technique is to create a link that is not a spoof site, or sending misleading URLs. A misleading URL can be an address embedded in a descriptive field, using HTML text that sounds similar to the target URL (Citi-Bank), or using obscure URL formatting that includes the target's name (citi.bank.com@geocity.com/updateyouraccount). An end-user that clicks on this page will be taken to a phish site.

However, this is a very large vulnerability. As spam filter technology improves, so will the technology of the phisher. The higher the level of defense, the more the problem proliferates. In essence, this is an Internet con which is based on social engineering and end-user general naiveté. It is unlikely that spam will ever cease to be a problem as every proposed counter measure has immediate weaknesses, and in some cases those weaknesses have even been demonstrated. Spam filters of today have a heavy reliance on text analysis, which can be defeated by either encoding HTML messages or basing the entire message in graphics. There are no existing Artificial Intelligence engines good enough to reliably decipher what is contained in an image-only message.

THE NEW PHISHING TECHNOLOGIES

Phishing has evolved as rapidly as the techniques used to attack it. Spoofers now use frames, pop-ups, and more technical implementations. In addition, they have become more knowledgeable. They now steal legitimate marketing lists from a target and use that to "validate" a phishing attack and improve the odds in their favor.

For example, an end user that has just signed up with a bank would be more susceptible to a "request" from that bank to verify information. Increased knowledge about a target improves the effectiveness of phishing attacks.

Spoofers are now also utilizing pictures and messages that are difficult to distinguish from those from legitimate sources. They have also begun to use instant messaging as a medium to get users to spoof sites, which is referred to as "spim." Finally, new tool kits are now readily available to help the spoofer wannabe build fake websites. However, the majority of spoof sites are still unsophisticated.

BLENDED ATTACKS

Increasingly, phishers are combining malicious code with their phish pages. Up to 10% of the recent phishing attacks were found to have a malicious code component. Remember the goal is always theft. Thus, the people the bad guys can't trick into giving away their information could

Insider Notes: To stop phishing, a behavioral approach must be employed. Using behavioral technologies that are installed locally on the machine, like a toolbar, will catch the attack in real time and block it.

THREAT TO GLOBAL EMAIL SYSTEM AND BANKS GROWING

By Stephen Lange Ranzini

Junk email is becoming a global menace.

According to data released at a recent meeting of the Organization of Economic Coordination and Development (OECD), the global cost of junk email messages was estimated to be $200 billion in 2004, while the number of junk messages exceeded 3 trillion, roughly triple the number in 2003.

Mark Sunner, Chief Technology Officer of MessageLabs, a global out-sourced hoster of email services for large businesses which handles 70 million emails for its clients per day, released data at the OECD meeting that indicates in July, 2004, fully 94.5% of all email globally was junk email.

MessageLabs data also indicates that between 1 in 10 and 1 in 14 of all emails globally are viruses. More ominously, MessageLabs indicates that every virus launched this year has a zombie network backdoor, or "Remote Access Trojan" (RAT). Once activated, a RAT allows malicious spammers to seize control of compromised PCs and load key-logging devices to detect passwords and user ids typed by PC users. The latest version of RATs also are enabled with software that allows the nefarious criminal minds that control the RATs to load additional software to compromised PCs, creating networks of zombie PCs called Zombie Bot Networks.

MessageLabs' Sunner also asserted that one major ISP informed him that 30% of all users are harboring Remote Access Trojans. This would mean that 200 million PCs globally (30% of the 665 million global email users) are controlled by Remote Access Trojans. Potentially up to 30% of all PC users who use Internet banking are also compromised.

Several experts at the OECD meeting indicated that they were quite impressed by the technical quality of these Next Generation RATs. The newer Remote Access Trojan key-loggers are down to just 2 kilobytes in size. They are being placed not just in malicious junk emails but on compromised websites and even innocent looking websites that offer brand name products at low prices.

A recent example purported to sell bicycles cheaply, and had a high placement in Google price-based searches as a result. It is not recommended that consumers use any website that is not fully trusted. However, even trusted names may be compromised. ICANN, the rules making body of the Internet, recently changed domain transfer rules to eliminate the requirement that changes of domain registration must be confirmed with the domain administrator of record. German hackers used this vulnerability recently to take over the German eBay website. If consumers become widely aware of these threats, they are likely to discontinue use of search engines such as Google or Yahoo to shop online or to search online for useful information. Linking to an untrusted website from a search engine is also not recommended. This will greatly reduce the value of the Internet to all users.

Enrique Salem, SVP Network & Gateway Security Solutions of Symantec, one of the leading virus and junk email blocking technology vendors, estimates that a majority of all junk email is generated through these Zombie Bot Networks or open relays. When compromised, each zombie PC in a Zombie Bot Network turns into an open relay. The value of a compromised zombie PC grows dramatically if it is connected to a high-speed Internet network such as a broadband network. Therefore, cheap broadband Internet access is driving the growth of junk email, theft and the utility of Zombie Bot Networks. Microsoft has formed a working group to try to combat these Zombie Bot Networks, but faces an uphill battle.

Symantec's Salem estimates that the typical spammer generates 200 million junk email messages per day and only requires 400 purchases at $20 each to generate the $8,000 in revenue required to break-even on a commercial offering.

However, we note that the value of a stolen credit card number using a trojan key logger averages $100 in the black market, so only 80 credit cards need to be stolen each day to generate a profit for the malicious spammer. Each identity theft can cause between $2,000 and $10,000 in losses to consumers and banks. We postulate that the theft of an entire online identity via RATs could be worth $500 to $1,000 on the black market. Therefore, a RAT-based identity theft would only need just 8 to 16 per day to generate a profit for the malicious spammer.

WHAT CAN BANKS AND CORPORATIONS DO NOW?

For companies, internal misuse of corporate networks by employees to generate junk email is also on the rise. To determine if your network is a source of junk email, register with America Online's free Complaint Feedback Loop tool at http://postmaster.aol.com. Besides keeping up with the latest required patches, which is admittedly a near impossible task due to the frequency with which they are released, corporate users should ensure that email server programs typically used are up-to-date.

For example, Sendmail version 8.9 or later is required to block open relay attacks. Corporate users should also ensure that Port 25 is always closed (this prevents a corporate email network from becoming an open proxy, which is highly sought after by spammers because it allows them to send junk email from your corporate server).

Spammers don't believe that they will be caught, they believe that they will get off even if they are caught, and can cover their tracks very effectively due to the security holes in the underlying architecture of the Internet. A new paradigm to rescue the global email system is urgently required.

The author is President of University Bank, Ann Arbor, Michigan. He is also the U.S. delegate to the United Nations global standard setting body for the financial services industry, UN CEFACT TBG 5 (Finance) and a member of the Security Committee of the Financial Services Technology Consortium, the R&D collaborative of the nation's largest banks.

still be victims of a keylogger or Trojan attack. Recent browser vulnerabilities have made Trojans a strong weapon for the phishers, because some vulnerabilities will allow malicious code to be planted just by the act of browsing to the phish site.

WHAT CAN COMPANIES DO?

The Internet is too highly a profitable way to conduct business for companies to give up on it. They have responded to these attacks as best they can. Many have established an incidental response team within their organization. When they are attacked, they can at least analyze the site itself, work with the ISP to shut it down and contact the FBI. Typically they can do little more. Attacks not only are common, but they are fast. By the time that a company reacts to shut it down, it has already accomplished its goals and identities have been compromised.

One important tool in this campaign against phishing is based on the fact that a website is copyrighted. Therefore, a spoof site does infringe on copyright laws. This allows legal action to be taken against the person managing the site and is referred to as a Digital Millennium Copyright Act (DMCA) complaint.

There are also anti-phishing organizations. Financial Services Technology Consortium (FSTC) is a group of banks focused on stopping phishing for the financial services industry. There also is antiphishing.org, which sponsors anti-phishing working groups of vendors and customers who get together to develop standards and techniques to fight this problem.

A promising approach is a behavioral technology that can detect phish sites as soon as the user encounters them and then blocks them real time. One such technology is currently used inside of eBay's Account Guard, which is a part of its toolbar.

The industry will also have a new powerful tool at its disposal, and it is called the Phish Reporting Network. This site is a place where companies who are victims of phish attacks can submit sites and large ISP's can block these sites. Blocking sites wherever possible and as soon as possible is important because shutting sites down is just not fast enough.

Unfortunately, protecting against phishing attacks often comes down to having the most sophisticated defense, so that spoofers will attack and steal from another target. Phishing attacks are technologically simple for criminals to carry out, so it would be unwise for a company to be considered the "low hanging fruit."

It has been said that some of the most successful businesses on the Internet simply applied a tried-and-true business model and created an online version of it. Unfortunately, age-old crimes also seem to be gaining success with the help of the Internet. The bad guys are using the Internet to steal, and quite frankly they are, for the most part, getting away with it. The current defenses do little to prevent the techniques used to commit online identity theft.

Malicious code is a powerful weapon for criminals. Everyday, there are more and more computers with antivirus software loaded and updated, fully patched operating systems, and firewalls built straight into the OS, but the attacks only increase. Malicious code writers can defeat all of our current countermeasures. Catching malicious code with signatures is too late; they have already spread around the world and done their damage.

Phishing attacks are at their root an almost laughably simple trick. Fake an email and fake a website and, sure enough, some users will hand over their credit card number and then some. The fact is that phishing works, and the phishers are evolving their techniques real time to be more advanced and harder to stop. Companies trying to battle the problem are finding that they have a tough place to start — they don't know how many phish sites are out there trying to victimize their customers. Some analysis of this problem has showed that there are three times as many sites out there as are being found. Shutting these sites down after they are found is too late; they have already done their damage.

THE ANTI-FRAUD TOOL OF THE FUTURE

The only way these problems can be solved is with effective behavioral technology. Using behavioral technology on new or modified malicious code will stop the attack from ever doing damage to the local machine or allowing it to propagate to others.

Behavioral technologies can be fast and small, because they don't have the weight of a large signature list slowing down their scan times and bulking up their file size. To stop phishing, a behavioral approach must be employed. Using behavioral technologies that are installed locally on the machine, like a toolbar, will catch the attack in real time and block it. As distribution of these types of tools increase, the number of sites found and shutdown will increase dramatically.

Behavioral approaches are the future.

■ ■ ■

As the Chief Technical Officer and Founder of WholeSecurity, Tony is the visionary behind the patent-pending behavioral technologies that drive the company's endpoint security solutions. He is considered an expert in information security and specializes in the areas of malicious code and phishing. In recognition of his contributions to the security industry, Tony was recently named Information Technologist of the Year by the Austin Chapter of the Association of Information Technology Professionals (AITP) and he serves as a member of the InfoWorld CTO Network. As a sought after public speaker, Tony often addresses executive forums, speaks at security events and serves on conference panels. He actively advises lawmakers, industry analysts, financial organizations and corporations on cyber-threats and how to defend against them.

Tony can be reached at 512-874-7451 or tony.alagna@wholesecurity.com.

Howard A. Schmidt has recently joined eBay as Vice President and Chief Information Security Officer. He retired from the federal government after 31 years of public service. He was appointed by President Bush as the Vice Chair of the President's Critical Infrastructure Protection Board and as the Special Adviser for Cyberspace Security for the White House in December, 2001. Prior to the White House, Howard was Chief Security Officer for Microsoft Corp., where his duties included CISO, CSO and overseeing the Security Strategies Group.

[8]

PREEMPTING DATA WARFARE: THE ART OF COMPREHENSIVE VULNERABILITY MANAGEMENT

Instead of simply waiting for a data system attack, and then performing a desperate form of triage, you must prepare for unpleasant surprises by continually assessing vulnerabilities. Here's how to stay several steps ahead of the enemy.

"WHO CAN SURPRISE WELL, MUST CONQUER."

- John Paul Jones, on the eve of battle

by MARIA CIRINO

In postindustrial warfare, computers are the weapons and information is the spoils of victory. Hackers and unscrupulous competitors constantly probe your corporate defenses, looking for weaknesses. The only way to stop these remorseless cyber warriors is to assess your own vulnerabilities before they do.

The Pentagon regularly reviews enemy threats, real or imagined,

YOU DON'T HAVE TO BE A HOUSEHOLD BRAND NAME LIKE AMAZON.COM OR YAHOO TO GET HIT WITH HUGELY EXPENSIVE BREACHES OF DATA SECURITY.

honing its capacity for war. You must do the same. InfoWar is not waged with bullets, tanks and bombs, but it is still a brutal conflict, and the winner takes all. That is where comprehensive vulnerability management comes in. It is your strategic battle plan for stopping attacks before they happen. Your corporate survival depends on it.

You need to act now, because IT vulnerability is steadily worsening. You do not have to be a household brand name like Amazon.com or Yahoo to get hit with hugely expensive breaches of data security. Every year, billions of dollars are spent on combating worms, viruses, Trojan horses and denial-of-service (DoS) attacks, and hackers are only getting more resourceful with each passing day.

Plugging the security holes in corporate systems used to be a relatively predictable task to manage. A company put its corporate security policy in place, conducted annual penetration tests, or "pen-tests," and plugged whatever vulnerabilities were found in servers and other systems. In those days, there was time to identify problems on a point basis and react to them at a normal systems-upgrade pace.

Today, however, the window between when a vulnerability in operating software or other systems is discovered and when it is exploited has closed dramatically, and now, the best defense is a good offense. Hence, the concept of comprehensive vulnerability management, a fairly new strategy that offers great promise in helping companies lock out malicious attacks before they happen. Simply put, comprehensive vulnerability management involves implementing a recurring program of identifying and addressing vulnerability issues. This strategy addresses everything from discovery of the vulnerability, to prioritizing the vulnerabilities most critical to address, to the process of actually fixing the problem. It then extends beyond the fix to remediation and boosts a company's proactive information security posture through comprehensive monitoring.

Comprehensive vulnerability management involves a process of continual vulnerability discovery, prioritization, remediation and monitoring of applications and networks. These processes are critical because IT infrastructures today are like ecosystems — changing and growing every single day, and morphing several times a day. These changes are driven by new devices that are continually being connected to the Internet, by mobile workers plugging laptops into docking stations, and by a wide variety of factors and events that affect the IT infrastructure on a daily basis.

A comprehensive vulnerability management process is also very important because it reduces the time between inspections of the state of vulnerability of the network, critical servers and applications so that organizations can prioritize and remediate (or patch) these vulnerabilities more quickly. This reduces exposure and risk from security incidents that might otherwise occur as a result of having longer time intervals between inspections.

The four components of comprehensive vulnerability management are:
- discovery
- prioritization
- remediation
- monitoring

Discovering vulnerabilities is crucial because they cannot be fixed if they are not identified. Prioritizing vulnerabilities is necessary because of their sheer number and the fact that they are increasing rapidly. It is the rare organization that actually has the ability to stay on top of all vulnerabilities as they occur.

On any given day, a company has to undertake "triage" decision-making to ensure that the most threatening vulnerabilities are addressed first — these two steps are taken so that the third step, remediation, can occur. (This step

Insider Notes: Discovering vulnerabilities is crucial because they cannot be fixed if they are not identified. Prioritizing vulnerabilities is necessary because of their sheer number and the fact that they are increasing rapidly. It is the rare organization that actually has the ability to stay on top of all vulnerabilities as they occur.

SECURITY MANAGERS MUST AVOID AS MANY PROBLEMS AS POSSIBLE, RATHER THAN CLEANING UP AFTER THE DAMAGE IS DONE. THEY NEED TO FOCUS ON PREVENTION, NOT THE CURE.

often takes the form of patching.) The fourth step, monitoring, is actually ongoing, and provides a "closed loop" in the system; monitoring not only enables the first three steps, but it also ensures that the company fixed what it intended to fix. Through continuous monitoring, new vulnerabilities are detected that may have occurred while previous vulnerabilities were being addressed, and this starts the cycle all over again.

IMPORTANCE TO EXECUTIVE MANAGEMENT

Comprehensive vulnerability management is important to executive management for two reasons:

- It allows organizations to incorporate business objectives into their security plans, a cornerstone of truly effective information security programs.

  Increasingly, executive management is looking to information security as an enabler for achieving business objectives, and as an important means for preventing unplanned outages, additional costs, lawsuits or other interruptions. Comprehensive vulnerability management is emerging as one of the best vehicles available to maintain a strong proactive security posture for meeting business objectives, while reducing risk and disruption.

- It assists in the compliance of regulatory requirements, forestalling the high costs and legal ramifications of being non-compliant. Today, companies face myriad regulations, with the Health Insurance Portability Accounting Act (HIPAA) and Sarbanes-Oxley requiring the most attention.

  HIPAA affects any organization handling sensitive patient records, such as healthcare companies, payers, providers or even a supermarket that operates a pharmacy. Any organization that handles information the government deems sensitive is liable for maintaining the privacy of that data — if a company cannot demonstrate that it is taking continual "best efforts" to maintain confidentiality, then the senior executives and officers associated with that company run the risk of federal criminal prosecution. This liability has emerged as the main driver for executive management commitment to a more proactive, programmatic approach toward information security, which is at the core of comprehensive vulnerability management.

Similarly, Sarbanes-Oxley mandates that information security and privacy risk must be considered a factor in a company's overall business risk. Executive officers and directors of public corporations are held personally responsible for ensuring that this section of Sarbanes-Oxley is carried out within the required standards.

Recent regulatory requirements are now capturing the attention of managers who historically were not concerned about security and privacy, which were once considered more within the CIO's purview. The potential for personal liability has made them very concerned about ensuring that adequate measures are being taken.

The acceleration of inspection intervals and the implementation of a comprehensive vulnerability management program is one of the best ways to ensure that executive management understands what is happening within their security infrastructure, while also controlling that risk.

Successfully implementing comprehensive vulnerability management requires executives to embrace a new managerial paradigm, by which they view data security not as an isolated, linear function but as an integral part of the entire enterprise.

 Insider Notes: Comprehensive vulnerability management has emerged as one of the best vehicles available to maintain a strong proactive security posture and enable the attainment of business objectives, while reducing risk and potential disruption.

Alvin Toffler, in his brilliant and seminal book, *The Third Wave*, aptly describes the new perspective that executives must adopt:

> *"The multipurpose corporation that is emerging demands, among other things, smarter executives. It implies a management capable of specifying multiple goals, weighting them, interrelating them and finding synergic policies that accomplish more than a single goal at a time. It requires policies that optimize not for one, but for several variables simultaneously."*

IMPORTANCE TO SECURITY MANAGEMENT

At the end of the day, security management bears responsibility for executing an effective information security program. Security managers must avoid as many problems as possible, rather than cleaning up after the damage is done. They need to focus on prevention, not the cure.

Comprehensive vulnerability management is a more proactive approach that security managers can invest in, rather than adding yet another layer of security technology that generates reports that often go without review. This lack of review typically stems from lack of sufficient staff. Through comprehensive vulnerability management, an organization can reduce its risk and enhance its overall security posture. Therefore, these services have become increasingly popular and are fast becoming a staple of most corporate security programs.

ACTION ITEMS

Executives need to ask what kind of comprehensive vulnerability management programs are in place in their organizations. If one is not established, immediate efforts to install vulnerability management will greatly advance an organization's existing security program.

If the security staff is running programs internally, they should look at the output of those programs and determine if there are effective measurements and reporting in place. They then need to compare the current approach they are taking with an outsourced approach. They need to undertake an analysis of what is being spent on information security and consider reallocating portions of the security budget to more preventative measures, such as comprehensive vulnerability management, instead of adopting new point security solutions or hiring more people to monitor existing technology.

MANAGING PATCH MANAGEMENT

Patch management is a challenge. It solves some problems but, in the process, creates others. The closed-loop system of comprehensive vulnerability management involves trolling for vulnerabilities in short enough intervals to discover the ones that have been fixed and identifying new ones that have inadvertently cropped up as a result of a new patch.

Such systems are complex. No one vendor, which is under constant pressure to get these patches out as quickly as possible, can design for every possible contingency in all IT environments. Because patching is an imperfect science at best, companies need an approach to help catch those unintended vulnerabilities as soon as possible.

COMPREHENSIVE VULNERABILITY MANAGEMENT DEFINED

In general, a vulnerability is a weakness in software that can be exploited by an attacker or malicious user. Vulnerabilities can also be assessed based on an individual company's security policy, since not every organization requires the same level of security. The definition of a vulnerability in practical terms depends a great deal on what a company's security policy defines as acceptable use. Anything that violates the security policy, whether it is a weakness in software, process or a technology can be viewed as a vulnerability that can compromise security.

Comprehensive vulnerability management is an important component of a corporate security policy because it establishes a recurring program of monitoring for vulnerabilities, rather than the occasional checks that historically had been normal procedure for most organizations. There are

Insider Notes: Successfully implementing comprehensive vulnerability management requires executives to embrace a new managerial paradigm, by which they view data security not as an isolated, linear function but as an integral part of the entire enterprise.

CASE STUDY: PROTECTING THE DMZ

The Problem: Plan and implement a comprehensive vulnerability management program that would address the areas of greatest risk to the company.

The Solution: The following components of the VeriSign Managed Vulnerability Protection Service (MVPS) were selected by the company and implemented:

- Monthly External Automated Scanning
- Quarterly Internal Automated Scanning
- Quarterly External Network Vulnerability Testing
- Quarterly Web Application Testing

The Process - Monthly External Automated Testing

The initial testing and scanning phase uncovered major weaknesses in each of the company environments that were assessed. The monthly external automated scan detected hosts that were un-patched for several recent Microsoft vulnerabilities. Since exploit code for these buffer overflow vulnerabilities was freely available on Internet websites and underground Internet Relay Chat (IRC) channels, timely detection and remediation was critical in protecting the Demilitarized Zone (DMZ) environment from compromise. The compromise of any of the affected hosts could have resulted in exposure of confidential consumer data, which would have led to loss of consumer confidence, a breach of regulatory requirements and ultimately significant financial loss.

Once the flaws were detected, the company implemented patches to protect the environment from attack. During the quarterly network vulnerability assessment, VeriSign verified that the patches had been installed and the exposure had been eliminated. In addition, this assessment uncovered some configuration weaknesses that resulted in high-risk vulnerabilities.

The Process - Internal Automated Scan/External Network Vulnerability Testing

The internal automated scanning process detected a large number of critical vulnerabilities on the network. These could have possibly been exploited by insiders or by worms introduced by mobile users. Security incident statistics show that the majority of security breaches occur on the internal network. They are often carried out by disgruntled employees, or by the spread of malicious worms. Hosts on the internal LAN also tend to be much less protected than externally facing hosts, often providing easy targets for technically capable users. Hosts that were identified as highly vulnerable included several internal financial application servers and a database server hosting the human resources management database.

The internal scan results prompted the security team to implement a program of regular patching and improving the security posture of new desktop and server build configurations. Subsequent monthly scan results illustrated the improved internal security posture as the numbers and severity of vulnerabilities detected decreased significantly over several months.

The Process - Web Application Testing
The company had never previously implemented a web application testing program, and recognized that security was not a primary consideration during its in-house development cycle. While the company had implemented firewalls to protect its DMZ and internal environments from external attacks, it had previously failed to recognize that each web application provided an avenue of attack and could not be protected by a firewall Access Control List (ACL).

VeriSign discovered critical vulnerabilities in several of the web applications that were tested. By testing the application from the perspective of a user without any login credentials and as a valid user of the application, VeriSign identified Structured Query Language (SQL) Injection and Cross Site Scripting flaws that could result in the exposure of confidential data and provide an attacker unauthorized direct access to the application database.

Additionally, session management weaknesses were identified that could allow an authorized user to obtain the privilege level of an application administrator, thus compromising all user accounts. Successful exploitation of any of these flaws would have resulted in significant financial loss due to fraud, loss of customer confidence and exposure of confidential consumer data with regulatory ramifications.

As a result of the findings from the web application assessments, the company initiated a program to educate its development team on secure programming practices. The development lifecycle was also modified to include security reviews at each phase of application development. Subsequent quarterly web application tests demonstrated the ongoing success of the secure development initiative, as application vulnerabilities were reduced over time due to the elimination of root-cause insecure programming practices.

The recurring nature of the vulnerability management program implemented at this company has resulted in measurable improvements in the overall security posture. Vulnerabilities have decreased in every area that is comprehensively assessed by the VeriSign MVPS team, and security processes have been implemented that ensure the security posture continues to improve.

multiple points of entry on a network, and each of these offers multiple areas of potential attack. It is necessary to craft a program that addresses each of those susceptible points on a regular basis.

For example, when designing a recurring program for an internal network, the enterprise would first schedule an audit of that network quarterly or even monthly. Other technologies that are good candidates for this program are phone systems, wireless systems and web applications. When creating a comprehensive vulnerability management program, each of these areas must be addressed and audited frequently. A vulnerability may have been discovered and patched in January, but a new one may be released a couple of months later; that vulnerability needs to be discovered and patched in a timely fashion, as well.

THE GATHERING STORM

The driving force behind the rapid evolution of comprehensive vulnerability management has been the lightning-fast pace of vulnerability exploitation. During the past two to three years, the rate of discovery and exploita-

THE DRIVING FORCE BEHIND THE RAPID EVOLUTION OF COMPREHENSIVE VULNERABILITY MANAGEMENT HAS BEEN THE LIGHTNING-FAST PACE OF VULNERABILITY EXPLOITATION.

tion of vulnerabilities has increased dramatically and the number of incidents and vulnerabilities discovered is increasing annually. Against this backdrop of change, it became clear that performing a one-time annual audit was not enough.

The loudest wake-up call to the industry was the reduction of the time between the announcement of a vulnerability and the unleashing of a worm that exploits it. Another ominous sign has been the development of exploits that just about anyone can use. In the past, people who were writing exploits were skilled individuals and usually they did not release those exploits for general use. Consequently, not everybody could run them, and the damage was limited. Today, worms are being released only days after a vulnerability is announced and exploits are made generally available so that anybody can run them, even those with very little technical skill.

A TALE OF TWO WORMS

A good example is to review the history of two notorious worms — SQL Slammer and MS-Blaster. The SQL Slammer worm was released a year after the vulnerability was announced. Blaster, on the other hand, was released only 23 days after the vulnerability was announced. This time period continues to contract with each new vulnerability that appears on the scene. Additionally, the next likely step will be the emergence of worms that

> **Insider Notes:** Patch management is a challenge. It solves some problems but, in the process, creates others. The closed-loop system of comprehensive vulnerability management involves trolling for vulnerabilities in short enough intervals to discover the ones that have been fixed and identify new ones that have inadvertently cropped up as a result of a new patch.

A COMPANY CAN DEPLOY MANY SECURITY TOOLS, BUT UNLESS THEY ARE PART OF AN OVERALL PROCESS, THEY ARE JUST PIECES OF THE PUZZLE.

spread by exploiting "zero day" vulnerabilities — vulnerabilities of which the software vendor is unaware.

While it is easy to assume that vulnerabilities have not been discovered if they have not been announced, anyone who attends a hacker conference knows that there are some very sharp people who are in possession of zero day vulnerabilities. Indeed, some industry experts believe that the vulnerabilities that exploited MS-Blaster were discovered long before they were actually announced by Microsoft. For a company conducting audits only once a year, the accelerated times in which vulnerabilities are being exploited makes it clear that a more comprehensive vulnerability management program is required to keep up with the pace of change.

EVOLUTION IN SECURITY TOOLS

Fortunately, the tools in the security arsenal have evolved as well. Today, when a vulnerability is announced by a vendor, a company can have extra protection if part of its security program includes having an outside expert conduct regular (i.e., monthly, quarterly, etc.) penetration testing on external hosts and scanning of internal hosts. Assuming the vulnerability is announced in January, a test performed late in that month will pick up that vulnerability on all hosts that are affected by it. If the security vendor is performing the testing, there is only a very small window of exposure to the company, in this case, a couple of weeks.

An important tool available today is vulnerability alerting. If a company subscribes to a vulnerability alerting service, it receives notification every time a vulnerability is announced by any vendor for any piece of software, as long as the vendor knows exactly what operating system and applications the client is running on its hosts. If the security vendor is given the client's asset information, it can provide alerts on these vulnerabilities. The security vendor can then match new vulnerability alerts against its asset database to say exactly which hosts are affected.

This approach reduces the window of exposure, because the company is able to find out about the vulnerability and its affected hosts. If there are practices to follow, those holes should be patched quickly. Then when the security vendor conducts one of its recurring assessments, it verifies the fixed vulnerability and also scans to find any missed holes when the patches were installed. The key value-add gained from this approach is the ability to identify which systems in a large configuration are actually affected by a specific vulnerability.

INDUSTRY-SPECIFIC RISK

When it comes to reducing the risks associated with such attacks, not all industries are alike. Companies in certain industries, like financial services and utilities, are higher value targets. It is not that financial services companies are designing their systems improperly as a highly regulated industry; on the contrary, they are often on the leading edge of technology development and deployment. The elevated risk is a combination of the lure of money and sensitive financial data. Many financial companies also have a large external web presence, including several external connections to trusted third-parties.

While companies in any sector are justifiably concerned about vulnerabilities, there is a potential for a substantial loss of reputation and brand if a financial services firm's server is exploited and credit card data is exposed. Financial companies are also high on any hacker's target list because of the data that they are holding, which promises a higher financial reward than any other industry.

A HIGHER LEVEL OF SECURITY THAN A SELECTION OF TOOLS

In evaluating comprehensive vulnerability management, it is important to differentiate between this strategic approach and the simple deployment of

Insider Notes: Today, the window between discovery of an operating software vulnerability and when it is exploited has closed dramatically. The best defense is a good offense. Therein lies the concept of comprehensive vulnerability management — a new strategy that offers great promise in helping companies lock out malicious attacks before they happen.

security tools within the organization. The key word here is strategy. A company can deploy many security tools, but unless they are part of an overall process, they are just pieces of the puzzle. A company needs to manage a program that includes security tools and processes to reduce risk.

A Managed Vulnerability Protection Service (MVPS) is a prime example of this type of holistic security program. An MVPS provides the customer with the security tools and expertise to effectively manage an organization's vulnerabilities. Other elements of the strategy include managing the entire lifecycle of vulnerability management, from discovery to prioritization of those vulnerabilities to remediation, and then moving to the next phase of the cycle, which is monitoring and assessment.

For any strategy like this to add the greatest value, top management needs to be involved. The best approach is when the security vendor works with the customer to identify exactly what they want to achieve with this program and what areas of their IT infrastructure they want or need to protect. From there, the vendor can come up with a program of services that addresses the various points of entry the company wants to protect.

Perhaps the most significant benefit organizations gain by implementing comprehensive vulnerability management is the ability to reduce the window of exposure across all sectors of attack. A company significantly narrows the window by continually assessing the different types of systems within its environment and remaining aware of new vulnerabilities.

This window can be reduced even further the more the vendor knows about the client company's assets. This additional information enables the vendor to notify the company within minutes of a vulnerability being announced and identify which hosts are affected. Armed with this intelligence, the organization can prioritize which hosts need to be addressed first. Once it prioritizes and patches these holes, the window is closed.

Consequently, the company's own internal change management processes are important at this stage. Companies must be able to quickly test patches and apply them. In any case, this boasts significant advantages over the more traditional method of assessment or vulnerability management. If the company is conducting a network penetration test once or twice a year, patches may not even be applied on any sort of regular schedule and hosts may be left vulnerable for weeks or months.

MANAGING THE PROCESS

While there is a lot a security vendor can do, there are important functions that companies need to address internally. Top-down management is essential to the success of any strategic technology deployment program, and is particularly critical in regard to vulnerability management. Just as with any security program, the policy has to be supported by the highest level of executives and cannot be managed just by a security group.

Also, there must be people who are dedicated to the vulnerability management program, either through an outside provider or a dedicated internal team. There must be a sophisticated change management process established, since a recurring assessment program will have patches and updates that need to be applied. If this is not a well established process, the remediation of vulnerabilities could become chaotic rather than a regularly scheduled event taking place during regular change management windows.

If a security services firm is providing the vulnerability management program, an internal person must oversee the project and communicate results to internal employees or upper management. Scheduling and running the vulnerability management program can be accomplished either by the vendor or an internal group. An internal group should handle the actual patching of machines, because typically an internal server group handles this function.

WHERE WE ARE NOW? WHAT NEEDS TO CHANGE?

As vulnerability management evolves within an organization, there will be a natural progression from very immature vulnerability management to a

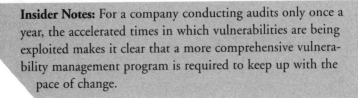

Insider Notes: For a company conducting audits only once a year, the accelerated times in which vulnerabilities are being exploited makes it clear that a more comprehensive vulnerability management program is required to keep up with the pace of change.

MANY ORGANIZATIONS EVENTUALLY REALIZE THAT IF THEY CAN IDENTIFY AND FIX VULNERABILITIES, AND IMPROVE THEIR SECURITY POSTURE PROACTIVELY, THEY MIGHT ACTUALLY ESCAPE WORM INFECTIONS.

more established business-oriented program. In this section, both ends of the spectrum will be compared and contrasted. This section will also address the ways in which a company can move from having no plan to having an effective plan.

Most organizations do not have an established vulnerability management program in place. Their security teams and IT operations tend to work in a reactionary mode. When a virus or worm hits them, they hurriedly patch their systems and clean up the problem. The reactionary method of vulnerability management incurs costs because it is inherently disorderly.

When Code Red hit, thousands of organizations went into panic mode and tried to patch infected systems. But first, they had to find Microsoft Internet Information Services (IIS) web servers that should not have been running on their network to begin with. In this case, as in others, what they did not know hurt them.

Code Red was followed in rapid order by Nimda, another piece of malicious code that required security groups to determine the servers on which IIS was incorrectly running. With no real proactive program in place to eliminate these IIS servers before the worm hit, the recovery task was made all the more difficult. When SQL Slammer came along infecting thousands of SQL servers in minutes, the impact was somewhat of a surprise. No one really expected that there would be so many SQL servers running on so many networks. Again, this incident indicates the lack of vulnerability management programs, since so many vulnerable servers existed.

THE SCHOOL OF HARD KNOCKS

Too often, companies must endure several devastating attacks before they realize that there is a better way. Typically, a company's security program consists of firewalls and antivirus software. While antivirus software is essential, it ultimately tends to be ineffective because most of the programs are signature-based and therefore identify malicious code already identified. When a new worm or virus hits, the updates are simply not published fast enough; organizations are infected before they even know what hit them.

Many organizations eventually realize that if they can identify and fix vulnerabilities, and improve their security posture proactively, they might actually escape worm infections.

At this point, many organizations begin to consider adopting a vulnerability management capability. They often begin with a limited or less mature program, one that perhaps only does ad hoc vulnerability scanning. With this type of program, a user within the security group runs the scan, identifies some non-patched hosts, and sends that list to the IT group for patching.

But there is a problem: this is not a repeatable method of preventing, prioritizing or fixing vulnerabilities. Repeatability is a key goal of a successful vulnerability management program. You want a repeatable process that is part of your business objectives.

In this early phase, companies often just do occasional scanning. Through this method, there is no way to measure how successful the program is because it is completely random. And even with this program, a company is still vulnerable to certain types of worms. Some level of success and improvement will be achieved, but they will not attain real success in terms of effective vulnerability management.

Insider Notes: An important tool available today is vulnerability alerting. If a company subscribes to a vulnerability alerting service, it receives notification every time a vulnerability is announced by any vendor for any piece of software, as long as the vendor knows exactly what operating system and applications the client is running on its hosts.

DATA SNAPSHOT

A proactive approach to security is more cost-effective than post-incident triage. Many of the survey respondents agree with this approach, as 51 percent of them indicated that they have implemented a formal vulnerability management program. Yet half of those who participated still lack a formal program. Understanding the benefit of vulnerability management

Does your organization have a formalized vulnerability management program?

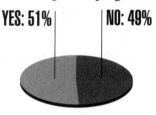

YES: 51%   NO: 49%

will move those organizations toward implementing a preventive approach as another layer of their existing information security program.

Download the complete research study for free at www.blackbooksecurity.com/research
Source: 2005 Larstan / Reed Infosecurity Survey

The ultimate goal of vulnerability management is to significantly improve the security posture of the organization. In these immature systems, this is not an established management process. Companies may run a scan one particular week for a certain set of machines and then not do it for a month or two, or until another worm infection, at which time they will just conduct more scans. In an immature company, the operator who runs the scans is the only one who has access to the results. Because of this, there is no way to measure whether the host that was identified as vulnerable was ever remedied.

MASTERING THE CONCEPT OF VULNERABILITY MANAGEMENT

To move from an immature to a more mature and effective program, organizations need to understand what vulnerability management is and what it requires to be successful.

In larger organizations, even with several people or groups conducting random scanning, there are too many existing vulnerabilities to treat them all as equal. This requires a way to prioritize certain vulnerabilities over others, so that the really critical issues can be addressed first. But to prioritize vulnerabilities, one has to combine vulnerability management with a risk management program, since the latter provides a link to business objectives. Although there are differences between vulnerability management and risk management, they both enable a company to identify critical assets through qualitative and quantitative analysis. It also focuses attention and resources on the threats to those critical assets.

An immature vulnerability management program is tool-driven and technically focused. There is no real connection to business objectives or critical business assets and it is not truly scalable. To establish an effective vulnerability management program, a company must combine vulnerability management and risk management in a way that assets remediation can be prioritized.

A critical part of vulnerability management is the discovery and accounting of all assets. To this end, tools are required to enable an organization to discover every asset on its network, and store that information in an asset database to identify what operating systems and what applications are installed on those systems. This type of database is essential for the success of a vulnerability management program because there are many ways that data can be used effectively to identify the critical assets. Once all the systems on the network have been discovered, then a company can focus on discovering their vulnerabilities. The discovery of vulnerabilities can be achieved with traditional vulnerability scanning.

BEYOND TRADITIONAL SCANNING

Even if a company has a recurring scanning program, this alone is insufficient. Traditionally, vulnerabilities have been thought of as software flaws that require patching. Scanners are good at finding software flaws, but this is only one of the causes of vulnerabilities.

Insider Notes: Perhaps the most significant benefit organizations gain by implementing comprehensive vulnerability management is the ability to reduce the window of exposure across all sectors of attack. A company significantly narrows the window by continually assessing the different types of systems within its environment and remaining aware of new vulnerabilities.

COMPREHENSIVE DILIGENCE IS CRITICAL BECAUSE ALL IT TAKES FOR A COMPANY TO BE VULNERABLE TO ATTACK IS AN ACTIVE MODEM OR A WIRELESS ACCESS POINT THAT NOBODY KNEW ABOUT.

Another cause is insecure configurations. For example, if file share permissions are incorrectly set, it will allow users to access data to which they do not have rights. An automated scanner has no means of identifying that type of vulnerability. In addition to scanning, a company needs other vulnerability discovery techniques, such as manual assessments. With this technique, a company may have a security analyst in the loop to identify vulnerabilities that scanners alone cannot find, such as insecure configurations.

Essentially, an organization needs to assess all of the potentially vulnerable technologies within it, including custom web applications. For example, if a company produces in-house eCommerce applications, they are typically developed on a very tight deadline with little consideration given to security. An attacker could exploit weaknesses in the application code that could grant access to sensitive information such as credit card data and customer records.

Web applications present another area that must be included as part of the ongoing vulnerability discovery. Other assets that should be included are modems, databases and wireless assets. Once all of these assessments (scanning, manual vulnerability assessments and web application auditing) have been implemented, a company must decide on a method to prioritize vulnerabilities, which is where a risk management program comes into play.

Risk management involves prioritizing critical assets and assigning a certain degree of criticality to those assets. In determining the criticality of a vulnerability, several questions are raised. Does the vulnerability result in remote administrative access? What is the criticality of the asset? What is the business impact if the vulnerability is exploited? These factors also must be considered when prioritizing vulnerabilities. If a large organization, with thousands of hosts, is performing regular vulnerability testing and has a database of thousands of vulnerabilities, they must be prioritized. Risk management will prioritize assets based on business criticality.

Once the vulnerabilities have been prioritized, a company must mediate and mitigate these exposures. The remediation of these vulnerabilities includes assigning them to asset owners. For example, if the database team owned a certain system, they would be assigned any database vulnerabilities and be responsible for addressing them. An effective tool for vulnerability meditation must allow recording and measurement on how quickly vulnerabilities are patched. A company should be able to compare how quickly different groups patch vulnerabilities within the organization to measure internal effectiveness. Part of this measurement should also include an analysis of whether business objectives are being met.

Ultimately, the vulnerability management program needs to be managed by the security group, although remediation of vulnerabilities generally belongs to the network teams or the PC server teams responsible for patching or administering these systems. The security team would not normally be patching systems because they would be charged with improving the company's security posture.

The security posture must be continually improved. This is the value of comprehensive vulnerability management. A company needs to test and scan comprehensively, and improvement will occur as a result of root-causes of vulnerabilities being systematically eliminated.

For example, if a company found that every server at a particular organization was running IIS, that would be the root-cause of why it was heavily infected by Code Red or Nimda. By identifying these root-cause issues, a company's security posture can improve over time.

Insider Notes: Most organizations do not have an established vulnerability management program in place. Their security teams and IT operations tend to work in a reactionary mode. When a virus or worm hits them, they hurriedly patch their systems and clean up the problem. The reactionary method of vulnerability management incurs costs because it is inherently disorderly.

An organization with a successful security program will establish a set of repeatable processes that can measure the results of the program, allowing the company to perform strategic thinking instead of knee-jerk trouble-shooting. Security must become part of each business process, rather than a bandage that is applied too late. The key to security is ensuring that vulnerability management is inherent to all daily operations.

It is essential to get buy-in from senior management. The Chief Security Officer (CSO) or head of information security needs to gain the support of the executive team to support the process.

ENFORCING COMPANY POLICY

The fundamental best practice for a company is to diligently apply a strategy of recurring security testing that includes complete and detailed testing of all parts of its systems that may provide unauthorized access to its network. These systems can include the network perimeter, internal network testing, phone systems (war dialing), custom web applications and wireless infrastructure.

Comprehensive diligence is critical because all it takes for a company to be vulnerable to attack is an active modem or a wireless access point that nobody knew about. For example, a user installs a modem in their company issued laptop at their local computer store. This action is against company policy. That laptop is then attached to a section of the network that also contains sensitive server data. This sensitive data has now been put in jeopardy through that modem. This is where a lot of damage occurs. A company's policies are only as good as the enforcement and measurement mechanisms supporting them. Comprehensive vulnerability management is intended to help a company enforce its policies because it helps the company to identify those unauthorized access points and practically enforce policies.

Many companies are not aware of the existence or number of unauthorized access points that they may have. A CSO may state, "We do not have unauthorized wireless access points in this building, I guarantee it," but an analyst standing outside in the parking lot with a rudimentary antenna fashioned from a Pringles™ can might ultimately prove him wrong.

Unauthorized wireless access points exist in companies all over the world and many go undetected for long periods. Again, having a policy is important and provides the vehicle that enables a company to take action when the policy is violated. However, it has to be accompanied by a mechanism to continually inspect the systems to see if and where those policies might be challenged or violated.

Another best practice is the enforcement of security policies. Employees will get away with whatever they are allowed to in the name of productivity. The extent to which a company will go to consistently enforce its policy is exactly how seriously employees will take that policy. Companies need to demonstrate that their policies are there for a reason and will be enforced.

HOW OFTEN SHOULD VULNERABILITY TESTING BE CONDUCTED?

Nothing takes the place of periodic testing and the reduction of time intervals between test periods. Often, the drivers of periodic testing are based on cost and how disruptive the program is perceived to be throughout the organization. It is important to find the optimal point at which this testing can be performed often enough to reduce company risk and maintain an appropriate security posture without breaking the bank or disrupting normal business activity.

The optimal time period between testing a security program has changed significantly. Five years ago, annual or semi annual testing was okay. A year ago, quarterly was fine. Now, the optimal time between tests has shrunk to monthly and even weekly.

These time intervals vary by industry and company size, and also as priorities change and new vulnerabilities are discovered. If a company tests

Insider Notes: While antivirus software is essential, it tends to be ineffective because most of the programs are signature-based and therefore identify malicious code already identified. When a new worm or virus hits, the updates are simply not published fast enough. Organizations are infected before they even know what hit them.

weekly or monthly, there are a set of vulnerabilities that will continue to pop up that the company's remediation group has not yet had time to remediate. Regardless, the company will at least know whether its priorities should shift, or whether or not it needs to work on higher-priority issues.

SECURITY AS A COMPETITIVE ADVANTAGE

Increasingly, companies are considering solid information security as a competitive weapon. At first it was viewed as insurance, and then as a business enabler. Today, companies are beginning to think that security is important to its customers, and if they can demonstrate a superior security posture, they may have a competitive advantage. With security becoming a competitive weapon, there may be less cooperation on security issues. This condition is set to get worse.

For example, the success of all phishing scams is beginning to have an impact. They have become so prevalent, so fast, and so effective that banks are beginning to not stand behind many of their customers, who may have lost thousands of dollars from their accounts by falling for these scams. Banks are pushing back and saying that the fault was on the user, not the bank. Their argument is that the loss resulted not from a failing in the bank's security infrastructure, but from user gullibility. Banks can't afford to cover customers who have been phished. This may result in customers pulling completely out of Internet banking, after losing. This step backward in eCommerce is a very real threat as a result of phishing.

CHOOSING A THIRD PARTY PROVIDER

First and foremost, choose a third-party provider that is a leader in providing comprehensive vulnerability management, and one that has invested substantial sums in the development of sophisticated systems that are far more comprehensive than the simple scanning engines that others may provide. It is not just the quality of the scanner that enables a firm to be excellent at providing this service; a provider's ongoing investments and overall expertise are also important considerations. All scanners do is point to the data. It is the analysis tools that are built around the scanning engine, the reporting tools and a rock solid process that really adds value.

Beyond the tools, it is the experienced professionals who know how to apply them. A provider must have experts who work with these issues every day, so they see vulnerabilities in companies worldwide and understand the commonalities. This makes them very good at quickly identifying tough issues and giving expert advice on remediation. By seeking out a specialist rather than a generalist, a company will get its problem diagnosed much faster and resolved more quickly

Finally, it is important to work with a company that has a strong track record, and a global presence can more readily identify threats that might be derivatives of, or related to, other attacks. A company running its own scanning engine and trying to perform its own analysis could easily miss such subtleties. It is the ability to correlate multiple data sources that allows an experienced security service provider to see what any one client can't see by analyzing activity beyond their single network.

Outsourcing enables a centralization of vulnerability data and allows a company to act quickly to mitigate vulnerabilities on behalf of a number of customers. In the growing interrelated economy, one company's vulnerability can easily become another's, so it makes sense to combine this knowledge and use it for the general economic good.

HOW VULNERABILITY MANAGEMENT SAVES MONEY

Comprehensive vulnerability management has become popular and is a fast growing security service, because it actually saves companies money by eliminating many of the root-causes. If a company can address its systemic issues and prevent security threats rather than simply reacting to them, it saves money. In addition, if a company goes to an outsourcer for this service, it will be able to leverage the investments that the provider has made and has amortized across hundreds of thousands of clients, rather than having to make all those investments individually. Not only does this translate on the value side, with global intelligence and aggregation, but also on the cost-savings side of the equation.

Continually prowling for potential vulnerabilities allows a company to take an incremental approach to ameliorating security problems. This is typically much more cost-effective than performing a massive remediation of vulnerabilities because the company has not tested in a long time. Prevention is much more cost-effective in the long run than reacting and responding to a crisis that could have been avoided.

Instead of thinking in either "military" or "corporate" terms, you should recognize that in today's 21st century economy, the two concepts have merged. These days, proprietary corporate data and national security are virtually one and the same. The new battlefield is cyberspace, and the most effective weapon in your arsenal is comprehensive vulnerability management. The more defensive barriers you install, the greater the chance that opportunistic hackers will get frustrated, move on and leave your company alone.

■ ■ ■

Maria Cirino has 19 years of technology leadership experience, including executive roles in worldwide sales, marketing and business development. As the Senior Vice President of VeriSign's Managed Security Services (MSS) division, Cirino is responsible for the end-to-end operation and marketing of the company's global MSS business. Cirino previously served as CEO and co-founder of Guardent, Inc., an early industry entrant and leading MSS provider. Prior to founding Guardent, Cirino was as a key member of the executive teams at Shiva Corporation (now Intel Corp.) and i-Cube, Inc. (now Razorfish, Inc.). In her management roles at Shiva and i-Cube, Cirino built new sales and distribution channels and helped achieve consistent revenue growth. Cirino's experience extends to principal roles with successful mergers, acquisitions and IPOs.

The Massachusetts Telecommunications Council recently named Cirino the 2004 "CEO of the Year" for her leadership role at Guardent. Other honors include her designation by Boston magazine as one of the top 100 Most Influential Women in Boston. She also was honored by Information Security magazine as one of the Top 25 Women in the field of information security, and she was selected by the Boston Business Journal as one of the area's top "40 Under 40" technology executives. She was inducted by Women's Business magazine into the "Women's Business Hall of Fame." She can be reached at 781-577-6500 or at blackbook@verisign.com.

[9]

COLLABORATIVE SECURITY: UNITING AGAINST A COMMON FOE

When it comes to corporate security, you're only as strong as your weakest link. Here's why a "collaborative" strategy that forms a chain of data-sharing sites is a strong defense against attack.

"WE MUST INDEED ALL HANG TOGETHER, OR MOST ASSUREDLY WE SHALL ALL HANG SEPARATELY."

- Benjamin Franklin

by PROFESSOR SALVATORE STOLFO

Human beings are social animals. Several millennia ago, we learned that banding together and sharing information conferred enormous advantages in our fight for survival. The same biological concept applies to technology, in particular the concept of "collaborative" security.

ORGANIZATIONS OUGHT TO FORM DEFENSIVE COALITIONS TO COUNTER THREATS FROM COMMON ENEMIES.

By collaborative security, I mean the good guys joining forces to defeat a common stealthy enemy. More specifically, sites that seamlessly, automatically, privately and anonymously work together with each respective security system, sharing information about a new attack that it may be experiencing precisely at the moment of attack. In this model, the first victims of a new attack inform all other parties that they may be attacked next, so they may take corrective actions and defensive positions, such as immediately deploying new blacklists or content filters to thwart and reduce the impact of new, zero day attacks.

Similar to the benefits of people joining forces, interconnected computers create efficiencies in which the whole is greater than the sum of the parts. I turn to Buckminster Fuller's concept of "synergy" to make my point:

> "Synergy means behavior of whole systems unpredicted by the behavior of their parts taken separately. Synergy means behavior of integral, aggregate, whole systems unpredicted by behaviors of any other components or subassemblies of their components taken separately from the whole."

Why must companies consider a collaborative security strategy? Malicious worm writers exploit newly discovered software vulnerabilities and launch their attacks far faster than systems can be patched to repair those vulnerabilities. One recent example, the "Witty Worm," appears to have been launched within a day after the public disclosure of a software vulnerability in a widely used firewall technology. The time between first discovery of a new vulnerability and widespread patch production and deployment is typically measured in days, which is too long to prevent exposure to a worm attack. Witty was launched far faster from the time of discovery of a vulnerability and indicates a new trend that may require renaming these threats as zero minute.

A worm is a self-propagating malicious program that infects host computers by exploiting a vulnerable software application or service on the host. Worm writers and attackers collaborate by sharing information about vulnerabilities and the tools to rapidly create new attack exploits. They launch attacks using many machines, often without the knowledge of the owners of those machines. It is now time that defenders among different organizations also collaborate to share information and prevent penetration and attacks on their systems. Organizations ought to form defensive coalitions to counter threats from common enemies.

It is important for readers to keep abreast of new technologies that aim to support collaborative defensive strategies. They need to seek out products and services that may distribute security information in real time.

Readers need to learn about and be actively involved with the Information Sharing and Analysis Centers (ISACs) for their respective vertical industries. The current cycle of information sharing is slow to react, and the patch management solutions are slow to be deployed. Neither can be relied on any longer to secure organizations. The ISACs will respond to industry leaders to provide needed new services such as real-time security alert distribution and collaborative defensive technologies.

Companies need to implement a fundamental re-architecture of network systems into secured enclaves and separable sub-nets, to avoid enterprise infections that often entail extremely expensive cleanup costs. Although an enclave architecture (common in secured military sites) adds IT costs for additional infrastructure (switches, routers and management systems), the value to an organization in protecting its assets far outweighs the incremental costs of physical network partitioning.

MARKET AND TECHNOLOGY TRENDS

Collaborative security differs from traditional or common security strategies. The new approach requires automated collaboration among protected sites with the integration of two ideas: collaboration and site-specific security systems.

Insider Notes: Companies need to implement a fundamental re-architecture of network systems into secured enclaves and separable sub-nets, to avoid enterprise infections that often entail extremely expensive cleanup costs.

COLLABORATIVE SECURITY AND ANOMALY DETECTION DEFENSES CHANGE THE EQUATION BY MAKING THE ENEMY WORK FAR HARDER THAN THEY DO NOW.

Collaboration is companies working together, by having their respective security systems share information about new attacks that each participant may be experiencing at the moment of attack. Site-specific security systems defend protected sites by use of anomaly detection, which is a technology that learns the normal behavior of a site and defends that site by detecting abnormal behavior. By first principles, a new, zero day attack is simply new, and hence abnormal for any site. It thus should be detectable if one knows how to look for its novel characteristics.

The integration of these two ideas, collaboration and specialized security systems, raises the bar against the enemy since the enemy would have to specialize and concoct an attack that looks normal to each of their intended victims, and each victim would look quite different. Hackers would have to spend significant time learning those site-specific characteristics, essentially creating attacks that are unique to each site they wish to attack. Furthermore, the appearance of the first zero day attack attempt would not go unnoticed to a large population of intended victims. The earlier all sites are warned of a new attack, the quicker that new zero day attack is eliminated by all sites.

These new security techniques that learn site-specific behavior, produce defenses that are specific to the site, and are unavailable to attackers for study, are the next technologies that will defend the IT infrastructure. Collaborative security and anomaly detection defenses change the equation by making the enemy work far harder than they do now. Hackers would have to build very smart attacks to penetrate intelligent and collaborative defenses, since each defensive position would be entirely distinct and unique to that penetration point.

This new solution, behavior-based security technology, detects and prevents the exploitation of host and network-based computer systems by zero day attacks. The technology can be deployed as a fully automated software solution operated by the end user without the need for frequent and slow-to-be-deployed updates of signatures. The security technology learns the typical behavior and data flow of a network system, and accurately and efficiently detects abnormal behaviors indicative of a zero day attack in time sufficient to filter and kill the attack in its tracks.

This core technical solution depends upon an innovative approach to network traffic, content-based anomaly detection and filtering, and a collaborative security architecture that provides for the real-time sharing of information among sites. The content anomaly detection technology consists of fully automated machine learning techniques. The collaborative security architecture is an efficient privacy-preserving and secured alert communication system that distributes suspect cyber attack information among cooperating sites to filter content and prevent the propagation of zero day attacks from victimizing other sites.

There is no commercial technology currently available to detect the first occurrence of a new worm exploit before its infection and propagation. The payload anomaly detector technology (PAYL) has the potential to solve this problem, delivering a solution that would substantially increase the security of all networks. PAYL models the normal application payload of network traffic in a fully automatic, unsupervised and efficient way.

However, the current generation of computer security systems and technologies has failed to adequately secure systems from zero day attacks. The problem will get far worse as systems advance in speed and capacity and are networked persistently via wireless and broadband networks. All computers will be under constant threat of attack wherever they may be located.

Insider Notes: The integration of these two ideas, collaboration and specialized security systems, raises the bar against the enemy since the enemy would have to specialize and concoct an attack that looks normal to each of their intended victims, and each victim would look quite different. Hackers would have to spend significant time learning those site-specific characteristics, essentially creating attacks that are unique to each site they wish to attack.

THE HIGH NUMBER OF VULNERABLE SYSTEMS GIVE WORMS UNPRECEDENTED OPPORTUNITY TO SPREAD WIDELY AND DAMAGE MUCH OF THE I.T. INFRASTRUCTURE. THAT IS WHY WORM WRITERS HAVE SUCH A GREAT EFFECT. IT IS EASY.

Furthermore, existing security practices require human participation to verify security incidents and to act upon such breaches to stop or repair the inflicted damage. This strategy is no longer feasible since host and network systems are becoming simply too fast to depend upon a "human in the loop" or slow patch deployment for their security. A new generation of fully automated and proactive security solutions is not only possible and feasible, it is inevitable.

The optimal solution to prevent worm infection is to detect and filter the worm on its very first appearance at a network gateway or within a Local Area Network (LAN) from an infected machine, prior to the injection of its exploit code into the first or next victim host. This prevents initial worm exploitation in the first place. Current approaches based upon signature string detection simply fail to detect zero day attacks. By definition, a zero day attack is new, and has no known signature available to detect its presence in network packets.

TRENDS DRIVING COLLABORATIVE SECURITY

Worms are becoming more virulent and damaging. This is because all victims currently look the same. They run the same services, suffer the same vulnerabilities and use the same general purpose security systems that are blind to the same attacks. The high number of vulnerable systems give worms unprecedented opportunity to spread widely and damage much of the IT infrastructure. That is why worm writers have such a great effect. It is easy. What they craft as an attack for one site is a useful attack against many other sites. They have immediate leverage and scalability due to the "monoculture" problem of IT. This monoculture dictates the writing of general software, by which vendors race to introduce software to the market, although it has embedded vulnerabilities, and they try to sell as many copies as possible. This is the core problem that also exists in security products — i.e., "general purpose, one size fits all." If one security product is blind to an attack, then many sites are also blind to that attack, which fails to secure anyone from that same attack.

A worm is launched from a source host computer against a new victim host computer and typically follows a sequence of phased activities from initial targeting, infection and subsequent replication to other victims. As stated previoulsy, conventional approaches to fighting worms that are predicated on signature string detection are ineffective at detecting zero day attacks. By definition, a zero day attack is new, and has no known signature available to detect its presence in network packets.

To prevent a worm from saturating other hosts on the Internet, it is recommended that a response be mounted within minutes of the first infection, and that numerous network service providers cooperate in the quarantine.

An optimal solution to the problem of worm detection and prevention is a multi-step process:
- detect the first appearance of a worm while its packets are in transit towards its intended victim
- filter the worm packets prior to infecting a host and initiating its damage and subsequent propagation
- distribute the information about the worm to other sites for content filtering

DETECTION STRATEGY

This detection strategy also has three parts:

❶ Place an inline payload anomaly detector within the perimeter of a network (e.g., as a network appliance, a host or a network interface card)

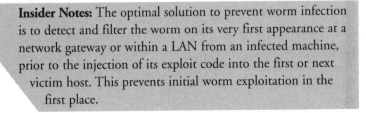

Insider Notes: The optimal solution to prevent worm infection is to detect and filter the worm on its very first appearance at a network gateway or within a LAN from an infected machine, prior to the injection of its exploit code into the first or next victim host. This prevents initial worm exploitation in the first place.

AMERICAN BUSINESSES CAN'T CONTINUE TO SUSTAIN THE MULTI-BILLION DOLLAR LOSSES OF NETWORK BANDWIDTH, DENIED SERVICES, AND COSTLY CLEANUP FROM WORM, HACKER, AND INSIDER ATTACKS.

to detect suspect worm payloads

❷ Verify the presence of the suspect worm by correlating other sensor data with the payload sensor alerts

❸ Filter the verified packets prior to delivery to other vulnerable hosts

In keeping with our mission to prevent a widespread worm attack, our system distributes the newly discovered suspect worm signature and source IP address to collaborating sites. This allows them to implement packet content and IP blacklist filtering at their gateways. Thus, coverage against the worm would be assured among the perimeter sites across a distributed enterprise.

By exchanging suspect worm signatures across multiple sites, the arrival of a new worm and its signature can be quickly validated and containment methods throughout an enterprise implemented. The means of verifying the existence of a worm exploit in a packet is performed either by a) correlating anomalous payload alerts received from other sites, or b) correlating probe alerts with the detected anomalous packets that have successfully penetrated a perimeter firewall.

Correlating detected worm probes with detected anomalous packets provides enough reliable information to filter such anomalous packets without fear of losing legitimate traffic. This is an entirely new way of detecting malicious packet contents, not only in providing a means of detecting new attack data, but also in providing a highly efficient and effective means of directly representing a "signature" of a new attack.

THE BENEFITS OF COLLABORATION

The performance objective to limit infection to less than 1% of the susceptible hosts on a corporate enterprise network depends on:

- the fast detection of worm propagation (within 10 seconds or less)
- reaction strategies operating at high speed. These include content filtering (i.e., identification of the worm packet content) and the distribution of content filters among collaborating sites

If the earliest victims that detect the worm are able to communicate a signature of the worm within 10 seconds to other susceptible hosts and networks, the worm will be contained to a small set of initial victims. The more organizations that are collaborating, the broader the network coverage to exchange this information very rapidly. The distributed sensors and the real-time sharing of attack alert information among distributed sites could provide an early attack warning system for all participating sites, who may respond by updating firewall defenses or other mitigation strategies.

The benefits of the technical solution to zero day worm detection and prevention are apparent. American businesses can't continue to sustain the multi-billion dollar losses of network bandwidth, denied services, and costly cleanup from worm, hacker and insider attacks. Raising the bar of protection to destroy zero day worm propagations quickly and effectively with a low-cost technical solution is of broad benefit to the nation and its critical infrastructure. The combination of two technologies — a fast packet content payload anomaly detector and filter, and a security alert distribution and correlation system — form the basis of this solution.

THE NEED FOR CULTURAL CHANGE

Collaborative security and content-based anomaly detection provide real-time and rapid dissemination of security information about zero day attacks. The approach lessens the need for third-parties to provide slow-to-be-delivered signatures. The diversity of each site's data and packet content make it far harder for worm writers and attackers to find one common

Insider Notes: Conventional approaches to fighting worms that are based on signature string detection simply fail to detect zero day attacks. By definition, a zero day attack is new, and has no known signature available to detect its presence in network packets.

DATA SNAPSHOT

The first two charts support the premise that "collaborative security" is a signifi-cant paradigm shift in thinking about corpo-rate security. The responders indicate that they are unfamil-

How familiar are you with the Information Sharing and Analysis Centers?

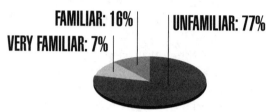

FAMILIAR: 16%

VERY FAMILIAR: 7%

UNFAMILIAR: 77%

iar with organizations in existence that provide a service to their own industry to share important security information. Clearly, the ISAC's have to do a better job of informing their industry to partner, but those potential partners need to proactively seek out information themselves in order to improve their security postures.

Download the complete research study for free at www.blackbooksecurity.com/research
Source: 2005 Larstan / Reed Infosecurity Survey

exploit able to penetrate all sites without being noticed. Hence, diversity thwarts the unfettered use of common vulnerabilities. Real-time alert shar-ing thwarts the exponential speed of widespread worm infestation.

The core principle is a change in mindset of current security practitioners within an organization. Today, each organization considers itself an "enclave" to be protected from all other sites. All other sites and organizations are con-sidered "the enemy." The fundamental culture change required is to recognize that a coalition of security forces provides better and deeper defense than any one organization can muster alone. Business partners, suppliers, customers and even competitors: all have a common interest in maintaining each other's security postures, to remain available to pursue commerce. It is in everyone's self-interest to collaborate. This is an entirely new way of thinking about security and requires a change in culture in how businesses relate and interact with each other for their respective protection and survival.

Information sharing today is a complicated issue with confusing regula-tions and inherent liabilities. Companies are challenged to protect their data, assets and customer information. Sharing any data or information with other sources, some of them anonymous, may cause concern and confusion about the legality of such sharing. These concerns need to be carefully understood, and the means of sharing attack information described herein must be seen as supplemental to internal efforts to protect corporate assets, rather than as a possible means of leaking information that may threaten an organization.

In a nutshell, sharing the right information about attacks and attackers enhances security and protects corporate assets. Not doing so may cause organizations to inherit even more liabilities in the future for not following best practices to secure their assets and data.

IMPLEMENTING COLLABORATIVE SECURITY

Here are the three steps necessary for putting in place a collaborative security system:

❶ **Determine sensor deployment.** Determine the number and strategic placement of distributed sensors (e.g., at the gateway of an enclave, or at a peering point upstream, or both) for an enclave of a given size in order to maximize coverage and minimize communication costs and time to detect propagations and attack precursors

❷ **Classify worm and surveillance activity.** Deploy the means by which different worms and scan/probe activity can be quickly classified into meaningful clusters and profiles according to their characteristics (destination ports, inter-probe delay and payload length, for example) and their behavior. This correlation function enables fast filtering with lower error rates

❸ **Implement a detection and mitigation strategy.** There are three parts to this implementation:

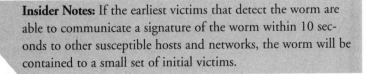

Insider Notes: If the earliest victims that detect the worm are able to communicate a signature of the worm within 10 seconds to other susceptible hosts and networks, the worm will be contained to a small set of initial victims.

EARLY DETECTION GETS THE WORM

You're probably well aware of recent cases of worm outbreak on the Internet, perhaps having expended your own budget and resources to clean up a mess you wish never happened. A collaborative security solution would have ameliorated this problem.

Readers may be lulled into believing that they no longer fear zero day exploit penetrations because they have built firewalls around their perimeters, shutting out a potential targeting of their internal systems. They believe this at great risk to their own organization.

As IT budgets are under constant scrutiny, and as security technology takes an increasing share of that budget, organizations seek cost cutting and operational expense reductions from new technology and IT services and applications.

Voice over IP (VoIP) is an excellent example. To cut telecom and operational expense, many organizations are inserting VoIP services into their networks. A close inspection of VoIP reveals that its collection of protocols and services requires that a significant number of ports (for signaling, data transmission and other services) be opened. This necessitates a reconfiguration of the firewalls to accommodate the traffic flow of the Session Initiation Protocol (SIP) server with client communications and the VoIP terminal. Presuming that firewalls are reconfigured properly, the opening of new penetration points must be regarded as opened windows of opportunity for attackers to exploit. This is especially true, given that there is no single market dominated solution but a collection of vendor offerings running on just a few standard platforms. However, as VoIP grows in popularity and is more broadly deployed, VoIP services, and their underlying platforms, will create more opportunities for a new generation of zero day exploits. Vulnerabilities will be found, and they will be accessible through firewalled perimeters, and they will be exploited.

The risks are very great. A "low profile" stealthy zero day attack that places a spyware program on a VoIP client can provide unprecedented access to an organization's telephone communications. The damage that an eavesdropper can do to an organization cannot be underestimated.

As it now stands, eavesdropping on standard telephony is very hard. A VoIP implementation makes this much easier. A collaborative security solution could mitigate this risk for organizations running the same VoIP services.

The payload anomaly detection technology field within the VoIP subnet would learn and model typical VoIP data traffic, along with the typical media and other data services an organization provides to its employees and members. The site-specific characteristics of the VoIP service would thus serve to detect unusual and abnormal VoIP traffic.

Detecting such events, and validating a zero day exploitation, would be followed by a real-time alert notification, with content-based signatures of the anomalous packet data, to the other collaborators running the same VoIP services. Rapid deployment of content filtering on the VoIP data stream will avoid a successful penetration, and prevent a zero day exploit from successfully saturating all susceptible VoIP servers and clients. Notice, too, that a content-based filter that drops bad packet data also allows good packet data to proceed through firewalls unabated. Mitigation strategies that quarantine whole servers or clients, and therefore kill VoIP transmissions (creating havoc with business operations that depend upon telephony), are not optimal.

In the end, each new generation of technology and each new widely deployed service or application creates fodder for new exploits. Security solutions for these new technologies always lag behind its deployment. During that crucial period where attackers study and craft new exploits, defenders are left to wait and watch until the bad event occurs.

Change is inevitable. The confidence one may have in their security posture at any point in time may give the reader a brief respite, but not for long. Collaborative security solutions can substantially reduce risk for each individual organization by leveraging a coalition of defenders. The unlucky first victim of a new attack serves to instantly forewarn all other collaborators who would avoid that same attack. Perhaps then attackers would find something more useful to do with their time and skill, and we can all breathe a bit more easily when talking on our VoIP phones.

a. place an inline payload anomaly detector within the perimeter of a network (i.e., on a host or a host's network interface card) to detect suspect worm payloads

b. verify the presence of the suspect worm by correlating other sensor data and signatures delivered by other remote payload sensor alerts

c. filter the verified packets prior to delivery to other vulnerable hosts

Thus, as previously stated, the means of verifying the existence of a worm exploit in a packet is performed either by correlating anomalous payload alerts received from other sites or correlating probe alerts with the detected anomalous packets that have successfully penetrated the firewall. This approach provides coverage against new worms, and that would appear among the perimeter sites across a distributed enterprise.

By exchanging suspect worm signatures across multiple sites, we can quickly validate the arrival of a new worm (and its signature) and implement containment methods throughout an enterprise. A graphical depiction of this architecture is displayed in the accompanying figure.

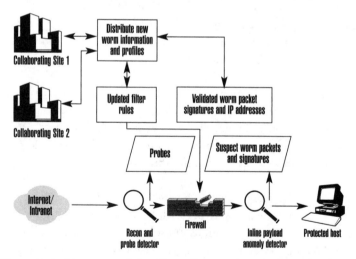

Figure 1. Architecture and data flow of proposed worm detection, filter and containment technology for cross-enterprise worm prevention.

EXPECTED OUTCOMES OF THIS APPROACH

No system has yet demonstrated the performance objective to limit infection to less than 1% of the susceptible hosts on the Internet. It is believed that ongoing research and development will produce technology that will achieve these goals for enterprise-level networks where collaborative sharing among all distributed sites within a corporation, and across participating organizations, is assured.

This worm protection technology would be accurate and affordable, not requiring expensive computational resources, and be able to operate at gigabit network speeds. This is accomplished via fielding of multiple sensors and using distributed/parallel processing to keep up with network speed without a negative impact on throughput.

The essence of the solution lies in parallel processing of multiple detectors, each operating on low-cost stock hardware that are dynamically load balanced. The technical solution consists of partitioning the network traffic among a number of processors to maintain network speeds without packet loss.

For example, if a core detector running on stock hardware is demonstrated to operate at 250 megabits per second, then at least four such sensors would need to be integrated to maintain gigabit-per-second speeds. This is accomplished by a system including a high-speed switch that directs network traffic to a single detector device. There are numerous strategies for partitioning traffic and executing the detection code in parallel. The nature of the problem described here is inherently "parallelizable."

A collaborative security system can grow with any size and speed network, and any organization can comfortably field a protection system able to

> **Insider Notes:** The fundamental culture change required is to recognize that a coalition of security forces provides better and deeper defense than any one organization can muster alone. Business partners, suppliers, customers: and even competitors: all have a common interest in maintaining each other's security postures, to remain available to pursue commerce.

DATA SNAPSHOT

The notional security enclave paradigm is further revealed in this plot. Half of the responders indicate they have no knowledge of their own external strategic partners upon whom they depend for their own commerce. Not knowing one's own dependencies implies that the corporate security strategy either suffers from myopia, or worse, is possibly mis-

I know who my strategic business partners are and my organization's dependency upon their IT services and transaction flows.

TRUE: 50% **FALSE: 50%**

aligned with the corporate core business strategy. If a modern corporation, dependent upon third-party suppliers in their own industry chain, does not know the state of this dependency, and the state of the corporation's ability to maintain their flows of products, services and transaction flows, a surprise cyberattack will easily reveal a significant domino effect of failures flowing throughout a supply chain. How can a corporation fully understand its risks of doing business, ignorant of the ability of its strategic partners to defend themselves and, thus, to guarantee survival of its own IT services to maintain business operations. Defensive coalitions between strategic partners simply makes good business sense.

Download the complete research study for free at www.blackbooksecurity.com/research
Source: 2005 Larstan / Reed Infosecurity Survey

grow with that organization, as networks continue to advance in speed and capacity. Exactly the same principle applies to Internet scale protection. As more sites field detectors and participate in sharing alert information and zero day attack signatures, the enemy have fewer and fewer opportunities to penetrate new victims. The tide will turn, leaving attackers with few opportunities to easily attack arbitrary sites.

CRITICAL FACTORS OF A SUCCESSFUL IMPLEMENTATION

A collaborative security solution from a single provider is unlikely. It is more likely for multiple vendors to offer products and services for collaborative security. Therefore, each will provide its own proprietary solution, setting their own standards, and making interoperation between competing solutions difficult, if not entirely impossible.

By its very nature, and by its core concept, collaborative security requires an industry-wide standard for information representation and sharing. Such an approach was espoused by The Defense Advanced Research Projects Agency (DARPA), which funded work to define the Intrusion Detection Message Exchange Format (IDMEF) standard. IDMEF is an XML-based representation for multiple IDS systems to seamlessly exchange alert information and to represent this information in a standard language with common semantics for each attack type.

Although the intent of IDMEF was laudable, and most vendors supported it, it did not have the kind of impact DARPA had hoped. Third-party Managed Security Services Providers and providers of SIMs soon offered products and services to share and correlate multiple alerts from distributed Intrustion Detection System sensors. Collaborative security solutions will require the means for all sites to easily and transparently share attack information (IPs and worm signatures) and avoid control for any one vendor.

Moveover, many corporate networks have grown over time in a fluid and somewhat disorganized fashion. Few network architects realized the value of partitioning and segmentation, and most corporate networks tend to be decentralized, whereby nearly every system can directly connect with any other. The better, more secured, approach is to physically and logically partition networks into "enclaves" that are protected by switches and routers that allow for rapid network quarantining of infected sub-nets. The quick discovery of an infection within one sub-net can thus quarantine the infection to a small contained subset of hosts, protecting enterprise-wide systems.

MAJOR CONTRIBUTORS TO FAILURE

- **False Positives.** The content-based payload anomaly detector has performed remarkably well in several laboratory tests and several network field trials. Unfort-unately, anomaly detection may generate too many false positives and be useless to secure networks.

Indeed, anomaly detection — in general — may not be 100% accurate, and may exhibit high false alarm rates. However, there are means to mitigate against false alarms, dramatically improving accuracy and reducing error. The solution lies in correlating other alert information, including precursor scan and probe alerts from an IDS sensor and exchanging alert information about suspect worm events detected among collaborating sites.

The correlated information exchanged among sensors and different domains via a real-time distribution system acts as confirmatory statistics, either to verify that a common worm attack has been detected, or to establish the likelihood that an alert is false and can safely be ignored.

■ **Communication Standards.** Collaborative security requires true collaboration among all participants and that all vendors supply core technical solutions. Vendors that compete by attempting to control the standard of communication between participants will cause confusion and delay in fielding a widely deployed solution. The standard will be established either by a sufficiently powerful organization (perhaps the IETF), or from a coalition of vendors who understand the gravity of the situation and the importance of securing the Internet, and who collaborate themselves to create a standard for collaborative security.

BEST PRACTICES

A collaborative security solution is applied as an addition to standard corporate security best practices. A fundamental re-architecture of network systems into secured enclaves and separable sub-nets is a key enabler to avoid enterprise infections with extremely expensive cleanup costs. Although an enclave architecture (common in secured military sites) adds IT costs for additional infrastructure (switches, routers and management systems), the value to an organization to protect its assets far outweighs the incremental costs of physical network partitioning.

Placing inline sensors and filters at each sub-net gateway is required to ensure collaborative security works best at defending all corporate assets. Think of this collaborative approach as the same protection commonly engineered for large seagoing vessels. The hold of a ship is partitioned into watertight compartments, limiting any breach of the hull to only that compartment. The partitioning of a ship's hull provides greater security for the entire ship. Corporate networks are best protected by the same principle.

To carry our nautical metaphor to its stark conclusion: an attack that results in the complete destruction of the IT network means the entire company goes down with the ship.

■ ■ ■

Salvatore J. Stolfo is Professor of Computer Science at Columbia University and co-founder and Chief Scientific Advisor of System Detection, Inc., makers of Recon. His research interests include intrusion- and anomaly-detection systems, data mining and distributed systems. He has a B.S. in computational mathematics from Brooklyn College and a PhD from New York University's Courant Institute of Mathematical Sciences. He can be reached at 646-775-6043 or sal@cs.columbia.edu.

[10]
MANAGING AND PROTECTING INTELLECTUAL PROPERTY IN A SHARED INFORMATION ENVIRONMENT

The Internet has ushered in a new and murky era of intellectual property rights. Proprietary data is slipping into the public realm, at great cost to companies that own that data. Here's how to protect what's rightfully yours.

> "IF THERE IS ANYTHING IN THE WORLD THAT CAN REALLY BE CALLED A MAN'S PROPERTY, IT IS SURELY THAT WHICH IS THE RESULT OF HIS MENTAL ACTIVITY."
> - Arthur Schopenhauer

by JIM NISBET

The phrase "industrial espionage" is uttered with increasing frequency in the marbled halls of Washington and the dark paneled boardrooms of corporate America. If your company invests 10 years and $5 billion in a new invention, your shareholders expect a healthy return on that investment. If a hacker steals the information required to make that

THE LOSS OF INTELLECTUAL PROPERTY IS NOW CAUSING DAMAGE THAT IS REACHING THE HIGHEST LEVELS OF MANY COMPANIES. THE GROWTH OF THIS PROBLEM IS SIMILAR TO THAT OF UNWANTED EMAIL (SPAM) WHICH WAS, AT FIRST, AN ANNOYANCE BUT HAS NOW BECOME AN EPIDEMIC.

product, he profits immediately — and your long-term investment goes down the drain.

Everyday we read in the newspapers that sensitive information has been accidentally or intentionally released, causing great harm. Recent studies show that U.S. companies are annually losing more than $59 billion in proprietary information and intellectual property. This is clearly a huge problem. Part of the solution is effective monitoring of sensitive content that exits the network.

We live in an environment today where high value digital content is replicated and transmitted as part of the normal life cycle of this information. Access control restrictions by themselves are no longer sufficient to protect this information. Digital Rights Management (DRM) systems offer the ability to maintain rights over distributed content, but such solutions are not practical for all types of data.

In this chapter I will discuss new content security techniques that allow organizations to effectively monitor the transmission of sensitive content. This is an evolutionary approach that builds on existing network infrastructures to inspect content when it moves, without requiring changes to applications and business processes.

What is Intellectual Property, and why is it important to protect against unauthorized disclosure? Webster defines Intellectual Property (IP) as intangible property that is the result of creativity (such as patents or trademarks or copyrights). Trade secrets, design rights and expression of ideas, such as in writing, music and pictures, are all examples of IP.

As companies diversify, so does the definition of IP. Financial organizations value customer account information, entertainment companies are required to protect third party licensed materials, and software companies regard Market Requirement Documents (MRDs) and source code as IP. The bottom line is that any company in possession of IP is expected to demonstrate reasonable efforts in securing this high-value information.

(Note: for the purposes of this chapter, other terms such as "sensitive data" and "high-value digital content" are used interchangeably with intellectual property.)

AN EPIDEMIC OF INTELLECTUAL PROPERTY LOSS

The loss of intellectual property is now causing damage that is reaching the highest levels of many companies. The growth of this problem is similar to that of unwanted email (spam) which was, at first, an annoyance, but has now become an epidemic. Companies have historically accepted the occasional loss of intellectual property. However, the level of losses, and the frequencies with which they are occurring, has grown from a minor problem to a crisis. These companies are now motivated by real pain. They perceive a need to monitor where sensitive information goes, to make it more difficult to lose that information. A further complication is provided by the growth in outsourced organizations. For example, offshore development partners must insure that data doesn't move in unauthorized ways.

Financial institutions that outsource personally identifiable information must convince themselves and convince the external regulators that they are

Insider Notes: Digital Rights Management (DRM) ensures that usage rights are inseparable from the information itself. Under most DRM implementations, access information is stored as part of the metadata for the file and managed by a rights management server. These solutions are being explored both for corporate data and also consumer entertainment, including movies and music.

not losing proprietary or confidential information. Technology companies that outsource software development or manufacturing may be outsourcing that intellectual property to countries that don't have strong IP protection laws, making it all the more critical to monitor IP in these environments.

THE TRENDS DRIVING THE PROBLEM

Two major trends drive the adoption of content security and content analysis: increasing federal and state regulation and the epidemic growth of intellectual property losses.

In the wake of high-profile corporate fraud cases such as Enron and Worldcom, both federal and state governments have passed legislation that mandates monitoring and controls for sensitive information. It seems reasonable to conclude that monitoring the actual movement of sensitive information will become increasingly important to achieve these goals.

Some of these regulations, including Sarbanes-Oxley and Gramm-Leach-Bliley Financial Services Modernization, require management to provide documentation as to why it has confidence that financial information is not being prematurely disclosed and that it is accurate. In healthcare, HIPAA regulations require that personally identifiable information not be transmitted unencrypted across the network.

In California, Senate bill 1386 requires that if a company has reason to believe that personally identifiable information has been compromised, it is obligated to notify everyone affected within 30 days of the breech. All of these regulations require that best practices be employed in its execution. If content security and content analysis of information leaving the network are the existing best practices, then a company will be required to provide this level of monitoring.

THE TRADITIONAL APPROACH

There are two traditional approaches usually deployed to protect intellectual property: Access Control Restriction and Physical Partitioning.

❶ **Access control restriction.** This is fundamental for all types of corporate information. Information access is managed through access control lists (ACLs). The management and monitoring of ACLs is relied on, so sensitive documents and database information are simply not accessible to all employees. Availability is provided either on a departmental (group or roles) basis or on an employee level basis where only executives at a specific level are allowed access.

❷ **Physical partitioning.** With this technique, sensitive data resides only on a specific network segment, where it is accessible only by a limited number of locations. The network is either physically separated, or network routing rules are established that do not allow connections between partitioned networks.

DIGITAL RIGHTS MANAGEMENT

DRM ensures that usage rights are inseparable from the information itself. Under most DRM implementations, access information is stored as part of the metadata for the file, and managed by a rights management server. These solutions are being explored both for corporate data and also consumer entertainment, including movies and music.

Consumer rights management solutions have focused on the need for documents or files to be accessed and read, but not copied. Such solutions can provide specific copy protection essential to mass media distribution. DRM solutions for the corporate environment have different objectives. A trusted computing infrastructure is required to identify who the requester is and from what computer the request originates. This involves the installation of a Public Key Infrastructure (PKI) and an identity management system. In addition, there are classes of data that do not currently lend themselves to DRM protection, such as software source code, binary data and database data.

Insider Notes: Trusted individuals need access to sensitive information on a frequent basis. However, access still must be monitored for events that can happen to and around this data. Continuous monitoring often finds numerous accidental and careless handling that allows sensitive data to get transmitted to places where nobody in the organization anticipated.

CONTENT ANALYSIS AND CONTENT MONITORING ARE A NATURAL EVOLUTION OF DATA CONTROL TECHNOLOGIES. IT IS RATIONAL TO MAKE SURE THAT SENSITIVE INFORMATION FROM AN ORGANIZATION IS NOT ACCIDENTALLY LEAVING THE ORGANIZATION OR BEING COMPROMISED IN SEEMINGLY INNOCENT WAYS.

The traditional "access control" approaches secure access paths to data. DRM, while providing protection for properties moving along the Internet, is restricted in application. Transmission monitoring provided by content security and content analysis technologies offer additional control over the transmission of sensitive information.

With content analysis, the technology learns from analyzing key pieces of sensitive data the types of information that require visibility, monitoring and alerting when that content moves from one domain to another. The information being transmitted is then scanned to see if it fits the same "DNA" or structure of the information that has been determined to be sensitive. It actually compares outgoing data to a linguistic profile of protected data. Rather than looking at specific words, it examines linguistic markers. It can also classify content containing key words or phrases or specific patterns.

This visibility then allows a more thorough assessment of the information to identify whether the data is leaving the organization, or just moving harmlessly from one group to another internally. Since it is the content that is being analyzed, it is irrelevant if that content is in a report, a spreadsheet or an unloaded database. It is identified as sensitive to the company and its transmission outside the network monitored.

Unauthorized access isn't the only problem addressed by transmission control. Trusted individuals need access to sensitive information on a frequent basis. However, access still must be monitored for events that can happen to and around this data. Continuous monitoring often finds numerous accidental and careless handling that allows sensitive data to get transmitted to places where nobody in the organization anticipated. This creates vulnerability. After the vulnerability has been created, it often stays vulnerable for a period of time, allowing someone to exploit it. That is when high-profile cases of theft occur, such as the loss of source code. It is worth noting that for every publicized case there are many cases that go unpublicized.

Content analysis and content monitoring are a natural evolution of data control technologies. It is rational to make sure that sensitive information from an organization is not accidentally leaving the organization or being compromised in seemingly innocent ways.

CONTENT SECURITY TECHNOLOGIES DEFINED

Content security has also been referred to as intellectual property protection, proprietary information protection, inside out security, insider threat prevention, reverse firewall, data firewall, secure content management and data leakage protection. All these descriptions refer to the continual monitoring and accurate identification of high-value information as it is being transmitted outside network boundaries, empowering companies to effectively gauge and manage their security policies.

Content security can be divided into several components, one being an email centric view, where content inspection is only done on data leaving the organization via email. This would be accomplished at the SMTP gateway or email server plug-in that would inspect everything, and if a violation occurs, send an alert, reject the email or quarantine it for further review.

Content security can also be looked at from the network level. In this method, the mechanism of transportation, whether email, instant messaging, file transfer or via web post does not matter. What matters is the con-

Insider Notes: The challenge of outbound content security is accurately identifying what and where the high-value content resides to identify it as "protected" information, meaning information that will trigger an alert and audit if transmitted outside of the network boundaries.

tent itself. This is extending the role of the network to include the control of the transmission of high-value information.

The challenge of outbound content security is accurately identifying what and where the high-value content resides to identify it as "protected" information, meaning information that will trigger an alert and audit if transmitted outside of the network boundaries. However, the benefit is accurate identification of your "protected" information up front, ensuring accuracy of the alerts, meaning few, if any, false-positives. This advantage provides a very attractive Total Cost of Ownership (TCO) for the stakeholders owning the audits.

CONTENT ANALYSIS – THE ENGINE OF CONTENT SECURITY TECHNOLOGY

A company can dictate, through corporate security policies, that it does not want its trade secrets leaving the organization. The difficulty is in determining that a document contains trade secret information. That is where content analysis technology becomes essential. A company needs to "instruct" the content analysis technology to only care about the information that has been tagged, and to disregard public information so as not to produce a string of false-positives.

There are three major ways of detecting IP loss:

❶ **Destination.** This flags anything going to a specific group of companies — competitors, for example. While effective in identifying communications with competitors, it also tends to clutter the security process with harmless message exchanges among friends who happen to work for competing companies. This can be especially troublesome in areas of industry cluster where a person can work for several fierce competitors during a career.

This method can also nurture an environment where employees feel that "big brother" is watching over them, in particular their email communications. Nonetheless, companies are often on solid legal ground if they educate their employees that the corporate network is restricted for company use only and that all network traffic is being continually monitored for the safety of the company. Monitoring content and not people is the key point to stress here in order to bolster corporate morale.

❷ **Keyword search.** This content analysis technique looks for a common string within a document, such as "confidential" or "do not distribute." This method requires stakeholders to define the specific text, or patterns of text, to screen and report. The more distinctive the text, the more accurate the results. However, this can be troublesome for financial companies that are expected and, more importantly, trusted to maintain complete control over their customer "account" information.

The search industry has long used the concepts of Recall and Precision to measure the accuracy of keyword search results. Recall measures how many of the documents that should have been captured were actually captured. Precision looks at the number of documents captured that should NOT have been captured. Poor Precision and Recall when analyzing content will appear as false-positives. Selecting keywords that deliver the highest degree of accuracy can be challenging. Ideally, you want to generate the least amount of false-positives to make the best use of the auditor's time. Many companies do not have the bandwidth to carefully sift through each alert, making accuracy a must.

Boolean "and/or" logic used to extend keyword technology provides the ability to refine the selection criteria. Care must be taken that the changes to the extended keyword queries really do improve precision and reduce the instance of recall errors. For example, a keyword query of:

"confidential" and not "birthday"
>   or
"sensitive" and "company" or "corporate"

Insider Notes: Selecting specific keywords that deliver the highest degree of accuracy can be challenging. Ideally, you want to generate the least amount of false-positives to make the best use of the auditor's time. Many companies do not have the bandwidth to carefully sift through each alert, making accuracy a must.

IT IS NOT PRACTICAL TO LOCK DOWN THE ENTIRE NETWORK TO PROTECT AGAINST THE LOSS OF HIGH-VALUE INFORMATION. YET, IT IS IMPERATIVE FOR SENIOR EXECUTIVES TO FEEL SAFE IN THE NOTION THAT THEIR TRUSTED EMPLOYEES ARE NOT ACCIDENTALLY, UNKNOWINGLY, OR PURPOSELY LEAKING VALUABLE INFORMATION.

is difficult to validate. It is all too easy to end up with an unmanageable set of keywords resulting in unacceptably low accuracy. Keyword Search is just one tool within the content analysis toolbox.

❸ **Partial match technology.** Partial Match Technology ("Documents Like This" Recognition) recognizes documents that share similar characteristics. A company provides a document that contains trade secrets, and says that it wants to stop that document from going out and also stop documents that are very similar to that document. The advantage of this technology is its improved precision. It is also easier to set up, since this content analysis engine only requires examples of the information that needs protection and it can recognize derivatives. As the information requiring protection changes, so does the information kept to detect similar documents.

NEXT GENERATION METHODS FOR SECURING INTELLECTUAL PROPERTY — THE NEED TO EVOLVE

To restrict access to high-value data, companies have traditionally employed an ACL (access control list), which is essentially a table depicting which access rights each user within a group has to a particular file directory or individual file. Unfortunately, ACLs on their own will not stop a user from transmitting proprietary information once they have been issued access rights.

This touches on a sensitive subject. Most companies would like to lock down their network without interrupting day-to-day business transactions. One method for access control that has recently been adopted is DRM, mentioned earlier, where metadata within documents and structured data will describe their access rights. When new DRM managed content is accessed, a rights management server must validate that a specific user is allowed to access that content. Any DRM system will require a trusted computer infrastructure, starting with PKI.

The promise of DRM is that content owners can essentially keep an electronic tether on their digital content. Of course, not all classes of data are good candidates for DRM. Structured database data (e.g., customer accounts) would be difficult to protect in this fashion. Certain types of textual content, such as source code, would be very clumsy to manage with a DRM system, unless that functionality is embedded in Source Code Management (SCM) software.

This poses a serious question: "How can I create a secure network environment in which my employees can effectively work?" It is not practical to lock down the entire network to protect against the loss of high-value information. Yet, it is imperative for senior executives to feel safe in the notion that their trusted employees are not accidentally, unknowingly or purposely leaking valuable information. The remedy to this exists today in the form of security solutions that continually monitor network egress (i.e., data exit) points specifically targeted at what a company identifies to be intellectual property. The key here is IP the company has identified to be "protected" information.

Anyone who has gone shopping for clothing has seen the anti-theft devices attached to high-value merchandise. A customer walking out of a store with the tagged merchandise in hand would set off an alarm alerting the employees to the theft. The employees then have to make a decision as to whether they want to stop the customer themselves, escalate it to a supervisor or escalate it even higher and contact store security. The anti-theft device provided the mechanism to alert the employees as the merchandise left the store, allowing them to proactively manage the situation instead of finding out later that evening that thousands of dollars of merchandise had left the building.

Security solutions that continually monitor network egress points for high-value information leaving the network provide visibility, similar to the store anti-theft devices. You should identify high-value information and mark it as such. In many cases, it is obvious where the bulk of the critical information lies. Most companies would start by placing financial, human resource, marketing requirement documents, pricing documents, customer and account information on the "watch list."

DEFINING NEXT GENERATION DATA CONTROL

Using content analysis techniques to continually monitor and identify the transmission of intellectual property across network boundaries is considered the next generation of data control.

Ten years ago, Internet connectivity was not the vital entity it has clearly become in today's networked world. Companies have become so entrenched that to threaten its removal would cause havoc. Thus, to conduct business as usual while remaining in control of intellectual assets, companies have engaged in strict network security policies, mostly focused at keeping the "bad guy" out.

The deployment of firewalls and other technologies have been relatively effective in keeping non-authorized people at bay. This model has assumed a high correlation between authorized employees and third-party users on a shared network. However, organizations have evolved away from this simple model.

Companies today have a large number of contractors both, off-site and off-shore, that VPN into the network. They also have a growing number of trusted third-party vendors that provide outsourcing support. This has resulted in a growing need to continually monitor and, in some situations, block the transmittal of high-value information. It is not realistic to stop every item leaving the network, because it would bring most businesses to a screeching halt.

SEVEN "BEST PRACTICES" FOR SECURING INTELLECTUAL PROPERTY

❶ Define your company's sensitive data:
- Financial
- Human Resources
- Research and Development
- Legal
- Business Strategy

❷ Establish where sensitive data resides on the corporate network

❸ Take these explicit steps to document that the company is treating the content as valuable:
- Spend money to protect sensitive data
- Properly document the defined data
- Create, implement and enforce sensitive or proprietary information corporate policies

❹ Implement a content security solution that will fingerprint, monitor and immediately alert when content has left the network

❺ Using a detailed audit report, begin researching transmission violations

❻ To prevent a repeat offense, immediately take corrective measures, such as:
- Employee consultation
- Reassessment or realignment of corporate policies

❼ Habitual violations may require further investigation via in-depth forensics, such as:
- Investigation to adequately prove violation
- Litigation

OPTIMAL IMPLEMENTATION AND MANAGEMENT

The initial implementation of a content security solution can start as a point solution. The value of this system rests in its ability to generate alarms with a high degree of accuracy. Once this solution is implemented, it needs to be integrated into a system management framework that correlates with other events such as network intrusion.

ASSET CLASSIFICATION – A NECESSARY FIRST STEP

Many companies do not have a clear understanding as to what information within their possession should actually be categorized as IP. Companies that recognize BS 7799 and/or ISO 17799 as uniform security management standards are subject to "asset classification and control," in which case they are obligated to document their assets, where they reside, how they are managed and what security mechanisms have been put into place.

Asset classification schema includes:
- Confidentiality — Can the information be freely distributed?
- Value — Is the information costly to replace?
- Time — Will this information's confidentiality status change over time?
- Access Rights — Who will have access to this information?
- Retention — How long must an archive exist?

Critical Factors for Implementation
- **Buy-in from content owners.** Content owners are the true beneficiaries of a content security strategy, and they also tend not to be aware of the latest technologies. Their input is critical in any initial program to identify sensitive content, such as asset discovery or asset vulnerability analysis. They will be important in the continual monitoring of interceptions.

- **A high-profile success.** A specific type of high-profile data that causes the most concern among the most important internal processes of a company needs to be identified for immediate action. This can be financial data or, for technology firms, source code or other types of data. Protect this data by implementing a very tight set of content security interception rules. The process is similar to rolling out a pilot program. Success in protecting one class of high profile data can be built on to cover other types of sensitive information.

- **Reporting.** Create and maintain a reporting structure that can monitor how changes in targeted content effect violations and whether new definitions of sensitive information are stopping the exit of data, as it is designed to do.

MAJOR CONTRIBUTORS TO FAILURE

There are several events or attitudes that will limit the success of a content security strategy.

- **Setting expectations too high.** The goal of a content security strategy cannot be to monitor the network and stop all sensitive information from leaving. The goal must be to provide evidence where certain "protected data" is going and develop policies that keep the owners and users of this data from allowing this transfer to occur to non-sanctioned recipients.

- **No content owner buy-in.** Content owners must not only buy-in, but be enthusiastic supporters of this strategy. They need to be motivated not only to identify the sensitivity of their content, but also willing to respond when provided visibility that a transgression against company policy is occurring. Very active content owners are essential. Without them, this strategy withers.

- **Lack of data differentiation.** If there is no clear way to separate and tag sensitive data from the rest of the information that populates the network, this strategy will not work. The number of false-positives will overwhelm attempts to isolate and address real problems.

- **Buy-in from the top.** A content analysis strategy can be neither a security nor an IT project. It will require cross-departmental sup-

> **Insider Notes:** Content owners are the true beneficiaries of a content security strategy, and they also tend not to be aware of the latest technologies. Their input is critical in any initial program to identify sensitive content, such as asset discovery or asset vulnerability analysis.

CASE STUDY: A HIGH-STAKES GAME
INDUSTRY: ENTERTAINMENT/VIDEO GAMES

The Problem: Perpetual Entertainment has been developing a software platform that it hopes will attract computer game players and entice them to pay a monthly subscription fee to play. The company also develops other games for the computer. Its chief assets are 15,000 files of source code, which the company views as the primary manner in which it makes its games superior to its competitors. With a growing amount of source code and a share of the $1 billion computer gaming industry at stake, Perpetual needed a 24-hour automated guard to keep this code from falling into the wrong hands.

Creative developers propel the video game industry. These individuals are often not in tune with, or even cognizant of, the value of their creations to the company. The president of Perpetual had to ensure that these developers were not putting this code at risk accidentally. Theft of this code could ultimately mean the loss of an edge in a highly competitive industry.

This problem was compounded by the culture of this industry. The computer gaming industry is defined by the freedom allotted to its skilled employees to be creative. Therefore, any heavy-handed lock-down of company assets could have major productivity and morale implications. Perpetual needed to ensure that its professional staff had access to all needed data, but that they were not unwittingly putting that data at risk.

The Solution: The security needs of Perpetual were to keep its high-value assets, in this case source code, protected from casual or involuntary risk exposure without restricting its trusted employees from accessing this source code in a responsible manner as part of their daily activities. Tablus provides a transmission control and content analysis solution for high-value assets, which allowed this company to address its concerns. The "monitor-the-asset-not-the-employee" approach that drives the Tablus product fit the Perpetual need for a light-handed, but effective, method to monitor the movement of its important intellectual property.

Time to Implement

The company used most of the time required to implement this system to determine which business documents to protect. This took the cooperation of several business departments that needed to be involved in this process. Deploying the product itself took only half a day, and setting it up less than an hour, after the president of Perpetual viewed the Tablus training video.

However, Perpetual is a small company. The process would be considerably more complicated for a larger company. A network administrator would need to identify the hardware on the network, and the directories containing sensitive data on the servers would also need to be identified. A security administrator would then be responsible for selecting the document files that required protection based on the company's security policies. This would substantially increase the time to implement, depending largely on how well the company has identified these important issues.

Benefits Realized

Perpetual reaped the benefits of this implementation quickly. A staff software developer working on a high-value artificial intelligence code wished to continue working at home. Consequently, he sent the application to his home account. The Tablus system recorded the file leaving the corporate network and posted a notification on the console which Perpetual's president views three times a day. This security breech was discovered within a couple of hours after the code left the network. The developer was then instructed to use the company's VPN and password protected files in the future. If that code had found its way to rivals, the AI component would have lost its competitive value, wasting months of development costs, along with the time of several high paid software developers.

By using content analysis, the company was made aware of its high-value property moving outside of the network. As an added benefit, it was also able to identify a potential hole in its security policy and provide instruction to a trusted employee on how best to access needed files in a secure manner.

A security implementation like this is especially appropriate in a company like Perpetual, where its "corporate value" is actually embedded within its intellectual property and this property must be accessed everyday by professional employees. As employees become familiar with sensitive information, it is human nature for them to begin minimizing its importance. Content analysis monitors and protects against such lapses.

port to both implement and monitor. Therefore, success is tied to a high level buy-in to insure the cooperation of all who create, use and distribute information.

STEPS TO IMPLEMENT A CONTENT SECURITY STRATEGY

This section provides detailed information on how content analysis can best be implemented within a company. It describes the required steps for an optimal implementation as well as the critical factors for success. It then identifies some pitfalls to avoid and offers the best methods to manage a successful implementation.

❶ **Get agreement on what will be monitored.** Identify the classes of information to monitor. These can include trade secrets, clinical trial data, personally identifiable information, as well as other types of data identified as sensitive and in need of protection. Identification of sensitive assets requires asset management and protection techniques. Many larger companies have already completed these tasks. Sensitive data may be whole documents or portions of documents. In addition, content often has a time limit. Some information, such as a press release, may be deemed sensitive prior to release, but not after release.

The same situation exists with aging information. After a period of time, some sensitive information is no longer sensitive. These time issues must also be kept in mind when identifying intellectual property. By identifying content as sensitive, the company can insure that it will be flagged no matter where it is going or in what context.

❷ **Identify the security processes and procedures already in place.** These include all processes and procedures agreed to by the content owners. These processes could have been implemented in response to an audit requirement, or as part of a solution pushed for by corporate security officers or privacy officers. They are intended to identify and prioritize high-value data and determine whether enough is being done to protect it. It is important to connect with internal staff that has the most to lose if their data is compromised, and understand existing processes that can support a content analysis strategy. Content analysis is a second-generation security strategy that builds on existing security efforts.

An identity management system that identifies content in need of prioritization, or a company directory management system, are good foundations for a content security implementation.

❸ **Understand the nature of the content to be monitored.** The company needs to determine if the content to be monitored is all of a certain kind, such as spreadsheets or MCAD files, so it can monitor for that specific type, or if several different types need to be included in a monitoring strategy.

❹ **Determine the kind of content analysis that will be able to identify that content.** Does the particular content lend itself more to keyword analysis, or to a linguistic analysis, or to completing a "document like this" type of Bayesian analysis?

❺ **Implement a discovery process to determine where the monitoring device or devices should be deployed.** The monitoring device should be connected to the network at the point where data leaves the corporate network and corporate protection. Then, this device must be monitored to determine whether it is identifying the types of content that it was designed to identify.

With this complete, it is important to stick to very static rules for content analysis. Fine-tuning should be avoided. Any privacy concerns that arise

> **Insider Notes:** Identify the classes of information to monitor. These can include trade secrets, clinical trial data, personally identifiable information, as well as other types of data identified as sensitive and in need of protection.

DATA SNAPSHOT

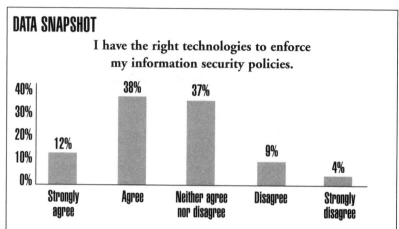

I have the right technologies to enforce my information security policies.

IT security professionals have access to a wide assortment of technologies to enforce security policies, but half feel that the technologies already available to them are sufficient.

Download the complete research study for free at www.blackbooksecurity.com/research
Source: 2005 Larstan / Reed Infosecurity Survey

internally about monitoring data in transit can be assuaged by a strict policy of identifying specific types of data that are being monitored for, and then monitoring only for that data.

In addition to these specific targets, the transit of other types of information can also be monitored to establish a baseline of data types that are leaving the organization. This may prove to be valuable forensic information.

MAJOR BENEFITS FOR COMPANIES WHEN THEY INTRODUCE TRANSMISSION CONTROL SECURITY

The loss of intellectual property is an understated problem. Many IT departments that experience a breach in outbound security often just keep it quiet, even from its own top management, and hope that the damage is slight. This tendency to cover up is a more important problem to solve than the inbound security problem. When a "bad guy" breaks in, the worry is about what was taken and what damage was done. However, the action is noted and counteractions can be deployed. Sensitive information put at risk accidentally can cause just as much damage to the

THE LOSS OF INTELLECTUAL PROPERTY IS AN UNDERSTATED PROBLEM. MANY I.T. DEPARTMENTS THAT EXPERIENCE A BREACH IN OUTBOUND SECURITY OFTEN JUST KEEP IT QUIET, EVEN FROM ITS OWN TOP MANAGEMENT, AND HOPE THAT THE DAMAGE IS SLIGHT.

company financially, materially or to its reputation, and often catches the company unaware or off guard.

If a content security, content analysis system stops three cases of sensitive or protected information from becoming vulnerable, it will immediately pay for itself in terms of risk minimization and could generate a hard ROI in the millions of dollars. In large companies, sensitive data that is accidentally put at risk happens with increasing regularity.

ASSET MONITORING, NOT EMPLOYEE MONITORING

Using specific content checks against items that are leaving the organization is less of a "Big Brother" censoring effort than generic types of scanning. If all outgoing items need to be read, it may create a hybrid IT/HR organization or security organization that could quickly create an environment of fear within an organization that cannot help but be detrimental to creative performance.

With a content analysis system, it may initially seem that all email will be watched. In reality, private use of company networks is not OK and companies have the right to monitor all traffic on its network. Many companies do this without good tools and actually assign an individual to sift through email. If a company has an inclination that an employee is doing something wrong, it can look through the mail spool and review all of

Insider Notes: If a content security, content analysis system stops three cases of sensitive or protected information from becoming vulnerable, it will immediately pay for itself in terms of risk minimization and could generate a hard ROI in the millions of dollars.

their email. An alert from a content security system will only catch things already established as sensitive by the company, and it only matches the fingerprints when sensitive content leaves the network.

However, in many companies, there still exists a problem with the professionals who create and daily manipulate sensitive or protected information. They tend not to appreciate its importance to the company or its legal ramifications and the need to restrict access to only those with a distinct need to know. There's a disconnection between what the executives believe that professionals need to do for security reasons, and what these professionals are willing to do. This issue is sometimes addressed successfully by company training, which emphasizes the importance of keeping certain types of information secure. However, the condition continues in most companies where what top management thinks is going on with respect to controlling the dissemination of sensitive or protected information is very different from what is truly going on.

EXPECTED OUTCOMES

An immediate payoff to a content security strategy is that it will catch the accidental and careless releases or transference of sensitive data. This involves data movement that is not sanctioned by management or that management is unaware of. For example, marketing may be sending competitive information to a distribution list and one person on that list does not work for the company anymore. The departmental use of this old list allows sensitive information to be sent outside of the company. Another example is the developer who is posting sensitive source code outside of the company that he either believes is not sensitive or because he gets source code in return.

The short-term objective is to get visibility into questionable activities like these so that the security group is not chasing ghosts, nor trying to educate everyone in the company when only a few are creating this risk. Often staff is involved in some type of data exchange or manipulation that seems to be innocent, but is either against company policy or creating vulnerability that could be exploited. Content analysis will provide visibility into these activities as well as those that may be harmless on an exception basis, but still be against company policy.

A good content analysis strategy will also enable the IT staff to prioritize the deployment of solutions that have the greatest impact. Most employees in a company are only interested in doing a good job. Therefore, if IT sees a tremendous amount of company proprietary information being sent using one of the free webmail providers, then it may point them towards the need to implement a better VPN solution or to deploy a corporate webmail solution that is easier to use.

A content analysis strategy also enables a company to construct a defined set of internal policies on the movement of sensitive materials. This will allow auditors to interact with security people and define a set of restrictions that satisfy all needs and provides visibility for audit controls.

A secondary outcome would be to enable the creation of a structure that will block the most egregious violations of moving sensitive information.

COST ANALYSIS SCENARIO

Most likely there is not a technology centric security solution provider in business today who has not been asked to illustrate an acceptable and believable Return on Investment (ROI) for their product suite. To ease the pain of getting a purchase order approved for a network security solution, definitive metrics are key for companies to justify the cost, which in many cases could be upwards of tens, if not hundreds, of thousands of dollars. The willingness to spend such significant budget dollars hinges on the finance officer's confidence that he or she will be able to demonstrate that the company is at risk, and in a deeper financial risk if the money is *not* spent on protecting themselves from accidental or deliberate security policy violations. It appears, at least according to a multitude of publications, that many companies tend to be reactive and only open their wallets when catastrophe strikes, and then the need to implement the necessary security solution(s) becomes painfully obvious.

Insider Notes: Unfortunately, the consequences of being reactive versus proactive can be devastating to your company, jeopardizing your shareholder value and public image. A hit to your competitive intellectual property can have a severe effect on the financial status of your company from that day forward.

Unfortunately, the consequences of being reactive versus proactive can be devastating to your company, jeopardizing your shareholder value and public image. A hit to your competitive intellectual property can have a severe effect on the financial status of your company from that day forward.

AN ALL TOO TYPICAL SCENARIO

How much is a company's confidential information worth? If compromised, how will it impact the company? How is the worth of data measured? The following worst case scenario attempts to provide a useful estimate as to the damage a company is likely to experience from IP loss. A financial institution has done its research and due diligence into the various means of building a solid network security infrastructure. In doing so, it has deployed what most companies would refer to as the "norm", including: firewalls, IDSs, VPNs, routers and network and workstation antivirus programs. It has also locked down Instant Message (IM) forums and personal email web access, "https" for intranet and online banking, file encryption and access control to the server room as well as to stationary and mobile workstations. In fact, the only recognized security hole that still needed attention was protection against someone walking out with the files in hardcopy or softcopy format.

THE CONSULTANT

An auditor, Tom, has been consulting with the institution and building trust with the employees, especially Ed, who happens to be closest in proximity to Tom's desk. Over the past few months, Tom has asked Ed to email various documents to his email account. Ed complies, not realizing that the institution security policy clearly states that confidential information (i.e., account information) never can be transmitted via email. However, Ed supported Tom's multiple requests because he was trained to be a helpful service provider. Besides, if the institution trusts Tom to audit their systems and thereby have access to critical data, why shouldn't Ed honor this trust?

While working within earshot of Ed, Tom overhears a conversation between Ed and one of the loan officers. From this, Tom discovers that there are hundreds of thousands of dollars in certificates that are about to mature within the week. At first, Tom doesn't think much about it until the loan officer comments that the list is worth a lot of money to the company's competitors. And for Tom, if he could get hold of that list and sell it to the highest bidder...

THE LOSS

The next day, Tom calls Ed and asks him to email a few files to his address to ensure he can wrap up his contract commitment by the end of the week, as scheduled. Ed emails him the requested files without a second thought. The list of matured certificates was now out of the institution's secure network infrastructure. Other than Tom or Ed, no one was the wiser.

With all the security solutions in place, there was still one giant hole: data transmissions leaving the network were not being monitored. Had they been in place, an audit would have been immediately generated the moment Ed accidentally violated the security policy, and the company would have quickly been able to address the violation and take corrective steps to ward off repeat performances. Instead, high-value data — client names, addresses, phone numbers, Social Security number, the amount of their investments and their maturity dates — are no longer within the confines and control of the financial institution

■ **Cost of Matured Certificates:** $600,000

THE USE

After receiving the email, Tom contacts a former client, a competitive investment firm. He mentions the list and sells it to them for a sizeable profit. The list is not emailed, but printed hard copy and all reference to the origins of the list are removed. Within days, the investment firm contacts the "prospects", enticing them to transfer their matured funds into this new company's special high-yield investment programs.

Insider Notes: Sophisticated content analysis techniques once only used by a handful of financial service organizations and government agencies now can be applied to the problem of understanding where intellectual property is heading.

■ **Cost of Lost Members:**
  Certificates: $600,000
  Members Who Lose Confidence: $275,000
  Withdrawal Of Funds From Other Accounts: $125,000

THE REACTION

Most of the members were surprised that it wasn't their financial institution contacting them about reinvesting their funds. However, many do not even think to question the contact and assume that the institution is aware and, consequentially, supporting this new investment firm. After all, how else would that firm have their personal information?

Those members who felt alarmed contacted their personal investment representatives and alerted them to the situation. Their representatives were shocked and outraged that this happened, but were at a loss as to how this breach of information could have occurred. They had all the latest and strongest network security devices in place; access to the office requires a key card or a representative signature, and the computer room could not be accessed without a key card and unique PIN.

Furthermore, prior to the institution hiring an employee, there was an extensive background check. Once cleared, each new hire is bonded, signs a non-disclosure form, a non-compete form, and must sign-off that they have read and will abide by the rules specifically detailed within the employee handbook.

■ **Cost to Reputation:**
  Negative Publicity
  Decreased Shareholder Value
  Decreased Member Confidence

■ **Cost of Possible Lawsuits:** $500,000 average settlement per member

THE RESPONSE

The financial institution hires a forensic security company to immediately investigate and resolve the information leakage. The goal of the forensics team is to provide clarity into where the breach took place, how it occurred

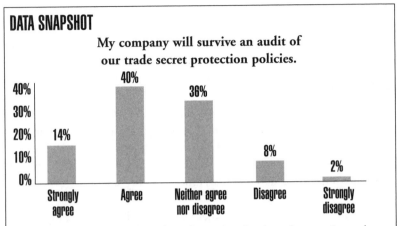

DATA SNAPSHOT

My company will survive an audit of our trade secret protection policies.

Given the highly visible breaches of security that have been written about in the press, it is interesting to note that the majority of security professionals feel that their companies would survive an audit of the procedures used to protect that information.

Download the complete research study for free at www.blackbooksecurity.com/research
Source: 2005 Larstan / Reed Infosecurity Survey

and how the company can plug the whole to reduce or eliminate future liability. Unfortunately, forensic investigations typically take place well past the violation, as was the case here. Weeks have passed; much data has been archived and backed up. Luckily, the data archive is the only major change to the network, preserving the quality of the investigative scene.

A typical investigation focuses on understanding the application and network infrastructure and business information flow. The team will begin gathering information by interviewing the key personnel to gain an understanding from their member's perspective. The investigation will continue with analysis of the backups and workstations within the institution, to find the source of the leak. An investigator might find a trace email, someone who has recently attempted to clean their hard drive to hide evidence, etc. Similar to police investigations, network investigations take time to gather the necessary sources of evidence in order to solve the case.

■ **Cost of Investigation:**
Forensic Company: $2,000/per day for 10 business days = $20,000
Two internal IT employees: $7,000 for 10 business days = $70,000

THE RESOLUTION

At the conclusion of the investigation, the forensics team advises the institution as to the common patterns of data leakage, such as insufficient monitoring, weak application-level security, weak network security and patch management. Most importantly, they recommend that the financial institution implement an outbound content security solution.

Implementing a solution like this at every egress point ensures a high level of accuracy, and elicits a quick response to infractions as they occur. If the institution had been alerted to the violation in real-time, its internal security team could have immediately reviewed the audit log details pertaining to the alert. The team could learn from where, who and when the loss was generated, and also to whom the data was sent and where it was being received. The ability to immediately act instead of react could have saved the institution hundreds of thousand of dollars as well as face with its members and business community.

It took two weeks, but the forensics team tracked down the source of the matured certificates leak to Ed, one of the institution's longtime, trusted employees. After many interviews with fellow employees and with Ed, the team believed that the data leak was not intentional. They were able to track down all transmissions sent from Ed to Tom. Based on the forensic evidence, and the interviews conducted with the members and the institution's employees, the institution decided to pursue Tom, but not press charges against Ed, and, in fact, to retain Ed. As a result, the institution now conducts biannual, mandatory security policy training for all employees, both old and new.

■ **Employee Training:** $250 per employee/125 total = $31,250
■ **Implementation of Continual Audit Requirements:**
2 employees at $5,000/month = $60,000 per year

THE RETRIBUTION

In order to make things right with the community and their members, and basically to clear the air, the financial institution held a press conference with one of the local television stations. Additionally, a personalized letter from the president of the institution was drafted and will be sent to every member, not just those whose privacy was directly affected.

- **Cost of Press Conference:** $3,000
- **Cost of Retribution Mailing:** $5,000

THE CONCLUSION

Charges were brought against both Tom and the investment firm who purchased the list. In the end, the cost to the financial institution was substantial. Since the accidental infraction, the institution has deployed content analysis technology at each egress point; updated its security policies to include intellectual property and privacy protection; and updated its employee training regimen. The financial institution biannually conducts an all-hands meeting emphasizing its success, while emphatically thanking the team for supporting its security policies.

SYNOPSIS

Though the preceding scenario is hypothetical, there have been many newsworthy episodes of proprietary information loss. Probably the most famous losses were those experienced by Cisco and Microsoft, which significantly impacted these companies' stock values. Valve Software also experienced IP loss in the form of source code, game maps and enough components that a skillful competitor could create a playable build of its game. It was estimated that the data leak would result in a four-month delay in launching the game to the public — a delay that impacts the company on many levels.

Unfortunately, it is all too common for a company to believe something like this would never happen to it. Companies trust their secure network infrastructure, which is focused on keeping out the bad guys, and they trust their people. However, instead of waiting for the loss of IP to occur before implementing an outbound content security solution, consider allocating a portion of your inbound security budget to protecting the most valuable assets from unnecessary loss. What is Intellectual Property worth to your company? Is millions of dollars in IP not worth paying 80K to protect?

If a company perceives that its security polices are being disregarded, and its employees are innocently or accidentally emailing out proprietary information, there is a good chance that it can correct the behavior and prevent the financial hit, the reputation blemish and the weakened shareholder value. After all, it is the company's business to know where its intellectual property is being transmitted.

Network security has evolved from simply prohibiting access to inappropriate destinations and stopping outlawed network protocols. The need now is to inspect the content itself, using sophisticated content classification techniques. Then, make the determination as to whether the transmission of this information is in accordance with existing company policies.

Sophisticated content analysis techniques once only used by a handful of financial service organizations and government agencies now can be applied to the problem of understanding where intellectual property is heading. Few security professionals today would feel comfortable without the protection of a corporate firewall. The time has come to deploy solutions that monitor the outbound direction.

■ ■ ■

Jim Nisbet is the founder and CTO of Tablus, Inc. He has worked as both a product architect and developer since the start of the company. Prior to Tablus, He was Senior Vice President of Products and Technology for Semio Corporation, which provided content categorization solutions. Jim was the founder and Chief Technology Officer of DataTools, a database software tool company founded in 1991 and acquired by BMC Software in 1997. Before founding DataTools, He worked for Stanford University at the Center for Information Technology for over 15 years. Jim can be reached via email at jim.nisbet@tablus.com.

[11]

RECOVERY STRATEGIES FOR THE "BOUNDLESS" ENTERPRISE

Distributed enterprises confer many obvious advantages, but their inter-connectedness also leaves them vulnerable to a multitude of insidious threats. Here is how to assure quick and effective recovery in the event that your extended enterprise is compromised.

"UPON THE CONDUCT OF EACH DEPENDS THE FATE OF ALL."
- Alexander the Great

by EVA CHEN

Few computer networks today exist in isolation; nearly every network is part of a distributed enterprise. While this "boundless" quality smoothes the way for greater commerce, it also exacerbates vulnerability and the risk of viral outbreaks. What's more, recovery becomes a harder challenge after an outbreak occurs, because effective response is significantly more complicated than in an isolated environment.

Outbreak recovery strategy is a crucial part of any overall business security effort. If you don't methodically plan for recovery before a crisis hits, your company could become dead in the water.

A comprehensive outbreak recovery strategy consists of creating four documents, each predicated on the following areas:

❶ Risk assessment
❷ Risk mitigation
❸ Damage control
❹ Damage recovery

THE RISK ASSESSMENT PLAN

To create a risk assessment plan, a company needs to first assess how and where its network is open to the outside, and what the risk of attack is from an outside threat getting to the network. Connection points must be identified and understood so that, when an outbreak occurs, the appropriate outside connections can be severed and the appropriate components isolated.

Corporate managers may be tempted to perform this step by digging up their existing network topology documents, but many times these do not accurately reflect the real world environment. There's no getting around the fact that a hands-on study of actual assets must be performed.

Many businesses, when they begin the risk assessment process, are shocked to see how open their "closed network" actually is. For example, they find that many employees have private broadband connections on their PCs, each of which can open up their entire network to the outside world.

Another "real world" aspect of this assessment is to determine and document the operating system of every piece of equipment, as well as what patch level has been installed. This must be implemented by actually checking each piece of equipment to understand which are vulnerable in the face of a particular threat.

MANY BUSINESSES, WHEN THEY BEGIN THE RISK ASSESSMENT PROCESS, ARE SHOCKED TO SEE HOW OPEN THEIR "CLOSED NETWORK" ACTUALLY IS. FOR EXAMPLE, THEY FIND THAT MANY EMPLOYEES HAVE PRIVATE BROADBAND CONNECTIONS ON THEIR PCS, EACH OF WHICH CAN OPEN UP THEIR ENTIRE NETWORK TO THE OUTSIDE WORLD.

THE RISK MITIGATION PLAN — AN OUNCE OF PREVENTION

Once you have determined where you are vulnerable, the second step is to create a risk mitigation plan, which entails putting in the proper protections to minimize a company's risk of being impacted by an outbreak. Some risk mitigation actions will be complex, while others will be as simple as realizing that, over the years, many open connections have been created that are not really needed and now must be closed. Perhaps the most important key to success in this step is to prioritize areas of concern. Graph the vulnerabilities on one axis, and the impact threat on another; the network aspects that are identified as high risk and high impact are the ones to address. Those should be mitigated first and most decisively.

The kind of chart that results will vary dramatically, depending on the business. A relatively low-profile small business may consider its risk of attack by a hacker to be trivial, regardless of potential consequences, and so may give installing an intrusion detection system a low priority. A financial institution may discover that its vital ATM network is fairly open to the outside and is running Windows XT. They may label this high risk and high impact and give it top priority for mitigation. One company

Insider Notes: Always keep in mind throughout the planning effort that the company network is part of a distributed enterprise and does not end at the company walls. At all points, dependence and interdependence of network components under the control of suppliers, customers or business partners must be considered.

IT'S ONE THING FOR EMAIL TO GET BACK UP, BUT IF IT'S NOT UP BEHIND THE RIGHT FIREWALL PROTECTIONS, THIS PRESENTS A VERY DANGEROUS SITUATION. EXPEDIENCY IS PRIZED, BUT IT IS UP TO I.T. SECURITY PERSONNEL TO PERFORM DUE DILIGENCE TO ENSURE THAT THE DEMAND FOR SPEED DOES NOT PUT OTHER ASPECTS OF THE ENTERPRISE AT RISK.

might consider its HR information important but supplemental to the core business. A human resources company, on the other hand, might be devastated by even a relatively short interruption in access, and institute mitigation plans accordingly.

THE DAMAGE CONTROL PLAN — THE POUND OF CURE

The third part of the effort is the damage control plan. This consists of anticipating an outbreak and planning on how the company will act to limit the damage, which usually involves shielding and isolating affected network assets to contain the outbreak and keep it from spreading to other areas of the network.

The network should be segmented to make this easier to accomplish, relying on the real world topography mapped out earlier. Companies can move quickly to put the infected segment into a special VLAN and isolate it from the rest of the network. A couple of caveats are worth mentioning. First, put the most critical servers on different segments, to ensure that at least some of these vital assets are likely to be available in case of segment shutdowns. Also, companies may want to avoid simply taking the easy road of defining segments by business function, such as R&D, human resources, marketing and so on. Doing so means running the risk of losing entire business functions in a shutdown. Remember, segmentation for security purposes is very different than segmentation for management purposes. Executives should balance these purposes when making network segmentation decisions, looking not only at the day-to-day operation but also worst case scenarios in an outbreak situation.

THE DAMAGE RECOVERY PLAN

The last component is the damage recovery plan. This begins by prioritizing which parts of the network are most vital and critical to the business and which must be brought back online fastest in the event of an outbreak. This is a lot more than simply recovery of information; it also includes getting vital network components back to normal operation so the business can continue going forward. Backup tape is important, but all components must be backed-up as well so they can be quickly reinstalled. Also important is making sure security-related systems are back up quickly so that the system (i.e., your extended enterprise) is protected and the network is not left vulnerable as it is rebuilt.

Always keep in mind throughout the planning effort that the company network is part of a distributed enterprise and does not end at the company walls. At all points, dependence and interdependence of network components under the control of suppliers, customers or business partners must be considered. Often a company announces something like "we were not hit by the x virus but our supplier in Malaysia was hit badly and therefore it cannot ship the components we need in time." But basically, the company was hit badly by the virus, even if company-owned equipment wasn't affected!

Part of any plan is to get input from other "owners" of the network as to how they will handle all of the issues discussed. A company should fully understand its dependencies and include them in the planning. These can become severe vulnerabilities. If a company's partners are not in sync, the company is left vulnerable and all its internal efforts will likely be for naught.

Organizations should consider spelling out the development of a recovery policy in key partnership and vendor agreements, when mission critical network components are being shared. They need to know where their

Insider Notes: Maintaining an up-to-date system change log is not emphasized at many companies. That's one of the biggest problems in outbreak recovery. It can take an extremely long time to recreate a company's entire network environment to the way it was before the outbreak.

MOST COMPANIES WILL CONTINUE TO PUT I.T. DEPARTMENTS IN CHARGE OF THESE PLANNING EFFORTS. THAT'S FINE, AS LONG AS SENIOR MANAGEMENT IS INVOLVED WITH THEM AND IS WORKING TO ENSURE THAT IT UNDERSTANDS THE CORE BUSINESS.

business resides, not just on their own network but also on all other networks with which it is connected. Incorporating all of them in company planning efforts is the only way to ensure that the business can recover quickly and effectively. Unfortunately, the ability to view the enterprise as an interdependent entity is not a perspective that all managers have. In this context, it should be developed.

Most companies will continue to put IT departments in charge of these planning efforts. That's fine, as long as senior management is involved with them and is working to ensure that IT understands the core business. IT professionals, understandably, tend to prioritize business from the perspective of technology as opposed to the corporate mission. But technology is a means to an end, not an end in itself. To be successful, IT personnel must pair their understanding of technology needs with a wider perspective of business operations. Senior management cannot afford to delegate this responsibility without remaining closely involved.

Every business must carefully consider its need for developing a full-scale outbreak recovery strategy. Many that are the most vulnerable do not do so. Every time there is well-publicized media coverage of a major outbreak such as the Code Red or Blaster incidents, there is a flurry of activity. Unfortunately, many companies pull back and don't follow through, leaving them — and their wider circle of partners, vendors and customers — greatly vulnerable to a severe disruption.

THE TRADITIONAL OUTBREAK RECOVERY APPROACH

The traditional strategy for outbreak recovery is largely ad hoc. Most companies do not have a formal strategy in place. When the system goes down, sectors are brought back online mostly at random, as IT gets to them, without concern for their priority or relative importance to the business. In the traditional strategy for outbreak recovery, business people and IT people aren't in sync. This is because they have not planned ahead, and with the outbreak, are working frantically, in emergency mode. Similarly, there are so many connections to the outside world that need to come back online, IT gets to them as they as they can, without planning ahead as to priorities and which connections are most important to the company.

Traditional recovery strategies tend to focus more on recovering specific pieces of data rather than recovering the entire system and therefore securing the efficacy of all data. Many companies are shrewd enough to ensure that data is backed-up or redundant but not many are doing the same with their systems. It is very common for companies to apply a patch, or make system changes or updates, but then neglect to do the same to the backups. Consequently, when the system crashes, it's not only a lot of work to go back and re-create the current configuration, often it is not readily known exactly what this configuration should be.

Maintaining an up-to-date system change log is not emphasized at many companies. That's one of the biggest problems in outbreak recovery. It can take an extremely long time to re-create a company's entire network environment to the way it was before the outbreak.

Sometimes it's a trial and error process. After the system is running again, you hear a lot of "Hey, how come this application worked before and it doesn't work now?" Or, something behaves differently than it did before. The system may be backed-up and working, but some patches might be missing or there may be applications that don't interact as they did before because of different versions, different builds, different permutations and so on.

Insider Notes: Understanding the business is vital because setting priorities is the single most important aspect of a recovery. The stages a company takes when bringing its business back, the assets made available and when, have an enormous impact on the revenues and business effectiveness during that period, and perhaps well into the future.

THE TRADITIONAL STRATEGY FOR OUTBREAK RECOVERY IS LARGELY AD HOC. MOST COMPANIES DO NOT HAVE A FORMAL STRATEGY IN PLACE. WHEN THE SYSTEM GOES DOWN, SECTORS ARE BROUGHT BACK ONLINE MOSTLY AT RANDOM, AS IT GETS TO THEM, WITHOUT CONCERN FOR THEIR PRIORITY OR RELATIVE IMPORTANCE TO THE BUSINESS.

Contemporary networks now have more connections than ever to the outside world. Typically, network administrators do not have formal documentation of these connection points nor a full understanding as to why they are there and their relative importance. This increases the complexity of the recovery in an outbreak situation. IT doesn't know if the VPN connection to that vendor or that remote employee has been backed-up, nor does it know if the restored link is configured to work the same as before. If it's not, the new configuration will cause changes in the way the business operates and shares information, which may be damaging.

THE CHALLENGE INCREASES

The emergence of the enterprise without boundaries has made the outbreak recovery process even more challenging. There are so many open ports and so many partners with so many connections in so many places and in so many ways — with wireless, IP telephony and so on. This has made it even more apparent that the traditional model as described is obsolete, underscoring the urgency of adopting a new one. It is imperative, for example, that an up-to-the-minute network topology, along with "maps" to every external link is included in the network recovery plan. Currently, the existence of this is a rarity, whereas it should be a necessity before an effective recovery is to be initiated.

THE NEW MODEL OF OUTBREAK RECOVERY

In the new model, an effective strategy for outbreak recovery begins with a good plan that is grounded in an understanding of what the network depends on. There are four basic aspects of the plan to consider:

❶ **Data backup.** Data that is critical to the business operation must be identified and backed-up. Data backup is a familiar practice, of course, but in this context it is particularly vital.

❷ **System configuration backup.** Remarkably, backing-up the system configuration is new to many companies, but it is as important as data backup and should become as ubiquitous. Every time a company adds something new to its system, even a patch, the recovery plan needs to be updated to include this fact.

❸ **Creating a connection map.** This map identifies the types of connections the company has to the outside world. Again, this will be new to many companies and the findings often amaze them as they see how "open" they really are and, therefore, how vulnerable.

❹ **Follow the outside links.** Trace these links out to the systems of business partners, supply chain members and any other stakeholder with whom your company maintains a valuable connection. A company needs to understand the recovery strategy at the other end of that link because it is an extended part of its network and, in many cases, just as valuable for ensuring business success. It should be noted that sometimes there is a challenge with meshing priorities between connected partners. One might be extremely dependent on a link that is of lesser importance to the other. These disparities need to be understood in advance.

This is all a change from the traditional strategy, which was only concerned with two things: a) data; and b) the enterprise in isolation. That's a model that is clearly obsolete today on both points.

> **Insider Notes:** For high-priority systems affecting core business functions or the ability to serve customers, isolate the infected network with a network virus wall to block suspect traffic, and apply a network administration tool to shut down network segments.

DATA SNAPSHOT

Do you currently have an outbreak risk management plan in place that is updated at least once a year?

YES: 38%   NO: 62%

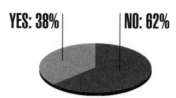

Download the complete research study for free at www.blackbooksecurity.com/research
Source: 2005 Larstan / Reed Infosecurity Survey

Another aspect of the new model is that, unlike the traditional model, it relies heavily upon a predetermined priority plan. Obviously, a business wants to restore the most important core components of its operation first, so whoever is offering input into this plan must have a keen understanding as to what makes the business run, where the value is being generated and what needs are most critical. It depends on the type of business whether these components are just-in-time delivery links, financial information, accounts receivable information or HR.

Contemporary recovery strategy also requires a technical understanding of which parts of the network work with specific other parts. Certain parts of the network must remain isolated from each other, as they are brought online according to priorities to prevent any reoccurrence of infection. Recovery efforts should try to simultaneously bring online those aspects which work together for the particular business goal. This needs to be mapped out in advance to allow optimum recovery. A company must determine what pieces of its network are impacted, what sectors need to be brought back up in tandem, and also how portions of the network that have been brought back up are to be partitioned from those which are still being "cleaned."

IMPLICATIONS FOR MANAGEMENT

It is critical that the executive management team is involved in all aspects of recovery planning. In the traditional model the CEO is often perceived as calling IT and saying, "What is happening to the network! Tell me what is going on!" CEOs can no longer afford this delegation and isolation. They must be more involved and make sure that their business priorities are reflected in the recovery plan or they won't get what they think is best for the business.

In addition, the new model requires the CIO to understand the business in a lot more detail than many do currently. They must understand how connections function from both a business and technology perspective. They need to understand which links are most critical to the business and why, and get a feel for real world business priorities.

When the CIO and the IT department are not involved in understanding the business operations of the company, there is no way they can help establish and then implement a truly effective recovery plan. The same can be said of the Director of Security or CSO. If they don't fully understand the business implications of the steps they are taking, there is a disconnection in planning and that weakness will show up in many ways during a crisis situation.

Understanding the business is vital because setting priorities is the single most important aspect of a recovery. The stages a company takes when bringing its business back, the assets made available and when, have an enormous impact on the revenues and business effectiveness during that period and, perhaps, well into the future.

This new role will be very beneficial for IT, especially during the crisis. Think of the environment in which you work now — hundreds of calls coming in from angry users, conflicting shouts and demands to "get my email up now," "get my sales interface up now," "get my inventory up,"

Insider Notes: As soon as you have gotten your internal system disinfected and operational, you will want to reestablish vital links with outside business partners that have been interrupted. Remember, you can't just flip a switch and reestablish these connections. Use a security assessment and vulnerability scanning tool to complete a final verification.

CORPORATE I.T. SYSTEMS ARE BEING TARGETED WITH SUCH INCREASING FREQUENCY THAT IT'S ONLY A MATTER OF TIME BEFORE YOUR BUSINESS IS HIT, AND THE BAD GUYS ARE BECOMING INCREASINGLY SOPHISTICATED.

"get my financial links up." It's all politics that wastes their time and keeps them from the situation at hand.

With priorities preset, this model becomes a thing of the past. The role of information security people is also changing. They are the ones who are aware of the protections that need to be in force, and they must work side by side with IT to apply the proper patches and inject the proper security measures as assets are brought back online.

It's one thing for email to get back up, but if it's not up behind the right firewall protections, this presents a very dangerous situation. Expediency is prized, but it is up to IT security personnel to perform due diligence to ensure that the demand for speed does not put other aspects of the enterprise at risk.

HOW TO RECOVER I.T. AFTER AN OUTBREAK

It is often thought that once a network is shut off, all that is required is to flip a switch and turn it back on. But there's a lot that needs to be done first. Not following a recovery plan and its procedures means risking re-infection, and a quick recurrence of the outbreak.

The first action to take for effective recovery after an outbreak is to notify the group responsible for defining IT security policy. These are the people who perform regular security assessments, audits, and manage security awareness and training efforts. Although there will be clamoring for immediate reconnection, an investigation is vital so that the actions taken in the aftermath of an outbreak are the right ones. Collect data for verification and solution, and investigate the type of outbreak and the potential risks. If it's a network outbreak and it's affecting core business functions, steps must be taken immediately to control the problem.

Deploy outbreak prevention policies to all machines that have antivirus protections installed. Isolate the network segments based upon their business impact and timetable. For high-priority systems affecting core business functions or the ability to serve customers, isolate the infected network with a network virus wall to block suspect traffic, and apply a network administration tool to shut down network segments. If needed, shut down the layer3 switch or router to prevent outbreak propagation internally.

For areas where there is no immediate impact to core business, users can manually unplug suspected machines from the network, use network virus wall to block suspect traffic, or unplug the switch or router and use a network administration tool to shut down the network segment.

At the same time, you need to identify and isolate infected machines and systems by reviewing overall network traffic, and identifying abnormal usage by tracing the traffic to the IP/host. You can also look to outside allies such as your antivirus software company and switch/router company to find out if proper scanning tools are available for specific outbreaks.

You will then need to use a vulnerability assessment tool to identify vulnerable machines and apply the appropriate patches. For application and operating system security patches, Microsoft Software Update Services (SUS) can be used for patch management, even if it is far from perfect to effectively update Microsoft patches. To patch switches/routers, reference the vulnerability announcements by organizations such as CERT, Bugtraq, Secunia and CVE. You can also access vendor Web sites, which are usually up-to-date when it comes to suggesting solutions such as providing patches or guidance on changing configurations. Do not forget to back up the new configuration, so it's ready to go when needed. This is a must in all cases.

Insider Notes: The emergence of the "enterprise without boundaries" has changed the way practitioners should view outbreak recovery. The computing world is now a big TCP/IP network, and the distinction between "my network" and "your network" is less distinct, and certainly less practical.

CASE STUDY: RUNNING WORMS TO GROUND

Background: This diversified financial services company had understood that anything that exists on the Internet can find its way onto their internal network and that its walls could be penetrated by a determined enemy. It had a strong belief and commitment to a layered approach to security. It also was committed to the approach that it is better to have products from two vendors (Symantec and Trend Micro) defending the network.

The Problem: At one point in time, several workstations were not patched. Two different groups within the company thought that the other group had taken care of this requirement, but neither of them did. Consequently, some workstations remained without patches. Another employee plugged into the network with a laptop that was infected with a worm that took advantage of these missing patches.

The Solution: Overall, the impact of this worm infection was small. As soon as suspicious activity surfaced on the network, the devices' network access was disabled. However, before then, it did cause some infection, with about 1% of the 80,000 workstations impacted. Cleanup of the

Then, clean up the damage by tapping into services such as antivirus vendors' solutions, referencing the OS vendor for information regarding cleaning up the system registry and files, and use a cleanup service to clean up virus or worm remnants. If clean-up fails, backup data first if possible and then reinstall the system from the image file.

TRUST, BUT VERIFY

Once cleanup is completed, verify everything. Perform a manual scan to ensure that you've achieved the result you wanted. Verify that all patches have been applied and are in effect (some patches may need machines to be rebooted before they take effect, for example).

Complete a final verification by using another scanning tool to ensure that no human error was made during this phase. When all verifica-

desktops occurred rapidly. Most of them were up again within two hours and the rest by the end of one day. Fortunately, no servers were infected.

The Process: When the infection occurred, the network-based router generated noisy network traffic that can identify a source to investigate. When the source was found that contained suspicious or malicious code, it was removed immediately and the network access of that device was disabled. This approach allows the company to keep things clean and handle events while they are still small skirmishes. It has a team of eight people that are focused on prevention, containment and recovery. The preventative role is considered most important. This company pays great attention to the rest of the computing world and what is going on with industry trends and threat trends, and it actively drives its patch management program to keep up with threats.

You'd be wise to follow the example of this particular company. When it comes to possible infections, it doesn't trust anybody or anything! It has constructed security zones and it even conducts virus scans on every piece of incoming mail.

tions have been made, you can recover your network and restore data and configuration as needed.

As soon as you have gotten your internal system disinfected and operational, you will want to reestablish vital links with outside business partners that have been interrupted. Remember, you can't just flip a switch and reestablish these connections. Use a security assessment and vulnerability scanning tool to complete a final verification. Also, cross review with

Insider Notes: When hackers attack email servers or a physical operation is shut down by a catastrophic event, that's not the time for you to leaf through a manual, trying to figure out responses. Practices should already be defined and tested, and those responsible for executing them should have a thorough knowledge of their duties in a crisis.

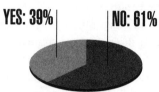

DATA SNAPSHOT

Is the extended enterprise taken into consideration when developing and implementing your outbreak risk management plan?

YES: 39%   NO: 61%

Download the complete research study for free at www.blackbooksecurity.com/research
Source: 2005 Larstan / Reed Infosecurity Survey

business partners so you understand what is being done at their end and are confident in their results.

You will need to monitor network activity by deploying outbreak prevention policies, and monitoring specific ports using sniffer technology. Alerts will be triggered when network traffic or port access is violating security rules; be sure to carefully monitor these events. Also, fully enforce updated security policy going forward, using technology to trigger alerts and block network access if not in compliance, and help partners update to the latest scan engine and security signature. Finally, before reestablishing connections, ensure that all machines have the latest patches and follow the latest policies so that reinfection can be avoided.

After all of the above actions are in place and the system is back in business, outbreak monitoring must be continuous to secure connections in the future. If needed, apply the latest security signature/patch, and the latest additional firewall or security rules, on routers/switches. Use sniffer technology for monitoring network traffic and particular ports.

New security architecture design should include multiple security layers to protect core services, so a single failure won't impact the main business. Similarly, isolate core services from regular networks when possible.

It is vital to keep communication open with security people at partner locations to share and update information, as well as maintain relationships with your antivirus support professionals, so you always know the latest threats and solutions.

THE ENTERPRISE WITHOUT BOUNDARIES

The emergence of the "enterprise without boundaries" has changed the way practitioners should view outbreak recovery. The computing world is now a big TCP/IP network, and the distinction between "my network" and "your network" is less distinct, and certainly less practical. eCommerce is further blurring the boundaries between consumer and enterprise networks. The risk of outbreak is greater, and the damage from outbreak is more severe. As network information speeds get faster, so does the speed of an outbreak.

New technologies such as P2P, Electronic Data Interchange (EDI), Personal Digital Assistant (PDA), Instant Messaging (IM), and web collaboration have closed network boundaries and enhanced network connectivity, but also created network complexities. The upshot is new security challenges. Today, an outbreak can come not only from "your network," but also through a VPN tunnel, P2P, IM, or even a wireless link. Network capabilities are greater than ever before, but so is the challenge of network control. The security collaboration between and among partners, service providers and customers, as well as control over roaming nodes, has become absolutely mandatory in this new environment.

Partners need to protect VPN, ERP and EDI connections. Service providers have the responsibility to provide protection from DOS attacks, spam and email NDR attacks. Customers must provide, for everyone's sake, the proper protection needed at their end during file sharing, web surfing, online ordering, information subscription, and other connected/shared

> **Insider Notes:** IT and IS departments must take the lead in developing the plan. If security is an issue, the director of security operations must be involved. But in the end, one person, and a backup, should be responsible for launching the business' recovery. Some organizations designate that person the operations recovery commander.

services. And, with needed response times shrinking, stronger relationships and better communications between network administrators and domain experts such as antivirus companies are required.

The old business way of fax/telephone/meetings has been supplanted by the new business way of email, VoIP, EDI, and web interactions. Network connectivity should be considered the number one priority for business success. In many cases, no network means, quite literally, no business.

BEST PRACTICES FOR IMPLEMENTATION

Corporate IT systems are being targeted with such increasing frequency that it's only a matter of time before your business is hit. And the bad guys are becoming increasingly sophisticated. Even worse, the reaction window between when IT systems are penetrated and when the bad guys do their damage is getting shorter. Perpetrators are becoming increasingly sophisticated in targeting a business' vulnerabilities. The time between patching a system that has been penetrated and restoring operations is getting shorter. That puts a premium on recovery plans that are well organized and maintained regularly.

Developing best practices in the IT department and immediately surrounding departments in support of a business continuity program poses no insurmountable problems. Yet frequently the practices either are not in place, or are inadequate. Even in instances where the practices were at one time well developed, they often have lapsed. To a large extent, that's because the management of these recovery teams also have other full-time jobs within the enterprise.

Government regulations increasingly require a business continuity plan that is more than a paper tiger. It is becoming necessary for all companies to develop and maintain a systematic strategy, and develop supporting practices to continue their business activities in the event of a catastrophic event that shuts down the IT department.

THE THREE STEPS FOR BEST PRACTICES

When hackers attack email servers or a physical operation is shut down by a catastrophic event, that's not the time for you to leaf through a manual,

RECOVERY ITSELF IS NOT A SPECIAL SKILL. THE SKILLS NEEDED FOR EFFECTIVE RECOVERY ARE RELATED TO THE DEVICE THAT HAS BEEN TARGETED.

trying to figure out responses. Practices should already be defined and tested, and those responsible for executing them should have a thorough knowledge of their duties in a crisis.

The practices should be built around these three steps that apply to any business:

❶ **Map the topography of the business and underlying IT support.** Include an up-to-date topography of IT systems that must include a list of servers, their locations and their functions. This sounds simple, but all too often company topographies are one or two years behind current configurations.

As servers, or server functions, are added and subtracted, it is critical to amend the topography. Otherwise, restoring operations becomes much more difficult and slower.

❷ **Establish a priority list.** IT and business people need to understand which parts of the business are most critical and which are most time sensitive. Both groups need to understand which part of the IT operation supports those critical business areas and would have the greatest financial impact if it went down. The answers to these questions will dictate the order of recovery. This priority list also needs to be updated and managed on a regular basis.

❸ **Personnel must be assigned to specific tasks.** This is somewhat like an emergency contact list. The function required, such as recovery of email, determines the qualifications of the personnel needed to patch and recover that system. Restoration of each function should be spelled out step-by-step. There should be a chronology of when systems will be restored.

Without this important third step, the execution of recovery is hobbled. Operations people, from the CIO down, must be involved in the assignment of personnel. It is important for a company to know and document the qualifications of everyone involved in the plan. If an email server is being attacked, then knowledge about the server ought to be easy to designate. But if the target is a special platform, then very specific and consequently less available skills will be required. Recovery itself is not a special skill. The skills needed for effective recovery are related to the device that has been targeted.

WHO'S IN CHARGE?

IT and IS departments must take the lead in developing the plan. If security is an issue, the director of security operations must be involved. But in the end, one person, and a backup, should be responsible for launching the business' recovery. Some organizations designate that person the operations recovery commander.

The operations recovery commander, or whatever title is bestowed on the plan leader, should be a decision maker fairly high up in the organization, with a broad knowledge of the enterprise and its business strategy. It's usually not the head of the IT department. There's no time to build consensus during a recovery. The commander will be put on the spot to make important decisions on guiding the company on the way back to restoring operations.

One of the most important responsibilities for the operations recovery commander and his immediate staff will be contacting the personnel responsible for accomplishing all the procedures. Many businesses still use call lists to reach the engineers needed to execute the plan. But other mobile technologies, such as phones with walkie-talkie features, are now being implemented with great success. Regardless of the technology, each plan should include a list of all the people involved in the plan, how they'll be contacted, as well as their role in the recovery and when they need to perform it.

STRATEGIC IMPLICATIONS

No recovery plan is complete without expanding its scope to include relevant strategic issues, such as how a catastrophic shutdown would affect an enterprise's relationship with it suppliers and business partners. There are different ways for a business to be proactive in addressing this issue. One way is to participate in professional groups whose charter focuses on security and recovery. These groups are often a valuable exchange of experiences and a way to gauge how others are performing.

However, IT managers and others involved in designing a recovery program also need to regularly meet with suppliers and partners. These meetings should be similar in frequency to marketing and sales meetings. It's a way for the company to reach an understanding of what to expect from its important partners in a time of crisis. Coordination and prioritization of systems recovery is essential for the resumption of full business operations.

■ ■ ■

Eva Chen, a co-founder and the CEO of Trend Micro, served as the company's Chief Technology Officer from 1996 to 2005 and Executive Vice President since May 1988. As CTO, Eva was responsible for overall product strategy and technology direction. Eva contributed heavily to seven patents, including those pertaining to the detection and removal of viruses in email and on computer networks. Under her guidance, Trend Micro has earned a reputation for innovation — from Trend Micro Enterprise Protection Strategy, an industry-first approach to managing outbreaks, to products including Trend Micro InterScan VirusWallTM, the industry's first gateway-based antivirus solution; Trend Micro PC-cillinTM; and Trend Micro ScanMailTM.

In April 2001, Eva was honored with a Lifetime Achievement Award from Secure Computing magazine, in recognition of her 13 years of contribution to the advancement of antivirus technology and computer security. Eva has written numerous articles on the subject of Internet security. In April, 2000 she won the Judges Award from Secure Computing for her article, "Poison Java." She also received the prestigious "Tribute to Women in the Industry" (TWIN) award from the YWCA. In 2003, she was named one of the top five most influential "Women of Vision" by Information Security magazine. She can be reached at 408-257-1500 or eva_chen@trendmicro.com.

[12]

CONTENT SECURITY AND THE EXPANDING NETWORK PERIMETER

As employees expand their computing horizons and the line between the corporate and public networks blur, your company's concept of security must expand as well, to account for networks outside the perimeter.

"SYSTEMS-THINKING IS A DISCIPLINE FOR SEEING WHOLES. IT IS A FRAMEWORK FOR SEEING INTER-RELATIONSHIPS, RATHER THAN THINGS."
- Peter Senge

by MICHAEL XIE

Information security officers tend to view systems outside of the corporate perimeter the way Romans viewed the Visigoths and Vandals: as Barbarians at the Gate. This simplistic perspective no longer reflects end-user habits. Today, an ostensible "friend" can be an enemy who's inside the perimeter.

THE USER OF THE NETWORK PROGRAM AND THE TECHNICAL STAFF VIEW THE NETWORK FROM VERY DIFFERENT PERSPECTIVES, AND EACH HAS A VERY DIFFERENT UNDERSTANDING OF A NETWORK'S DEFINITION. THIS AFFECTS THE APPLICATION OF NETWORK SECURITY.

Security deployments typically have been at the perimeter of the network only. IT managers are treating the public Internet as the untrusted network and all segments behind the perimeter as the trusted network. This train of thought must change as more sophisticated attacks are being developed to bypass conventional security.

The perimeter of security has changed, and is no longer just connection-based. Now, security is about content and data coming from trusted, untrusted and semi-trusted sources. Network security solutions must address this evolution, while still preserving performance and the network services that users want.

Complete content inspection applies to the security of network traffic. Users generally view the Internet as a medium for web browsing or shopping. They also use it to send emails to friends, and receive emails with messages and attachments. They may also use file-sharing protocols to exchange music files (MP3) or to download programs onto their computer (via FTP).

Companies have a different view of the Internet. They run applications that are much more complicated, such as Enterprise Resource Planning (ERP) and Customer Resource Management (CRM). This software runs on multiple computers and needs to interact with databases that are both inside and outside of the company. Consequently, they rely on Internet network transmission to complete their day-to-day tasks. However, both the corporate and the individual end-user view the network as part of the computer that enables meaningful work to be accomplished.

A CIO and the IT group have a totally different view from the users. All of an end-user's mouse clicks, transmitted graphics, web pages, databases and everything else displayed on a user's computer screen, consist of millions, or billions, of pieces of code.

To the user, the graphic file, or spreadsheet, is continuous content, but the web or applications server views this file as millions of little pieces of code, that goes through a very complicated routing and switching infrastructure to arrive at a user desktop. The user desktop computer then will run a program to reassemble all those pieces and display it on user's screens. This complicated process is practically transparent to the user.

The user of the network program and the technical staff view the network from very different perspectives, and each has a very different understanding of a network's definition. This affects the application of network security.

Traditionally, network security did not consider the end-user viewpoint. Network security has always been about bits, bytes and packets, not about applications, databases, files, graphics, emails/attachments and downloaded music. Typically, one network packet, at maximum, consists of 1,500 kilobytes. Network security, during the old days (before the ascent of the Internet), was just about how to make sure that these packets, and all of its bits and bytes, got routed to its destination without error. Complicated routing, switching and other types of equipment were developed and installed to make this happen.

Security products and systems were basically about how to protect this one network packet. Although there are millions of these packets traveling at the same time within a network, as long as the equipment can protect one of these single packets, it can apply the same algorithm to all the other packets and ensure that all traffic gets protected. That is how the traditional network security worked.

> **Insider Notes:** Not only do traditional security devices need to change, but also how network segments are designed. Developing security zones to move and layer security closer to corporate assets are now mandatory to safeguard corporate resources within the corporate network.

WITH THE ADVENT OF LAPTOP COMPUTERS, PDAS, MOBILE USERS, TELEWORKERS, REMOTE ACCESS, INSTANT MESSAGING AND SO FORTH, THE TRADITIONAL PERIMETER IS BEING BYPASSED IN MANY WAYS.

Based on that assumption, companies only needed to worry about what type of firewall they should install, and whether they should run network address translation (that would play tricks with the packet headers and thereby hide certain information from hackers and make part of their network inaccessible to the external user).

Internet Protocol Security (IPSec) and IPSec VPNs are another part of traditional network security. IPSec can take several forms. A digital signature can be used to sign the packet; encryption can be used to make the packet unrecognizable to anyone except the two end points of the communication; and authentication can be used to make sure that one packet is sent from the person who claimed to send it. All of these technologies are based on the IP packet. If the packet is secure, then the whole thing is secure.

Conversely, it also means that if a hacker can get access to a single packet for that IP address (e.g., from www.hacker.com), it will allow him to get access to everything from that address without encountering further protection mechanisms.

The concept of firewalling the corporate network from the "big bad Internet" and treating all internal networks as a "continuous trusted network" is compounding the problem. With the advent of laptop computers, PDAs, mobile users, teleworkers, remote access, instant messaging and so forth, the traditional perimeter is being bypassed in many ways. Mobile employee laptops may become infected while they're away from the office, and transport the virus or worm onto the corporate network when they return to the office. Not only do traditional security devices need to change, but also how network segments are designed. Developing security zones to move and layer security closer to corporate assets are now mandatory to safeguard corporate resources within the corporate network.

THE NEW ENVIRONMENT

With security based on this IP packet focus, the arrival of the Internet with its email, web browsing and sharing made the security issue substantially more complicated. As an example, there are web sites, such as Yahoo, allowing thousands of users to post their own home pages. Many of these pages have personal information, such as pictures of children and dogs. But, unknown to the browser, they also may contain scripts that can, without the browser being aware, put some programs on their computer to spy, or even to operate as a Trojan horse. This changes the situation because single network packet security cannot be relied upon. In a case like this, what is being transmitted from the web hosting company has both benign and malicious content within the same IP packet. This benign and malicious content looks very similar to the traditional security technology.

In another example, a lot of the people within companies that didn't do anything obvious to compromise their systems, find that their network has all types of viruses that generating lots of the pop-up windows and advertising on the desktops, and they don't know how it got there. These are the result of the serious limitations of IP packet based security.

Complete content security goes much deeper than looking at just one packet. It looks at the stream of the network content. It provides a mechanism in a place where all packets delivered to one particular desktop are put into sequence. Inspections are provided before all of these packets reach the user's desktop to determine whether they are good or bad. And if it's something bad, it is stopped from going to the desktop. A virus is one example of a "bad thing" that will be stopped. Another example is pornographic material. Many companies have policies that do not allow pornographic web sites to be browsed. There is also legislation about the type of programs that should not be accessed during working hours, which will encourage many other companies to set up policies to regulate

Insider Notes: Security management needs a method, at a gateway level, to distinguish bad from good content. Bad content doesn't necessarily have to be anything that is "bad" in a moral or subjective sense. It should be defined as anything inconsistent with corporate policy.

DATA SNAPSHOT

Over time, security threats have evolved. Content based attacks are gaining a larger share of the total number of attacks. Attacks are getting harder and harder to detect, and the potential financial loss because of the attacks are getting bigger and bigger.

Are your current security defenses HOST-based or NETWORK-based?

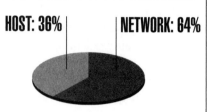

HOST: 36% | | | NETWORK: 64%

Download the complete research study for free at www.blackbooksecurity.com/research
Source: 2005 Larstan / Reed Infosecurity Survey

employee browsing. Security management needs a method, at a gateway level, to distinguish bad from good content. Bad content doesn't necessarily have to be anything that is "bad" in a moral or subjective sense. It should be defined as anything inconsistent with corporate policy.

The concept of complete content inspection means that there is a control implemented at the gateway level that assesses the packet, where it came from and what the protocol looks like (email or HTTP). It also drills down into these protocols and assesses if it's HTTP, what kind of web page and what type of data it is, or, if it's email, what type of attachments it has.

Complete content inspection will enable a company's CIO to set up and enforce policies that regulate what employees should and should not browse on the Internet, as well as at what times. An Internet usage policy like this has to be developed in great detail. For example, it needs to distinguish between different times of day. A company might have strict limits during work hours but may allow some loosening up after hours, or on the weekends.

A policy also needs to consider the department and the employee level. For example, the CFO will probably require more liberal Internet access, since he may be working on company financial issues and will need to do some financial research. However, this same liberal access cannot be offered to the CFO's support people because they might spend a lot of their time trading their own stock portfolios. An access policy needs to provide a multitiered level of authentication, and distinction by company, departmental, personal and group level.

All sides must plan policies and find technological solutions to make the execution of those policies possible. A company needs to analyze how many violation attempts happen during certain hours and then put into place systems to monitor and regulate access.

As technology continues to develop, traditional security devices will give way to a new breed of security device. To provide modern security against blended attacks, security devices must perform more than just firewalling or intrusion detection. Proactive security, with the ability to be deployed inline with the network traffic flow, is needed to inspect the entire conversation (not just the individual packets). Providing techniques to find malicious viruses, worms and Trojan applications, as well as malicious activity with the ability to terminate the conversations in real time, is becoming a mandatory security feature in modern networks.

ORIGIN OF LATEST ATTACKS

Several years ago, it was very easy to separate the network into trusted and untrusted segments. The typical firewall prior to 2002 connected three networks: one trusted internal network, a second untrusted network (usually the Internet) and a third network, often called DMZ, a demilitarized zone where some servers would be hosted. This configuration had been stable for almost 10 years, so it was very easy to differentiate what was trusted traffic, what was untrusted traffic and what was somewhere in between. But in recent years, things have become much more complicated. At first, threats entailed theft of phsyical property, so locks and keys were

Insider Notes: All sides must plan policies and find technological solutions to make the execution of those policies possible. A company needs to analyze how many violation attempts happen during certain hours and then put into place systems to monitor and regulate access.

BLENDED THREATS ARE BEING USED TO BYPASS TRADITIONAL SECURITY DEVICES, SUCH AS FIREWALLS AND IDS/IPS SYSTEMS. MANY OF THESE ATTACKS EMBED MALICIOUS CODE INTO THE PAYLOAD AND THEN FRAGMENT THE PAYLOAD TO AVOID DETECTION BY TRADITIONAL SECURITY SYSTEMS.

used. Then, there were connection-based threats which were combated with firewalls and VPNs. Later on, more and more threats became content based, which were countered with intrusion detection and antivirus systems. Gradually, the clear definition of what is edge and what is internal network started to blur.

Now, attacks might first come from your internal network, which used to be the trusted network. Employee laptops get infections from viruses, Trojan horses and peer-to-peer traffic. Internal tags can disguise themselves to appear as if they came from trusted sources. Even traffic from trusted sources to untrusted sources can be attacked by passive assaults. Attacks can come from external or internal sources. They can arrive actively or passively. They enter into a server, a server farm or a web server, and can also come passively when an employee is web-browsing or receiving email.

The response has been to connect more and more networks on the firewall and begin to partition networks into different compartments. This is analogous to a submarine where one compartment has leakage and lots of water, but other compartments can still keep the ship afloat. Layer two is where physical partitioning starts, and continues to layer three and layer four. Firewalls now have more ports, and the boundary of trust has been converged into a smaller size. Consequently, the entire security architecture has become more complicated than the original one point with a three-port firewall. In many companies, networks have been divided into smaller cells. They form a union and, ultimately, they have multiple gateways to enter into the untrusted network. Therefore, the network infrastructure gets much more complicated, and the difference between trusted and untrusted becomes blurred. Currently, the trusted network is defined as a small set of cells off the network, but even those trusted cells can still be sabotaged by a virus.

THE NETWORK SECURITY SOLUTION: THE COMPLETE CONTENT INSPECTION DIFFERENCE

To implement a network security solution requires two activities:

❶ Defend the network compartment as much as possible, so it protects everything within your cell. One cell could, in reality, be five, 10 or more than 100 computers.

❷ Create a mechanism that will protect the other compartments if one compartment is attacked.

A company may have 10 compartments and 20 international sites. It can set up its policy to have full control over this domain. However, there are often complications, such as connections to other vendors and business partners, that weaken the control needed to secure the domain. The strategy then is to try to evaluate the risks, put the most critical resources into a single virtual compartment and place the heaviest protection around it.

Similarly, the company would put its less risky resources on the perimeter and have them interface with the network with which it has less control. For example, it's very common for a company to have a dedicated connection to an accounting firm. They would set up their own internal accounting network, which has the heaviest protection around the systems that run payroll and other sensitive information.

There is another challenge faced by corporate managers, which is the uncontrolled proliferation of technology. Users hear about a technology, and they want to use it. They want a VPN, as well as the software that

> **Insider Notes:** Attackers are also leveraging code produced by earlier attacks to reduce the time it takes to create a new attack. The time between when a new vulnerability is found to the time it is exploited by attackers is rapidly decreasing. IT professionals must move much quicker to patch their systems before the next attack on their network.

NOW, ATTACKS MIGHT FIRST COME FROM YOUR INTERNAL NETWORK, WHICH USED TO BE THE TRUSTED NETWORK. EMPLOYEE LAPTOPS GET INFECTIONS FROM VIRUSES, TROJAN HORSES AND PEER-TO-PEER TRAFFIC. INTERNAL TAGS CAN DISGUISE THEMSELVES TO APPEAR AS IF THEY CAME FROM TRUSTED SOURCES.

allows them to aggregate accounting records from 20 countries and generate sales reports daily.

In addition, there are systems that a company might have outsourced to engineering partners in a foreign country who now need to set up the source code control and bug-tracking systems there, so they can work closely with other developers locally. The company wants them to work closely and produce the new product as soon as they can. Users generally want all the access to everything they can get.

One of the jobs of the network administrator is to try to meet these requirements and ensure security. They might open up one little hole for a new IT service and let in a virus that takes down a major system. There is always that risk, and it becomes a deciding factor when the network administrator decides which solution he wants to use. Network administrators often have to compromise on functionality and performance, and decide first on filling the need. They then have to decide on flexibility and how it plays with the existing network, and then, finally, how it impacts the security mechanisms.

THE EVOLUTION OF ATTACKS

The first viruses were file viruses that appeared in the 1970s. The majority of people who got infected by these viruses were copying or pirating games and programs illegally.

As copyright laws were interpreted and implemented differently in other countries, virus outbreak patterns differed among countries using early virus infection technology. With early viruses, users who abided by legal software licensing were rarely infected. But as technology improved and file sharing became a standard method of conducting business, the virus landscape changed dramatically.

The first major change started with Microsoft in 1997. Word 97 started having macro capabilities, where users could overwrite what to do when a document is opened or after it is closed. This attracted a large number of viruses, mostly because they were able to attack all documents. A user may still create a document on a machine, open it for some editing, and then save it. However, the computer suddenly gets infected with a virus, so every word document created will have that virus — and the next group of viruses is spread over networks.

With network viruses, a user does not need to do anything to have their computer infected, or even have their hard drive erased. The network threat has been elevated to a much higher level after users started to connect computers together and files could move between computers without users knowing about it.

There has also been an evolution in intrusion technology. Initially, intrusion detection and intrusion protection system (IDS/IPS) companies were building very basic technology. They initiated exclusion technology, deciding which IP address or which networks they wanted to block, and then simply cutting connections when something bad was detected. IDS/IPS has changed into a technology that can now dynamically detect what's happening on the entire network. IDS/IPS techniques have evolved from a single point of attack to multi-point and simultaneous action. Rather than blocking one IP address or one server, IDS/IPS systems now conduct analysis on all devices connected to the network.

Insider Notes: Viruses are no longer targeted at individuals or single computers. Intrusions are no longer single-point, nor can they be traced back to a single IP address. They are now distributed and can originate from anywhere in the world, from a single source, or multiple sources.

An important change in attack patterns is the blended threat, which combines multiple attack technologies. Blended threats are being used to bypass traditional firewalls and IDS/IPS systems. Many of these attacks embed malicious code into the content and then fragment the content to avoid detection by traditional security systems.

Attackers are also leveraging code produced by earlier attacks to reduce the time it takes to create a new attack. The time between when a new vulnerability is found to the time it is exploited by attackers is rapidly decreasing. IT professionals must move much quicker to patch their systems before the next attack on their network.

ACHIEVING DEFENSE IN DEPTH WITH SECURITY TOOLS

Companies must first have a thorough understanding of the types of threats that exist. Initially viruses were considered solved by installing antivirus software on the computer. Hacker intrusions could be addressed by IP addresses from which they originated. Those are misconceptions.

To come up with a good security solution that fits a company's needs, understanding the modern virus or threat is critical. Viruses are no longer targeted at individuals or single computers. Intrusions are no longer single-point, nor can they be traced back to a single IP address. They are now distributed and can originate from anywhere in the world, from a single source, or multiple sources. Companies need to realize that there is a whole profile of attacks to pay attention to. There are also solutions available for every type of intrusion, as long as the company has a good understanding of what the potential risks are and what types of threats can attack its network. It becomes a matter of cost. If cost and performance aren't issues, pretty much any solution will work. Budget is the second key consideration.

The third key consideration is performance. It is easy to install many different security solutions to secure the corporate network. You can get the best of each— the best router security, the best switch security, the best network security—and put them together. Ultimately, without good planning and design of the network and security infrastructure, a company may find itself paying for a high-speed fiber connection, only to obtain a slow connection due to all the different security devices used to secure the network. Thought and care must be used throughout the planning process to ensure that all crucial factors are met in a way that satisfies the company's objectives.

MAJOR BENEFITS OF CONTENT INSPECTION SECURITY

The most important precaution for a company is to provide a feature-rich and integrated solution. "Feature-rich" means a solution that handles evolving and complicated networks. These networks may still contain workstations running Windows 95, as well as the latest versions of Windows XP, various versions of Linux and a vast array of new and older systems. The network security solution cannot dictate what can and cannot be used. It needs to enable network browsing and support a majority of technologies.

The security solution should be used without sacrificing existing functionality. If a company is conducting business with an NFS (Network File System) and Lotus Notes, it still needs to be able to operate when new security measures are implemented. It is imperative that the security solution be compatible with the existing technologies that the company has already adopted.

The security solution also needs to be cost effective. Depending on the solution(s) selected, the cost may be a one-time purchase, and support costs may or may not be included with the original price. Support costs are also usually continual, with an annual renewal cost. Companies must evaluate their requirements against the features provided by the security solution and gauge its effectiveness for their needs. With many modern security platforms providing multiple security functions, support costs can be lowered by not requiring companies to purchase support contracts from a number of different vendors.

Performance is crucial. A security solution can't induce so much latency that a high-speed fiber connection resembles a slow T1 or DSL connection. That would be a tremendous sacrifice of productivity for security.

Insider Notes: The most important precaution for a company is to provide a feature-rich and integrated solution. "Feature-rich" means a solution that handles evolving and complicated networks.

DATA SNAPSHOT

The number of network connected computers has increased dramatically over the past decade; a non-networked computer is nearly useless, in most cases. As a result, management of the security defense on host level is becoming more and more difficult. This is why, more and more, network based security solutions are getting popular.

Has your company been attacked in the last 12 months?

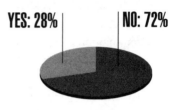

YES: 28%   NO: 72%

Download the complete research study for free at www.blackbooksecurity.com/research
Source: 2005 Larstan / Reed Infosecurity Survey

The best solution is to utilize as few components as possible. It is best to have an integrated solution, rather than having a best of breed solution for each security service. The reason is twofold. First, the probability of something going wrong is in direct proportion to the number of devices on the network. If 12 devices must be managed and each of them does different things, then the network is 12 times more likely to experience an error than if one device does it all.

Multiple single-purpose solutions complicate the network security topology, because single-purpose security devices are only built with one function in mind. In addition, a lot of integration work may need to be done so that many single-purpose security devices can work together. As you add more devices, problems increase exponentially.

A company with one or two vendors providing both firewall and VPN functions will avoid this problem. With a dozen different devices or security solutions, it might take an organization half a day just to figure out which device caused a problem. An integrated solution also makes it much easier for a company to keep its security devices up-to-date. A company that has to manage many different devices needs to go to each vendor to check for security patches and updates. It then has to ensure that each vendor patch works with every other vendor's patch, or incompatibilities may arise and disrupt network service.

THE THREE STEPS FOR DEPLOYING CONTENT INSPECTION

Security technology must now perform better than ever to catch the new breed of blended threats. Traditional security devices, such as firewalls, and IPS and IDS/IPS systems that only perform security tasks based on simple header information, or by performing "deep packet inspection" — are no longer adequate against the newer and more sophisticated threats.

To begin, a company must have a good understanding of its network typology. This usually involves both high-level strategic diagrams and low-level tactical configurations.

Below are the three steps to effectively implement a complete content inspection strategy.

❶ **Build up perimeter defenses.** The company needs to build up its perimeter defense to provide packet-level protection. Most companies already have this technology in place, but they will need to understand how it interfaces with the Internet. Companies will also have to assess the new protection upgrades, including new router switches, firewalls and antivirus solutions that have network edge blocking capabilities. In addition to these security functions, intrusion detection and intrusion prevention must also be assessed to see how these systems respond to both known and unknown intrusion attacks.

Companies also need to evaluate where their resources are in the perimeter and how these resources serve both internal and external customers. Rethinking and regrouping servers, applications and services into perimeter security zones that require the same level of protection can help organize and minimize the complexity of firewall rules. For example, grouping all web servers together in a separate DMZ servicing your external customers, allows much tighter firewall rules, and IDS/IPS monitoring.

Insider Notes: Performance is crucial. A security solution can't induce so much latency that a high-speed fiber connection resembles a slow T1 or DSL connection. That would be a tremendous sacrifice of productivity for security. The best solution is to utilize as few devices as possible.

334 ■ LARSTAN'S THE BLACK BOOK™ ON CORPORATE SECURITY

DNS servers, email servers and other semi-trusted applications should be separated in the DMZ to provide more granularity and tighter security policies. This approach may also help the logging process and allow the identification of suspicious activity quicker, as services are separated. To provide this form of infrastructure, companies need to evaluate firewall, IDS/IPS, antivirus and anti-spam solutions that can connect to multiple networks to support the security zoning required.

❷ Deploy a network management solution. As the network grows, companies will need to manage devices from many different vendors. There are several methods to accomplish this. A company can purchase network management software from all the major vendors. Typically, these licenses are included within the price of the software. Large companies with a distributed back office often customize their own network management solutions. They may use generic network management software that each vendor can interface with. Telecom companies often write their own applications that are customized for their own needs.

Either way, good network management software is necessary to monitor and manage all existing and new security devices.

Larger companies, with more assets to protect, will generally have more security solutions. These solutions will most likely be spread throughout the corporation, from the perimeter, to remote offices, to the network core and into the server farms. Having a system that can manage these security devices can be of great help in coordinating logs, reports, provisioning and to providing consistency across the enterprise. A tiered management approach is critical for non-centralized IT departments that need to share management responsibilities throughout the corporate infrastructure. The ability to assign read access or read/write access to other sub-administrators is critical to large IT departments with a decentralized management model.

❸ Institute data logging and reporting. Another important function of network and security devices is to log and report all security events. The analysis of these reports may aid in predicting future attacks and also provide the means to conduct forensic analysis. Reporting, monitoring and having people dedicated to analyzing these reports are crucial in real world security operations. Large companies may have use for a security events management solution. This tool does data mining and can automatically assess the event logs, determine patterns and correlate events.

The ability to provide log and event correlation is critical to spotting attempted attacks, and critical to providing evidence that an attack has occurred. Security systems must have the ability to send SNMP traps, syslog events and email alerts for all critical functions. Centralized correlation and reporting systems must be able to accept traps and syslog events from each security and network device for tracking and correlation capabilities. The ability to support a centralized or external time server to time stamp and record events is important in large networks with dissimilar systems.

POST-DEPLOYMENT

After deployment, it is important that all operating systems, routers and switches be continually updated, and that all operating systems and router switches are updated with the security holes patched and the bugs fixed. This can be done manually, semi-automatically or automatically with the choice dependent on the size of the network and budget. There are software solutions on the market that can keep track of all the security update patches, implement patch management and provide ongoing auditing and analysis of the network. When new equipment or services are introduced, it must be determined if the existing infrastructure needs to be changed or accommodated for that system to inter-operate.

In today's world, filled with fast spreading attacks and threats, it is important to keep corporate security systems updated. Sophisticated, blended attacks are increasing each year, and new attacks are beginning to leverage

Insider Notes: Security technology must now perform better than ever to catch the new breed of blended threats. Traditional security devices — such as firewalls, and IDS/IPS systems that only perform security tasks based on simple header information, or by performing "deep packet inspection" — are no longer adequate against the newer and more sophisticated threats.

NO MATTER HOW DANGEROUS THE INTERNET IS BECOMING, IT IS UNREALISTIC TO CUT OFF INTERNET ACCESS TO PROTECT AGAINST VIRUS INFECTIONS.

the success of previous attacks. Companies that continue to rely on manual updating procedures will be at a great disadvantage against these threats.

Threats are evolving faster. The time from when a vulnerability is discovered to the time a hacker takes advantage of that vulnerability is diminishing. Slammer, Blaster and Welchia are a few examples of fast spreading blended threats that have attacked and spread worldwide within hours. Companies should look for solutions that can be updated in near real time, with the ability to obtain signature and attack profile updates automatically 24x7.

By using automated update systems, administrators can simplify the tasks of keeping critical security devices and platforms up-to-date. This is especially important for security systems deployed at the perimeter. If perimeter security systems are left unpatched, the risk of exposure is increased for all systems behind that security device.

EXPECTED OUTCOMES

The best practice for a company, after introducing additional services and security solutions, is to test it first under a controlled environment, such as the main office with several locations, and then gradually introduce it to the core, and then the backbone of the production network. Careful planning, testing and rollout are the ingredients of a successful security deployment and an important first step, as new security services shouldn't negatively impact the rest of the production systems.

After introduction, the company needs to understand the vendor's maintenance, update and patch management process for all solutions, as well as the reporting and data mining capabilities. To truly leverage the security solution, companies need to understand the post-purchase service options and what other tools are available for collecting logs, reporting and alerting. For example, if a company spends $30,000 to buy a network antivirus solution and places it on the Internet gateway to protect email, the first thing it needs to see is a report that shows how many viruses it blocked every day.

Having reports from the antivirus and intrusion detection functions are only one piece of the security solution. Companies must also rely on their users to inform them of how the security solution is performing, with respect to performance and false-positives or false-negatives. Users have to state whether it makes the company's computing experience better, or if it makes it worse.

CRITICAL FACTORS FOR SUCCESSFUL IMPLEMENTATION

■ **Assess required scalability.** A company needs to invest in a product that can provide it with the flexibility to expand. By the same token, it also doesn't want to over-invest in a product that it doesn't need. A company doesn't need a $100,000 dollar firewall that provides it with the speed of several connections when it has only one. On the other hand, if it does have several connections, the company doesn't want to buy a firewall solution that will only scale up to a T1.

A good analysis of current and future requirements is essential. Today a company may have a single T1, tomorrow it might have a T3, and several years down the road, it may have fiber to the desktop. Therefore, buying something that works for a T1 connection now, but not a T3 connection in the near future is wasting money, because the security investment will not scale.

Insider Notes: In today's world, filled with fast spreading attacks and threats, it is important to keep corporate security systems updated. Sophisticated, blended attacks are increasing each year and new attacks are beginning to leverage the success of previous attacks. Companies that continue to rely on manual updating procedures will be at a great disadvantage against these threats.

■ **Understand the level of threats**. On technical terms, a company must understand the level of threats it faces, what it is trying to protect and the risk associated with not having adequate protection. It's a money game in which companies need to understand the cost of the security solution verses the risk to the asset. A company only needs to spend enough to defend what it has. It has to determine the costs in a worse case scenario (if an attack has compromised the entire system, requiring a complete recovery from backup), and factor that into the cost of a new security solution.

There are different levels of security certification. A company can invest $10 million to build a completely airtight security system, but if it has only $1 million worth of assets, it is overspending. The assets must also be evaluated in light of the probability of being attacked. Hackers increasingly seek financial gain, not notoriety. They're interested in easy hits. That's why a company doesn't need to build a high caliber 99%+ security defense system that no one in the world can access. All it needs is a security solution that is above average for a company of its size. This will create a security solution to provide adequate protection for the company, since hackers will find it a lot harder to attack than other companies with the same value.

Both economically and technically, a company must have a good understanding of the likelihood of these attacks occurring. Viruses, worms, Trojans and spyware are fairly likely to occur and should be high on the list of things to protect against. It may be worth a $20,000 or $30,000 investment to protect against 95% of modern viruses, because having no antivirus protection may result in reinstalling infected systems every other week. No matter how dangerous the Internet is becoming, it is unrealistic to cut off Internet access to protect against virus infections.

Companies should assess their security needs at all levels of the network, not just the perimeter. As employee mobility becomes more common, the chances of mobile computers infecting the internal network when they are brought back into the company are very good. Not properly accessing these potential vulnerabilities will leave the company's network fully exposed, no matter how secure the perimeter.

FACTORS FOR FAILURE

■ **Not understanding the nature of the threat.** Companies generally don't understand how hackers think, why they want to attack companies and what approaches they are using. The majority of break-ins are targets of opportunity.

■ **Lack of network coordination.** Most networks are complicated architectures. They contain a plethora of vendors. Technology gets introduced at certain points in time to protect certain network components and services — all without reference to the other systems. Some companies might be using IBM architecture for their financial network, AT&T for their engineering department and other networks for their remaining departments. These distinct solutions, without good network management, often result in technological cracks and the lack of coordination and correlation between them. Another problem is a frequent inability to completely unify the disparate networks and systems; this creates a condition where attacks can easily happen.

■ **Not keeping solutions up-to-date.** Companies may install security solutions, such as firewalls and antivirus systems, and then forget to follow up or upgrade them. Busy with day-to-day functions, they forget to download the latest updates and patches to keep the antivirus systems up-to-date and inadvertently render the antivirus solution useless. They also forget to continually monitor and analyze reports and alerts, allowing infections and attacks to go by unnoticed, or responding slowly to attacks that have already happened days, or weeks, ago.

■ **Not taking security seriously.** As IT resources are stretched, companies tend to concentrate on fires. They put on hold proactive

Insider Notes: Hackers increasingly seek financial gain, not notoriety. They're interested in easy hits. That's why a company doesn't need to build a high caliber 99%+ security defense system that no one in the world can access. All it needs is a security solution that is above average for a company of its size.

activities like maintaining existing systems and the operational tasks to keep servers up and running. This practice eventually puts their security defenses way behind and increases the risk and exposure to being successfully attacked. Compounding this problem is the lack of monitoring systems and the ability to review critical logs, which allows probing to go unnoticed. Many successful attacks begin with probing activities. Hackers often first test the waters with some form of probing tools and other reconnaissance activities. These early warning signs go unnoticed until the attack is underway.

■ **Managing the implementation process.** There are a number of different corporate reporting architectures. However, usually the IS department reports to operations, and ultimately to the CFO. The challenge to the IS department is twofold: the management challenge and the technical challenge.

The major complaint from IS departments is, if they do a good job, nobody thanks them. But if they fail and there is down time, everybody knows about it. In addition, it's not easy keeping up with the latest threats and learning how the latest routers, firewalls and intrusion devices work. There are so many different devices, solutions and vendors to choose from because networks are getting more diversified. The IS department is partitioning itself in a logical manner. To meet budgetary requirements, it may employ low-cost personnel to perform desktop support, higher end resources to perform data backup planning and another group to perform strategic planning and network implementation.

The department also needs technical expertise, especially when selecting vendors. Because it is difficult to manage a network with many different vendor's solutions, IS departments tend to commit to brand name security devices to shorten the learning curve. That's because vendors usually maintain continuity in technology. Once an IS department acclimates to a vendor's solution, it is easy to migrate to the next version. With all the choices available, companies typically do not want to deploy dozens of security solutions from different vendors because these solutions must be integrated to perform well.

The demand today is for solutions that interoperate well with other solutions, but this is generally nonexistent with many of today's security solutions. If a company deploys 12 different security devices, one to handle traffic shaping, one for intrusion protection, one for firewall, one for CRM and so forth, it will require 12 times the learning time just to get it all to work. For many customers, an integrated security solution is becoming the obvious choice to decrease the learning and implementation times, as well as to simplify management and maintenance efforts

The complexity of attacks is growing, as is their ability to bypass traditional point-based security. Companies must rethink their security posture and design a solution that protects the corporation's assets and operates within budget. Appliances that combine multiple security functions are increasingly the answer. Managing one security device that provides firewall, antivirus and IDS/IPS capabilities is simpler than managing three separate systems. Savings accrue not just in the up front capital, but also in the ongoing maintenance of one device, as opposed to three.

BEST PRACTICES FOR CONTENT INSPECTION

The best practice for a complete content inspection security solution must be discussed with respect to a company's size and risk category — small to medium size, low-risk enterprises; medium to large size medium-risk enterprises; and large enterprises with high risk.

For medium to large companies in the medium risk category, a security compromise would affect normal business operations and could be a headache for many employees. For large enterprises with high risk, Internet presence is critical and high confidentiality is required. These categories may not just apply to corporations, but also to each individual office and facility. Some large national companies may have facilities that could be

Insider Notes: Companies should assess their security needs at all levels of the network, not just the perimeter. As employee mobility becomes more common, the chances of mobile computers infecting the internal network when they are brought back into the company are very good.

CASE STUDY: PUTTING VIRUSES AND WORMS IN A CAGE

The Problem: The Calgary Zoo had multiple systems problems. On one hand, it was being subjected to repeated attacks by viruses, worms, and grayware. These attacks were not being prevented, nor was protection being provided the Zoo's existing firewall and desktop antivirus software.

In addition, the Zoo needed to eliminate performance and functional bottlenecks within its security infrastructure. These were leading to frequent mail outages and creating an environment that prevented the implementation of new technologies, such as secure wireless service.

The Need: The Zoo required a solution that would provide both fire wall and antivirus protection. It also required that that these solutions function both on the perimeter of the network and at its interior.

The Solution: Calgary Zoo decided to implement the Fortinet Platform with complete content protection. This system provided the integration of antivirus, firewall, VPN and IDP that the Zoo required. It also provided the additional functions of content filtering, traffic shaping, and anti-spam protection. All of these functions could be managed from a central point.

The Benefit: After implementation, the Calgary Zoo experienced an increase in network performance and a renewed ability to implement advanced technologies. Network intrusions have also been radically reduced.

evaluated as having medium, or even low-risk, but some headquarters of smaller companies might be categorized as highly-sensitive facilities.

For example, some headquarters might have extremely sensitive information that must be kept secret, or some companies, such as online service providers like eBay, that obtain the majority of their revenues from services provided through the Internet, are at high risk. Any down time means immediate loss of revenue and degradation of their reputation.

In the wake of new federal and state regulations governing information protection, the need for a thorough security analysis is critical to all businesses. For example, California has more stringent requirements than many other states or countries. SB 1386 (California Breach Information Act) requires the public disclosure of successful attacks made against customer information. This can impact all companies and greatly hurt customer relations when incidents happen.

BEST PRACTICES FOR COMPANIES WITH LOW RISK

Best practices for small, medium and large businesses vary significantly. For the small office category, where people simply want to have Internet access to browse the web and exchange non-critical information, a tape backup solution for a disaster recovery mechanism is usually all that is needed. Thirty to forty percent of businesses belong to this category. For these small businesses, in a worse case scenario, everything can be restored back to a state before the catastrophe — with the users hoping that the disaster scenario will not happen again.

For many smaller companies, this approach works, but it also means that there is usually no dedicated person looking after the network systems. The person with the most technical expertise usually ends up supporting the IT responsibilities, reducing human resource costs. Equipment-wise, some form of low-end integrated security solution is all that is needed. A lot of vendors are targeting SOHO (small office, home office) and small enterprises for these very reasons. The most critical aspect is to have as much protection as possible within the allotted budget. But, unfortunately, many SOHO and small business owners usually implement nothing for their security needs.

Insider Notes: The complexity of attacks is growing, as is their ability to bypass traditional point-based security. Companies must rethink their security posture and design a solution that protects the corporation's assets and operates within budget. Appliances that combine multiple security functions are increasingly the answer.

CASE STUDY: AVERTING DOOM

INDUSTRY: SEMICONDUCTOR MANUFACTURING

The Problem: Atmel had begun to experience sophisticated content based attacks against its networks. These attacks had been disguised as web (HTTP). Email (POP3, SMTP, and IMAP), as well as other legitimate traffic.

The Need: Atmel required a sophisticated content analysis solution that could stop these attacks without crippling network performance or requiring a large amount of IT resources to manage.

How Fortinet Helped: Atmel implemented the Fortinet platform that provides content protection at the perimeter of the company's network. This system provided insulation against both viruses and worms without impacting network performance.

Benefits: The solution was put to the test when the MYDOOM worm hit. The Fortinet solution stopped the worm before it entered Atmel's corporate network or impacted network performance.

As the level of threats and number of attacks increase with greater sophistication, so does the use of social engineering methods such as phishing and spyware, and the traditional methods that were once good enough may no longer be adequate. The low-cost DSL router/firewall appliance cannot detect the new breed of viruses, worms and Trojans. Couple this with sophisticated attacks such as spyware, and smaller companies are at greater risk without dedicated IT and security resources. A new breed of service provider is emerging to fill this void. Managed Security Service Providers are becoming more popular as the need for more sophisticated security defenses arises. These service providers offer much more than just Internet connectivity and bandwidth. They also offer security services for firewall, intrusion detection and prevention, antivirus, spam filtering, web content filtering and VPN.

BEST PRACTICES FOR MEDIUM RISK COMPANIES

Losing Internet connectivity will not cripple medium-sized companies with an intermediate risk category and sensitive information processing (such as R&D departments, accounting services and several hundred employees sending and receiving sensitive information via email). No immediate revenue loss would be incurred, but the company would suffer from loss of productivity. The down time would be a real nuisance, but would not be disastrous, because the productivity loss is still recoverable. Fifty to sixty percent of businesses belong to this intermediate risk category.

The advent of the Internet has caused many modern businesses to rely on their web presence to conduct business. With the complexity of modern business systems, reflected by financial systems and CRM, smaller to medium-sized businesses are starting to contract out these services. For companies that rely on their external connections to conduct business, outages can be severely harmful, especially if they occur during a critical part of the business cycle.

BUDGET AND STAFFING

Enterprises that conduct business on the Internet often have larger budgets for staffing and will have dedicated information system experts, contracted experts from their service providers or external consultants to help them with the planning and maintenance of network security infrastructure.

Medium-sized companies tend to focus on price-performance ratio. Because they have dedicated — or partially dedicated — IT resources, these companies are often familiar with many of the security solutions on the market, and usually have enough security infrastructure to address the majority of security problems they face. They have firewall solutions, VPN solutions, antivirus solutions and IDS/IPS solutions. These companies often deploy

Insider Notes: Managed Security Service Providers are becoming more popular as the need for more sophisticated security defenses arises. These service providers not only offer bandwidth, but security services for firewall, intrusion detection and prevention, antivirus, spam filtering, web content filtering and VPN services.

CASE STUDY: A DANGEROUS BLEND
INDUSTRY: AUTOMOTIVE

The Problem: Honda had traditional antivirus and firewall protection installed. The company was concerned that it may be vulnerable to blended attacks. The increased volume of these attacks encouraged Honda to deploy a comprehensive solution before critical information was compromised.

The Solution: Fortinet implemented its Fortigate complete content protection solution. This solution integrated multiple security functions and provided Honda security against blended attacks with coordinated and centrally managed firewall, antivirus and VPN protection as well as intrusion diction/prevention and content filtering.

Benefits: Honda was able to upgrade its network security protection against combined cyber attacks.

best-of-breed technology from each security category and tend to understand what is necessary to secure their networks.

One important item to point out for medium-sized companies with intermediate risk exposure is the cost of maintenance. Many security solutions are single purpose point-based solutions (such as software-based firewalls, IDS/IPS and gateway antivirus products). These require the company to piece the solution together on a general-purpose system with a common operating system. Depending on the product, the complexity may be fairly high and require a dedicated security expert to maintain the system. This approach may seem more cost-effective in the beginning, but once the time, human resources, capital equipment and maintenance is totaled together, the cost and effort may be higher than a simple security appliance approach.

When companies consider the best-of-breed solutions, they often compare only the one-time cost of purchasing the product. However, it is important to combine the product purchase price with the ongoing operational cost (that includes maintenance fees and the dedicated resources required for implementation and management). This applies not only to firewall solutions, but also to IDS/IPS solutions, antivirus solutions, anti-spam solutions, web content filtering and any other security function.

Human resources required to implement the solution often play a big role in the overall cost factor. For example, to set up and maintain many single purpose products, a company may require several consultants, each experienced with a different product in the overall solution. The cost of implementing and managing single purpose security solutions is expensive, and that's why the security appliance approach is gaining popularity. Many security appliances are now virtually plug-and-play, with installation wizards and adequate default configurations to help secure most basic security requirements. This dramatically decreases the implementation and ongoing maintenance costs associated with single purpose solutions.

Security appliances not only offer multiple solutions in one chassis to save on capital expenditures and continuing maintenance costs, but they also offer more sophisticated detection and blocking mechanisms. Examples include reactive IDS/IPS systems that also include a firewall. The IDS/IPS system is reactive and uses internal signaling to create a firewall rule to perform the blocking of malicious traffic. This approach creates latency between the time the threat was seen and the time it is blocked, exposing additional risk to the enterprise.

Other forms of multi-function security appliances are designed from the ground up to be an integrated solution with pro-active detection and blocking to ensure the highest level of protection. Sessions that are deemed malicious are identified and stopped immediately without having to create firewall policies dynamically. Customers must fully assess the technology as well as the cost savings to select the best-of-breed security appliance to suit their needs.

There are technologies that are similar in function but differ in the degree of solution completeness required. A good example of this is disaster recovery. For a low-risk facility, disaster recovery can consist of copying important files from one computer to another. For medium-risk facilities, industry standard automated backup systems and processes are required. If 90% of the computers in a protected medium-risk facility get a virus

DATA SNAPSHOT

Network based security threats have been dealt with by traditional security vendors for a long time. Now the solutions have been more or less standardized at a service provider level. That's why in this survey, the percentage of these types of security technology (stateful firewall, IPsec VPN, Intrusion Detection) only represent a small percentage. The content-based threats are new and there are various competing technologies available today. This is also the area where end-users need to worry about the most.

Do you agree that content level threats are gradually becoming more of a threat to your business than some of the traditional threats?

YES: 77% | **NO: 23%**

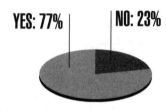

Download the complete research study for free at www.blackbooksecurity.com/research
Source: 2005 Larstan / Reed Infosecurity Survey

infection, the facility can reformat the infected hard drives, restore backed up files, and not lose a lot of their intellectual property. For many enterprises, it is also not a big deal to lose Internet access as long as their intellectual property is not lost or compromised. But it can be really costly not to have a good solution for disaster recovery.

Having good disaster recovery is critical to survival for most companies that conduct business through modern computer and network resources. They need to set up their systems to ensure that the company's most critical resources can be recovered and preserved in the event that they are lost or compromised. A good example of disaster recovery planning is the terrorist attack on the World Trade Centers on September 11, 2001. Many firms in the World Trade buildings had remote off-site backup systems that preserved the information lost in this catastrophic event, and as bad as things were, they were able to continue to conduct business afterwards.

BEST PRACTICE FOR HIGH RISK COMPANIES

The high-risk category companies usually have a core team of IT and security experts to look after their networking infrastructure and security requirements. These companies should budget adequately to allow them to evaluate different security and networking solutions before putting them into their production network. Many mission critical systems will even have multiple setups and facilities to replicate the production environment. For example, eBay has two or three labs that contain the same servers: one to backup the network, one for testing the network and a third for network development.

The most critical activity for these high-risk companies is redundancy. Their systems can be compared to systems in other mission critical applications, such as the design of an airplane with redundant systems that back each other up in case of a failure in one component. In the airplane example, engineers designed the system to be extremely foolproof. Even if one engine fails, safety and backup systems allow the pilot to land the plane safely.

For mission critical data centers, the same design principle applies. Cost isn't the number one concern for these installations and neither is functionality; reliability is. With these architectures, there are two of every critical component in the network: at least two outside connections to the Internet, two routers running the BGP or OSPF routing protocols, load balancing between multiple servers or firewalls, multiple power connections, redundant power, and so forth. Uptime is so important, even system upgrades are affected. As one system is upgraded, the other maintains connectivity and service. The upgrades or new systems are fully and thoroughly tested on a replicated system beforehand to ensure no new surprises to the production system. When a new solution is introduced, not only will there be new features, but also bug fixes that add new code to fix the previous release's system deficiencies. These changes may introduce new and unexpected problems.

The production environment must be as "bug free" as possible, putting tremendous pressure on new solutions. IT and security professionals must understand the risk of introducing new technology into stable production environments and design this factor into their security and redundancy planning.

In today's information economy, there's widespread connectivity and people are sharing information more than ever before. However, as I've shown in this chapter, greater connectivity also breeds greater danger. All companies are now vulnerable to attack. Information may appear to come from a "trusted" source, but in cyberspace there is no Bill of Rights. Everyone is guilty until proven innocent.

■ ■ ■

Michael Xie has more than 10 years of experience in the network security area, having successfully designed many industry-leading security products for companies large and small.

Xie currently oversees all development, engineering and support for Fortinet's products, which include the company's ASIC-accelerated FortiGate antivirus firewalls, FortiOS operating system, and management and reporting systems. Under his guidance, Fortinet has successfully introduced more than 25 innovative products since 2002. These products have garnered numerous prestigious industry awards — including the 2004 Security Product of the Year Award from Network Computing magazine and the 2003 Networking Industry Awards Firewall Product of the Year. These have helped Fortinet become the leader in Unified Threat Management solutions.

Previously, Xie held positions as Software Director and Architect at NetScreen, and Security Architect for Milkyway Networks. He holds multiple U.S. patents in the computer and network security area. He can be reached at 408-235-7700 (x 802) or mxie@fortinet.com.

[13]

THE RISE OF CONVERGED NETWORKS: A NEW THREAT TO SECURITY

Networks that share both voice and data pose a new danger to corporate security. Here's how to protect your systems, without compromising efficiency.

"EVERYTHING THAT RISES MUST CONVERGE."
- Law of Physics

by JOSEPH SEANOR

Voice and data networks are no longer separate, distinct entities. They are "converging" into one interrelated network, a trend that creates new and profound security dilemmas. Problem is, most corporate executives are unaware of this convergence, and if they are, they underestimate the risks it poses.

Strictly speaking, a converged network is a combination of the voice and data networks within a company, where both networks share the same connection and transfer data back and forth. Converged networks are increasingly prevalent, and corporate managers must adjust their security systems accordingly.

Unfortunately, most managers still think this way: "My voice network is my voice network, and my data network is my data network. All the security possible has been installed to protect my data network, such as firewalls, intrusion protection, antivirus, and anti-Trojan devices. And why would a hacker even try to break into my voice network, other than to listen to voicemail?"

This complacent and outmoded attitude is reminiscent of the French in 1940, who thought their "state-of-the-art" defensive perimeter, the Maginot Line, would protect them from German invaders. We all know how THAT turned out.

In today's environment, the majority of voice networks run on a computer system of some type, unlike the old mechanical telephone switches of the past. The newer PBXs (Private Branch Exchange) run as an application on a proprietary operating system, a Windows system or a Linux system, but underneath the PBX application and these systems is still a computer.

With that being the case, many companies have a computer system running a telephony application. This means that the voice network is a computer system running voice, and has some type of data connection back to the data network, whether that is voicemail, some sort of customer list or SQL (Sequential Query Language) database. Therein lies the security dilemma within a Converged Network: the connections between voice and data compel security officers to guard against threats that may apply to both voice and data. These two networks were once considered separated, but now they've converged and they share resources, data and information.

Most companies are unaware of this level of convergence and the security problems it poses. Most consider a converged network to be a Voice over Internet Protocol (VoIP) network. This is a true converged network because it is running voice as data packets. However, before this even occurs, there is a transition period where seemingly pure voice applications are sharing data with the data network. Most people don't realize that they are in a converged network, and this is where the security risk is. Below, I will examine the nature of this risk and how to combat it.

COMPONENTS OF A CONVERGED NETWORK

Typical components of a converged network are an IVR (interactive voice response) CMS (call management system), call centers, voicemail and PBXs that run on a computer instead of a mechanical switch. These are the standard components that would populate a converged network. Any company running an IVR, CMS or voicemail that has been purchased within the past three years has a good chance of already being in a converged network. Most of these systems are running on Windows, Linux or proprietary operating systems. Any company running voicemail today will find that these voicemails are stored on a server.

In the future, these systems will become even more converged. All voicemail will go to a Storage Area Network (SAN), and soon there will be the need for more data storage for these voicemails, because of regulatory compliance issues. That means companies will need to store voicemails for the long term. This will be done on big SANs farms or on giant Redundant Array of Independent Devices (RAID) drives, but there will be large storage facilities that will contain voicemails and ways to track, protect and manage this mass storage network.

SECURITY IMPLICATIONS OF THE CONVERGED NETWORK

The first issue is mindset. Corporate managers still think of voice and data as separate entities. They have had data security assessments completed by third-party organizations to ensure a high level of security and full compli-

Insider Notes: A company that worries about data tends to only protect web, application and file servers. However, on the voice side, a company's IVR, CMS and voicemail are now running on a server, and it is not being protected at the same level as data. That is a big problem. Any threat today that can attack your data severs can work equally well on your voice network.

COMPANIES DON'T REALIZE THAT THEY HAVE CONNECTED A VOICE NETWORK TO THE INTERNET, BUT THEY HAVE, THEREBY ALLOWING ANYBODY TO INSTALL WORMS, TROJAN HORSES OR SNIFFERS INTO THE ENTIRE INTERNAL DATA NETWORK.

ance with all federal regulations. When it comes to voice networks, they assume security is not a big issue. This is not true any longer. The voice network is now converged; it is running on a server. Anything that can be done to a server on the data side that concerns management or keeps them awake at night can now be done on the voice side.

A company that worries about data tends to only protect web, application and file servers. However, on the voice side, a company's IVR, CMS and voicemail are now running on a server, and it is not being protected at the same level as data. That is a big problem. Any threat today that can attack your data severs can work equally well on your voice network. If a company is running a voice network on a Windows 2000 server, every single problem that can attack a Windows device can attack the voice network.

There are many ways that a hacker can gain access to a data network through the telephony servers. Companies have not considered securing or protecting its voice network by sub-netting it, partitioning it or building a fire wall around it. If this is not the case, then they not protecting their voice network.

There is more concern today about locking down every way that someone can attack the data network, such as hackers attacking from the Internet, and then there is always the chance that someone could slip in through the back door of their voice network. Once a system inside of that voice network is compromised, it is possible for a hacker to gain access to any other part of the network through multiple avenues, including direct connections from the voice network to the data network.

While a company sees its telephony system as voice that does not need protection, in reality it could be a Windows 2000 server running a telephony application. This server could have an Internet connection to run Microsoft updates. When this happens, it will create a connection to the Internet, through the voice server that has not been protected. Someone can easily break into that system, and once they are connected inside, odds are that they can get another connection into the data network.

This threat has evolved because of the legacy mindset that exists in most companies. Most companies have a director of telecom who is in charge of the telecom system, and a director of data who is in charge of the data network. These two people have completely different jobs and completely different mindsets. Once they get together and start talking, they realize that voice is connected to the data network, and they recognize the fact that they are sharing resources.

Today, most people think there is a clear separation between voice and data. They think of the telephone as copper wires and not a data jack. Until people see an Ethernet cable coming right up to the telephone, they won't think that this is a data phone. They will think that everything is protected because their data is protected.

HOW CONVERGED NETWORKS ARE INTEGRATED

Most telephony systems today are running on a computer system. These telephony systems are no longer a mechanical switch. When a company buys a PBX, a call center or an IVR, it is buying an application that runs on a server. When the system is delivered it is plugged into the company network and begins to run the telephony applications. But it also runs things like SNMP (Simple Network Management Protocol) for monitoring and additional connections for patching and updating the system.

Insider Notes: Take a proactive stance for a converged network security posture. Consider voice threats such as social engineering, war dialing or weak pass codes. If a hacker gains access to the root of a voice server, the damage can be considerable.

WHAT NEEDS TO BE UNDERSTOOD IS THAT THE THREATS FROM THE VOICE WORLD ARE NOW TRANSITIONING INTO THE DATA WORLD, AND THAT THERE EXISTS, IN ESSENCE, ONE BIG NETWORK THREAT.

These activities are needed to monitor the voice applications, and for voice uptime and updating the system with security patches. Companies don't realize that they have connected their voice network to the Internet, but they have, thereby allowing anybody to install worms, Trojan horses or sniffers into the entire internal data network.

FIVE ACTION ITEMS

❶ **Gain knowledge.** Know what a converged network is. It is today's network environment that has data servers, voice servers and voicemail all connected to a single network.

❷ **Change mindset.** Develop a converged network mindset. By understanding the fact that you are working in a converged network right now, even if not a VoIP, you will start to recognize the existence of all of these new network connections.

❸ **Identify the converged network.** Identify the voice and data networks, and develop a brand new converged network diagram. This will open up visibility into the systems network.

❹ **Map out the converged network.** Develop one converged map that documents the entire network (voice and data) as one picture.

❺ **Take a proactive stance for a converged network security posture.** Consider voice threats such as social engineering, war dialing or weak pass codes. If a hacker gains access to the root of a voice server, the damage can be considerable. The hacker would be able to launch a scan against the entire internal network; he could compromise that server and set up voicemail boxes for all of his friends, and he could set up his own private web server. What needs to be understood is that the threats from the voice world are now transitioning into the data world and that there exists, in essence, one big network threat. Companies need to think proactively. They must transition all the security that they have established on the data side over to the telephony side. They need to put up firewalls and intrusion prevention systems, and apply the same security strategies and guidelines that were applied to their data network onto their voice network. This will help to prepare them for future attacks.

HOW A CONVERGED NETWORK DIFFERS FROM A DATA NETWORK

This section discusses how the traditional data network and today's converged networks differ. I will then explain how the threats associated with data networks are now just as much of a threat to the voice network and what the implications of this change in security risk are to management.

In a pure data network, the network is transmitting TCP (Transmission Control Protocol) UDP (Universal Data Protocol) packets that are transferring computer based information, whether it is web traffic, database traffic, email traffic or other general TCP/IP based traffic. There is no voice information, voice connection or voice packets, it is just pure data.

A converged network, on the other hand, inserts connections to a voice network into this data network. That is the main way in which data networks differ from a converged network. A converged network maintains voice information of some type or some form in its network architecture. That voice data could be voicemail, it could be VoIP phone calls, it could be an IVR, it could be a CMS or it could be a call center. The real issue is getting telecom and IT staff to overcome their antiquated attitudes and to recognize the cross-network connections between voice and data networks.

Normally, a company has a set of voice applications, VoIP, IVR, voicemail, CMS or Call Centers in their voice network. Nobody has a pure VoIP network running and no other telephony applications. When a company

Insider Notes: The real issue is getting telecom and IT staff to overcome their antiquated attitudes and to recognize the cross-network connections between voice and data networks.

DATA SNAPSHOT

Looking at the results of this graph, we see that more and more coporation executives are looking at the voice and data networks for security. However, the question is how much of an assessment is done on the voice side? Is it as detailed as the data network assessments? Having a detailed assessment of the voice side is the issue with the converged network.

Do you conduct assessments of both your voice and data networks?

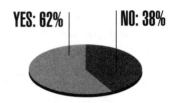

YES: 62%   NO: 38%

Download the complete research study for free at www.blackbooksecurity.com/research
Source: 2005 Larstan / Reed Infosecurity Survey

implements a VoIP network, it already has a PBX, either on premise or they lease one from another provider. The company normally has a voicemail system, and often some type of call center. Very rarely does a company have just one tiny voice application running in their voice network.

Traditionally, networks were pure data or pure voice, because voicemail was stored on proprietary operating systems that were not running Windows or Linux. But in today's environment, these voice servers are using Windows or Linux as the base operating system of the server and the server can also do additional functions other than just telephony.

HOW DO THREATS TO A CONVERGED NETWORK DIFFER FROM THE THREATS TO A DATA NETWORK?

A pure data network is subject to legacy threats, with which we are all very familiar. A data network is running IP packets, and there is a long history of knowledge and information about IP networks and their weaknesses. Information about how these data packets are created, put together, what they do, where they go and how they can be exploited are all out in the open. You can discover on the Internet all the information you want about how to attack a data network.

In a converged network, the situation is different because there are some proprietary operating systems and specific telephony applications that store voicemail or an interactive voice response system, or provide call center activities. With additional packets floating around a converged network, hackers can gather even more intelligence about the company. The new problem with a converged network is that even more confidential data is transmitted across the corporate network. Think of how much more sensitive information is discussed on a voice network, as opposed to email!

A data network threat is usually perpetrated by hackers, crackers, disgruntled employees and others. This is one level of threat, attacking the IP layer only. In the converged network, a voice side is added which provides a new level of attack, so there are now two levels of threats: the standard hacker threats, and a second level of threats. (For example: attacks against H323, a VoIP packet; sniffing VoIP packets; and attacks against Session Initiation Protocol, or SIP.)

This new level of threat in a converged network enables a new type of attack that is unusual because it is twofold. It is attacking the traditional data network and attacking the voice network at the same time, and in a new and unusual way. Not only are there threats from hackers that are attacking the data networks, but also hackers that are now becoming crackers or phone phreaks who can social engineer their way into the network. These voyeurs are listening in on voicemail and on VoIP phone calls, as well.

This is the new breed of attacker, one who is becoming more sophisticated in the nature of his attacks on the converged network. They are betting on the corporate mindset of two different networks, and the securing of two different networks. Usually a hacker who wants to break into a network will scan the network, and then go after a web server or other Internet facing device. But in today's converged network environment, he has multiple avenues of attack: he can attack the web server, but if he scans and finds a voicemail server or scans and finds a modem built for remote diagnostics

Insider Notes: The new problem with a converged network is that even more confidential data is transmitted across the corporate network. Think of how much more sensitive information is discussed on a voice network, as opposed to email!

MANAGERS TEND TO THINK THAT VOICE NETWORKS CAN NEVER BE ATTACKED BECAUSE HACKERS GO AFTER DATA, BUT IN REALITY THESE HACKERS GO AFTER THE SERVER.

and is able to hack that modem, he can then attack the voice network. Once he gets into that voice network and starts to run his normal modus operandi (MO) attacks, the attacker would start to try and elevate access, and gather intelligence about what type of server he has gained access to. But if he has compromised a newer voice server, he might find he is on a Windows 2000 server! Meanwhile, further scans might show that he also gained access to an entire data network as well. This is the danger when a hacker breaks into a converged network.

The target of a hacker in the system is not so much the data that is there, but the system itself. The hacker may or may not know he is attacking a voicemail server or a PBX. All he knows is that he found a system that he can attack. Once he gets into the system, he eventually finds out that he is in a voice network. Then he can find the connection to the data network and run any series of attacks, such as a "man in the middle" attack against the network, and forge credentials to get from the voice side to the data side, because that information is being piped over the same server.

HACKING TOOLS FOR THE CONVERGED NETWORK

If the voice side of this converged network has Internet facing devices, then standard scans from a hacker on the Internet will find all the ports that are open and conduct traditional attacks on the network. However, once he breaks into that server and does the standard poking around, he sees the telephony application running as a process on that server. That's when he knows he is on a telephony network, and that's when the real fun for an attacker starts.

There are tools that can gain hackers initial entrance into these systems during attacks, such as Nmap, which is a port scan that can find out a lot about a system. There are other assessment tools, such as Retina or Nessus, all of which are readily available. It depends on where the hacker comes into the network as to what he finds out. If he finds a way in with a phone sweep program when war dialing, he may initially lean a little more towards the voice network. If a hacker finds a way in by conducting a port scan on the Internet, he will focus first on a data network then, once inside, find he is on a voice network. How you will first notice the attacks all depends on how the hacker comes into the system, whether by modem or by port scanning.

KEY DIFFERENCES BETWEEN THREATS

The difference in threats is that a data network does not maintain any type of voice information whatsoever, whether that's a VoIP phone call, voice-mail or an IVR system. A converged network maintains both voice and data, which is traveling across this network architecture without restraints. In other words, voice data can be going across from the pure voice system into the data system via SQL pipes, RAID storage devices, voicemail or some sort of interactive system. A voice network maintains voice data only. It maintains voice phone calls, PBXs, voice routing information (where calls go to) and voicemail systems.

The convergence comes in when both of these existing networks that were once thought to be truly independent are now sharing information back and forth: storage of voicemails, a "do not call" list (federal compli-ance) or voicemail systems. Any system that is voice responsive is a con-verged system.

IMPLICATIONS: EXECUTIVE, I.T. AND SECURITY MANAGEMENT

The problems that exist in a converged network for executive management is that without a mindset of convergence, and without being proactive about security for a converged network, they are leaving their voice area, which contains valuable information, unprotected.

Insider Notes: Not only are there threats from hackers that are attacking the data networks, but also hackers that are now becoming crackers or phone phreaks who can social engineer their way into the network. These voyeurs are listening in on voicemail and on VoIP phone calls, as well.

A COMPANY HAS NO CHOICE BUT TO DEAL WITH THE EXPLOSION OF POTENTIAL AVENUES OF ABUSE FROM NOT ONLY EMPLOYEES, BUT ALSO FROM THE OUTSIDE WORLD. THIS REQUIRES MANAGERS TO TAKE A NEW APPROACH TO THE STRATEGY OF PROTECTING THE CONVERGED NETWORK.

Employees leave voicemails about everything to each other; if they leave something of a highly sensitive business nature, then these executives put that information at risk. This is one of the biggest problems for executive management. They don't understand the risks. Managers tend to think that voice networks can never be attacked because hackers go after data, but in reality these hackers go after the server. Executives believe that they can leave sensitive conversations on voicemail because no hacker will go after that. They do not realize that their voicemail is running on a server, and servers are what hackers look for. That's a big problem for executive management.

The problem for IT and telecommunications management is they do not understand the new nature of voice. They say, "It's voice, so it's my voice person's responsibility to deal with it. I don't have to protect the voice network because it is voice, it's not a web server, and it's not a database. I firewall my data network, I put all my IP end point devices on my data side. Voice — that's somebody else's problem to deal with."

The implications for telecommunications management are that they understand voice, but do not understand IP. They do not understand what a TCP packet is, or a UDP packet, or how hackers break into an IP network, or how viruses are let loose. All they know is that the data guys have all these viruses and worms, but their telephone system continues to work. In their voice world, it is copper-wired, a good solid technology, and it will never have these types of problems.

In the converged environment, telecom staff quickly discovers that PBX and voicemail run on a server, with connections to the data world or the Internet. Now, the same threat that can attack the server on the data side can now attack the voice system. That's a huge problem, because the telecomm staff does not understand the nature of security.

Security management is still focused on only defending the data network. That is where all the hype, all the media, and where all the press is focused. They tell us all about the threats to the data network, like the latest worm that is tearing up servers all around the world. Well, those same attacks can now occur in the voice world. They must open up their minds to the fact that voice and data are converged into one environment, and the threats that are prevalent in the data world, such as worms, viruses, Trojan horses, hacker attacks and scanning by hackers, can occur in the voice world as well. They've got to take the same powerful stance to protect voice as they've taken to protect data. If they don't, they have left a giant hole in their network security.

GROWTH OF CONVERGED NETWORKS

By 2009, VoIP will be the predominant form of enterprise voice communication. In 2003, PBXs accounted for over 95 million of the 111 million extensions in the commercial telephone network. In 2003, enterprise Legacy PBX had over 54.1% of the market; VoIP had 9.5% of the market. Legacy hybrid and KTS systems were 36.4% of the market. In 2008, it is projected that VoIP will be 45.5%, legacy PBX will be 31.0%, and legacy KTS hybrid will be 23.5%. By 2008, VoIP will definitely be the predominant telephony system. By 2010, VoIP is projected to totally take over the entire marketplace. The predominant communications system will be VoIP. This shows how the current trend in the communications market is moving to a truly converged network. This should be viewed as a wake up call for all owners and managers of voice and data networks.

Insider Notes: If a hacker finds a way in by conducting a port scan on the Internet, he will focus first on a data network then, once inside, find he is on a voice network. How you will first notice the attacks all depends on how the hacker comes into the system, whether by modem or by port scanning.

That's a growth rate of more than 200% over five years — about 40% a year. This growth is expected because VoIP provides such a cost savings for companies and gives them more control, as well as the ability to leverage their existing network infrastructure and allow them to get the most bang for their buck.

WHAT ARE THE SECURITY ISSUES ASSOCIATED WITH VoIP BECOMING THE DOMINANT TELEPHONY SYSTEM?

The major problem with a VoIP system is that it will double or triple the number of IP endpoints. Right now, a company has a set number of IP endpoints that establish the perimeter of its network. These are things such as your routers, web servers, DNS servers — anything that faces the Internet. The corporate network today minimizes the number of Internet facing equipment as part of current security practices. A move for a company into the VoIP arena turns the whole network architecture inside out. So, instead of four or five Internet facing devices, a company may have 1,000 IP enabled devices that can be abused or misused by anybody if the network is not correctly designed and maintained.

What a company needs to do now is plan for this inevitability and be proactive about its approach to security. A company needs to understand asset management and understand the evolving converged network, and the fact that a proactive stance will allow a company to become more secure. It is on this "true" converged network that a company will run its VoIP environment, as well as all of its IP.

AN EXPLOSION OF VULNERABLE POINTS

A company has no choice but to deal with the explosion of potential avenues of abuse from not only employees, but also from the outside world. This requires managers to take a new approach to the strategy of protecting the converged network. Previously, a company needed only to consider its data devices: routers, firewalls, DNS, Web servers, database servers and users, and how to protect those IP endpoints. Now, with the merger of the voice network into the data network, a company needs to apply security that will not only protect the data network, but must include the voice network as well. However, those changes must allow telephone calls to go through. A company must rethink security and start building this new type of security into their converged network now.

A company must also consider conducting asset management because of the growth in equipment connected to the Internet. In other words, the tracking and maintenance of devices must be a priority for the company. For example, in a normal office today, with 1,000 employees, a company will have to track 1,000 computers. With VoIP, it now has to track 2,000 devices, because everyone has a telephone. If some of those people are also doing remote work, this can triple to 3,000 devices. This is the problem of a converged network moving into a VoIP network. The need to deal with items is growing exponentially, and a company also has to deal with such issues as:

- keeping track of all these devices
- patching all these devices
- updating all these devices
- determining company policy in dealing with each of these devices
- verifying the security of these networks on a weekly, if not daily, basis

The security issues in such a network complicate quickly. Are separate policies needed for VoIP devices? Probably yes. Are separate policies needed for remote users using a soft-phone type of application where they can use their computer as a telephone? Definitely yes.

Before converged networks, companies were in this nice, neat little box where they could say that they were protecting their data from evil hackers, or from employees doing bad things. Security was a relatively direct issue; throw on some ID access, throw in some firewall rules and put in an antivirus.

Insider Notes: The convergence comes in when both of these existing networks that were once thought to be truly independent are now sharing information back and forth: storage of voicemails, a "do not call" list (federal compliance) or voicemail systems. Any system that is voice responsive is a converged system.

CASE STUDY: Rx FOR DATA VULNERABILITY

The Problem: This is a growing life science company with a mission statement to protect its medical data and patient information, and maintain compliance with government regulations, as well as to have its networks assessed on a regular basis.

HOW AVAYA HELPED:

Avaya introduced BioFirm to the concept of a Converged Network, where the voice and data network used the same Internet connection. Prior to this, the company had addressed each network independent of each other, which left a hole in its security infrastructure.

Avaya conducted a converged assessment of the entire Biofirm voice and data network. Avaya's Security Consultants reviewed the security devices and provided a vulnerability assessment on the network. During this vulnerability assessment, Avaya found a new hole not noticed in the network and was able to demonstrate how to mitigate the problem, which allowed Biofirm to reconfigure the monitoring of its network to allow it to check for policy violations as well.

Avaya looked for vulnerabilities on the data network, but also on the voice network, and provided a list of the vulnerabilities found on the voice network. These were not the standard toll fraud issues that a PBX might have, but included areas of additional concern with the voice network in regards to a converged environment. Voice and data vulnerabilities affecting each network were new items for the company to consider. Avaya reviewed both the voice and data network, and its comparison of the two networks identified new, and as yet, unidentified security issues for Biofirm. Given BioFirm's highly distributed global network, the company was particularly interested in possible entry points for external intrusion. Avaya was able to address this issue from both the data network and the voice network, assessing all of the new technologies used in a voice and data network, such as PDAs, wireless, bluetooth and other IP enabled devices.

Biofirm was not only concerned with the security of their networks from a technology point, but also in making sure it met all relevant federal regulations. The Avaya assessments met the needs and requirements for HIPAA, SOX and GLBA.

BENEFITS FOR BIOFIRM

First, Biofirm sought a return on investment for the work performed. Avaya issued an assessment report that demonstrated an immediate ROI. The new set of vulnerabilities that were discovered by combining both the voice and data network together exposed holes never seen before. And the new Converged Network map constructed as part of this project allowed Biofirm to clearly see its "real" network for the first time. Biofirm's investment provided a safer, stronger and more reliable network that enveloped the voice network as well. A second major benefit was that Biofirm learned that a number of its network monitoring systems were not correctly placed to provide an overview of the state of network security.

The converged network assessment also provided Biofirm with the ability to meet a number of the requirements for the Security Rule of HIPAA (Health Insurance Portability and Accountability Act). The Security Rule of HIPAA does not take effect until April, 2005, but this assessment allowed Biofirm to meet a number of requirements that are called for under the Security Rule. This, on its own, will save Biofirm tens of thousands of dollars. In addition, the company was able to check off a number of requirements for HIPAA, SOX and GLBA with one assessment.

This security assessment also enabled Biofirm to validate the integrity of the data that it stored on the network. For a company in the medical industry, the security, and more importantly, the integrity of the data stored on patients and research projects is critical. In essence, Biofirm employed Avaya to complete a standard assessment of its security infrastructure with a special look at compliance with federal requirements. Avaya demonstrated that Biofirm had a converged voice and data network that needed to be assessed jointly to truly understand system vulnerabilities. After completing this assessment, a number of vulnerabilities were discovered on the voice side that may have led to serious issues. By conducting a fully-converged network assessment, Biofirm was able to create a security environment that met all best practice requirements.

Conventional security structures are not all applicable to the voice world because voice uses different protocols, and different ports must be opened which require far more complex firewall rules. A company will have to have IP endpoints segmented off, or sub-net an entire section of telephones. This will require another methodology for protecting and monitoring that network for security problems. An Intrusion Detection System (IDS) or Intrusion Prevention System (IPS) will not work in a voice network because telephone calls cannot be stopped like incoming data. A call must go through.

Therefore, the entire convergence dilemma is becoming more and more complex every year. The company will need to look at something along the lines of an IDS to allow calls to go through, and be alerted to attacks on the voice network. At least this will be the case until new technology emerges to deal with voice attacks.

Some VoIP vendors adopt an incremental approach to security implementation. A company may migrate 100 telephones to VoIP now, then gradually move to 200, 500 and 1,000, but only over time in a phased approach. In this manner, companies are slowly adapting their security to the new converged environment. This slow migration policy will provide companies with the time to understand and work out the problems with the technology, and allow security to come up to speed. They can take their time and migrate slowly and build up. A migration plan of a year to two should give them enough time to acclimate to convergence and the issues it raises.

However, the problem is that in the security world the majority of all companies are living in a firefighting environment. They are fighting today's fires today; they are dealing with viruses, worms, hackers and crackers, all of that stuff. They do not have the time to plan things out because they are constantly under attack. So, for them to be proactive, they need to take a proactive stance. That may mean outsourcing some of their security services to take the load off their shoulders so they can better plan and strategize. Or, they may bring in a consultant to help them strategize for the future.

If a company takes all security measures on its own shoulders, odds are it won't be able to handle it. It will get stuck, it will get hit and it will get hit hard because it has not planned a strategy for migrating to the new world of convergence. Compounding the problem is that companies are now living in a converged world, but many just don't realize it. As soon as companies realize that even if they do not have VoIP, they do have a PBX, voicemail and IVRs, and they are running on a Windows 2000 server, so they must consider how to protect the network.

ASSESSING VULNERABILITY IN A CONVERGED NETWORK

To assess the security vulnerabilities in a VoIP or converged world, a company has to look at each of its telephony devices, whether it's voicemail, PBXs, IVRs, call centers or CMS and find out on what system it is running. If that is a Windows 2000 server, a company knows how to secure it and knows what to lock down. The same principles applied in protecting the existing data network need to be applied to the voice network.

However, in the voice world, you must consider the ports that need to be left open for calls to go through and updates to be enacted. If a company follows everything that is mandated by an NSA guideline for managing a secure computing system and locks down a Windows 2000 server, the telephony applications will not run on that system, because it closes too

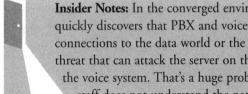

Insider Notes: In the converged environment, telecom staff quickly discovers that PBX and voicemail run on a server, with connections to the data world or the Internet. Now, the same threat that can attack the server on the data side can now attack the voice system. That's a huge problem, because the telecom staff does not understand the nature of security.

I.T. MANAGEMENT NEEDS TO STOP THINKING THAT THE NETWORK IS ONLY "VOICE" AND IT DOESN'T AFFECT THEM, BECAUSE IT DOES. THEY MUST LOOK AT THE NEW VOICE ENVIRONMENT AND SEE IT AS AN EXTENSION OF THE DATA NETWORK. THEY NEED TO THINK OF THESE NEW TELE-PHONES AS SERVERS AND COMPUTERS.

many ports and too many options needed to operate a telephony applica-tion. Some parts can be locked down, but not all.

The same principles used in securing a data environment can be used in securing a converged environment. The process is just more intensive. A company can't just run a scanner, find all open ports and close them. Some of those open ports are needed in a telephony application. A compa-ny needs to be able to look at the security policy and change and modify it, to keep the voice and telephony applications running.

A NEW BREED OF PROFESSIONAL?

One individual is needed to serve as the overall security officer of both voice and data. That is lacking today. Typically, there's a director of tele-com and a director of data; companies typically don't have a director of converged networks. The security officer might not be the right person for the job. With a security officer, the focus is on protecting corporate assets. He needs to be able to protect the entire network from all sorts of attacks. He is more of the visionary for the group. Companies still need to have somebody who will be the final decision maker in arguments between the data and voice mangers. The CSO has a lot more issues to deal with than that. This subject is an area of confusion that provides hackers with major opportunities.

SECURITY ISSUES WITH VoIP INSTALLATIONS

This section provides a structure against which readers can understand the strategic concerns associated with protecting converged networks, and pro-vides best practices in securing a converged network.

Currently, companies view the converged network in a piecemeal fashion. When VoIP is installed, the VoIP companies consider security only for its VoIP product. They do not look holistically at the entire network, and if the whole system is not protected, it can be ruined. Considering only the security measures needed for VoIP will protect that one small part of the network. However, to install VoIP, a company must have remote call-out, which requires big holes in the firewall to accomplish. If VoIP vendors were looking at the entire network, they would understand that they might have missed important issues associated with monitoring the network, such as intrusion detection and intrusion prevention capabilities.

VoIP providers need to be prepared to address the converged security issues of the future. They are bringing in a converged network at full speed when they put in an implementation of VoIP. If they do not suggest to the customer that they get a converged security assessment done or, at least, discuss the issues of converged security and converged security assessments, they are doing their customers a disservice.

STRATEGIC CONCERNS — EXECUTIVE MANAGEMENT

A major strategic concern in implementing new telephony applications into a voice network, whether it is VoIP, a new call center, a new PBX or a new telephony application, is that all of these applications now run on a server that runs on either Windows 2000 or Linux. They no longer run on the proprietary operating systems of the past.

These standard-based servers that run Windows 2000 or Linux must have the capability to update, troubleshoot and allow monitoring of that device by its network operating center. In other words, these devices will be running SNMP, to make sure that the server is up and running. If they do this, however, there is a definitive connection between their voice network and their data network. And that is a strategic concern.

 Insider Notes: Conventional security structures are not all applicable to the voice world because voice uses different protocols, and different ports must be opened which require far more complex firewall rules.

DATA SNAPSHOT

We are now seeing a growing trend in that security policy is becoming more of a business issue then it has ever been in the past. Corporate policy is now starting to address the newest advances in technology, which is critical to cover the converged networks from attacks.

Does your security policy cover the Converged Network?

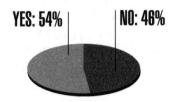

YES: 54%   NO: 46%

Download the complete research study for free at www.blackbooksecurity.com/research
Source: 2005 Larstan / Reed Infosecurity Survey

Managers must identify these connections and modify security policy to protect them. A lot of the companies that are now installing VoIP systems are expecting the vendor to tell them how to secure it. However, even if the VoIP network is secured, the rest of the network may not be. Routers, media gateways and firewalls have been installed to protect against denial of service attacks, and virus and worm attacks to the voice network. But to make a phone call out, a hole must be punched in the network to allow this VoIP call to go across the Internet. How is this protected?

It is the responsibility of the VoIP company to provide the best end-security for its product and allow the customer to have the services needed to protect its entire corporate network.

VoIP IMPLEMENTATION QUESTIONS

Questions you should ask about any VoIP implementation:

- What protocols does the VoIP network utilize? The standard answer is that it is H323 compliant. This is insufficient. A company needs to provide all protocols that will be used in this VoIP network. This may include TFTP to update files and UDP to run packets.
- What is being done to prevent denial-of-service attacks against the VoIP network? The company needs to explain to the customer what in their product line helps to prevent denial-of-service against a voice network. Since this VoIP system is now running on a data

network, if the data network gets infected, a denial-of-service attack occurs. How will this impact the VoIP network?

■ What is being done to prevent monitoring or eavesdropping on conversations? How do they deal with internal problems, such as someone plugging in their laptop computer and using a program like Vomit to listen in on a VoIP phone call? What are the capabilities for monitoring and prevention of eavesdropping on VoIP phone calls?

■ How do they handle updates of the VoIP program and the base operating system? Most VoIP providers will commit to having a technician come out and update the software when there is a major upgrade. But the VoIP system runs on an operating system. What about the updates to that base operating system? How are those handled? How do they handle Windows updates? Linux updates? Where do you find information about security alerts? And, how and where do you find information about the latest security alerts and updates for your VoIP product? How does the vendor update you on maintenance, operating system and security upgrades?

STRATEGIC CONCERNS — SECURITY MANAGEMENT

Security management should consider the following strategic concerns:

■ How do I secure this VoIP network? Is all the security work done before it's installed on the network or after? Does security cost extra? Can this be done in-house with internal personnel?

■ How is a VoIP network, the call center and the new PBX monitored for security concerns?

■ How is the security of these devices and applications assessed? If a third-party must do all of these assessments, that may be a problem since the people that are doing this work need to be trusted to do it for the right reasons. How are the VoIP and the PBX evaluated?

> **Insider Notes:** A major strategic concern in implementing new telephony applications into a voice network, whether it is VoIP, a new call center, a new PBX or a new telephony application, is that all of these applications now run on a server that runs on either Windows 2000 or Linux. They no longer run on the proprietary operating systems of the past.

THE CONVERGED NETWORK IS HIGHLY POLITICAL BECAUSE THERE ARE TWO DIFFERENT GROUPS, THE VOICE SIDE AND THE DATA SIDE, WHO ARE OFTEN IN CONFLICT.

Are there specific tools to use or that need authorization, so work on the network can be certified?

STRATEGIC CONCERNS — I.T. MANAGEMENT

IT management's major strategic concerns are to determine how this new VoIP network, this new call center, this new PBX and this new telephony application, connect to the data network. They've got to realize that this telephony application is connecting to the data network, and they need to be concerned as to where. They need to know the protocols being run because they need to put that into their IDS and IPS designs for monitoring and firewalls.

IT management needs to stop thinking that the network is only "voice" and it doesn't affect them, because it does. They must look at the new voice environment and see it as an extension of the data network. They need to think of these new telephones as servers and computers.

A server is the telephony application, whether it is a PBX, call center or voice-mail, and the telephones are desktop computers. As long as they look at it that way, they will have an idea of what's going on. They will need to know what applications will run, what ports will open, what protocols are being run, what ports in the firewall need to open up and how the heartbeat program can be put on those application devices so they can be monitored.

TEN BEST PRACTICES OF SECURING A CONVERGED NETWORK.

Best practices are straightforward and as follows:

❶ **Start out with a security assessment that covers the following areas:** an external assessment, an internal assessment, network discovery of all devices on the internal network, rogue modem scanning, PBX assessment and telephony application assessment. You also need to look for rogue wireless modems and rogue bluetooth devices. A converged network security assessment covers those eight areas. This must be completed on a biannual basis at the minimum. Anytime somebody goes in to make a change to a telephony application, they could be opening up a new hole into your data network.

❷ **Find all your devices.** A network discovery must be completed on a regular basis — if not daily, then, at least weekly — so you can keep up-to-date on all these devices. What if somebody takes their laptop and plugs it into the voice network, unplugs one of those VoIP telephones, takes that Ethernet cable from that VoIP telephone and plugs it into their laptop? How is that discovered? There are a number of automated programs that will do this on a continuous basis.

❸ **Have your network reviewed by a converged network expert.** If this is not feasible, bring in a data expert and a voice expert from an independent company. This cannot be kept in-house because of the politics. If you can't bring in people to provide an independent assessment, then you've got to bring in some additional people that are independent and not tied down by those politics. The converged network is highly political because there are two different groups, the voice side and the data side, who are often in conflict.

❹ **Update your security policy to reflect the new converged environment.** If you do not do so, you are leaving your company open not only to attacks and denial of service, but also to liability because you are not addressing federal regulatory compliance issues.

❺ **Establish a security team structure for your new converged network.** Security can no longer focus only on the data side; it must focus on both sides of the network.

❻ **Monitor both the voice and data network with IDS or an IPS solution, or you will miss half the picture.** Most companies have an IDS solution running on their data network. Some smaller companies outsource this. A company with a managed IDS service needs to have its own portal that they can access and see all the reports seen by the outsourcing vendor. Many outsourcing companies won't provide that access. However, a company must monitor its network with an IDS box because it needs to know what else is going on. How else can it catch that employee that has unconnected the connection to their VoIP telephone, and connected it into their laptop and started transmitting illegal files? The only way this is caught is by running an IDS or some other monitoring system.

❼ **Wherever possible, use encryption to protect the security and integrity of your VoIP or voice network.**

❽ **Maintain password security practices**. Change the passwords on your systems, including all default accounts and passwords. This means finding out how to change passwords on the converged network.

❾ **Use multilayered, multi-vendor defenses on both the voice and data network.** In a multilayered, multi-vendor defense (a "melting ice" defense), a company has multilevel defenses in its network. This is fine, but if they are all from one vendor, then a hacker only needs to break through one level and they have the means to break through every other. With multi-vendor defenses, a hacker needs to break through firewalls from several different vendors, increasing his difficulty. It is the same concept behind the steering wheel lock on a car. Make it inconvenient for a hacker, and many will look elsewhere. A company needs to not only have a multi-layered defense but also a multi-vendor defense in a converged environment.

❿ **Place firewalls on both voice and data networks.** Do not limit the installation of firewalls to your data network only. In this converged environment, you need to place firewalls on both the voice and data networks. Your CMS, IVR and PBX's are servers of some version and therefore should have a firewall protecting it. Just ensure that you have mapped out the appropriate ports for the telephony applications that are being run on that device.

In addition, encryption should be used whenever possible. This will help stop many problems because people can't listen in on phone calls if encryption is running.

Don't underestimate the extent of the danger. A hacker could be a disgruntled customer, causing millions of dollars of damage, simply because he didn't get the free toaster you promised him with his purchase.

Or the attack could be on a grander scale. The futurist Alvin Toffler, in his book *War and Anti-War*, perhaps summed it up best: "Whatever the terms, it is now possible for a Hindu fanatic in Hyderabad or a Muslim fanatic in Madras or a deranged nerd in Denver to cause immense damage to people, countries, or, even with some difficulty, to armies 10,000 miles away." In the new converged environment, this immense damage can be — quite literally — phoned in.

■ ■ ■

Joseph C. Seanor is Security Consulting Manager at Avaya. Joe joined the Avaya Enterprise Security Practice after working in the federal government, intelligence community and private sector. He has been an instructor at Learning Tree Corp., teaching security professionals about IDS and firewall deployment. He is a licensed Private Investigator and Computer Crime Investigator, and was the Senior Technical Security Investigator for America Online for seven years. At AOL, he investigated several cases involving hackers, intrusions, email threats presidential threats, and other crimes committed by AOL users or through the AOL network.

Joe also worked for the Department of Justice, Telecommunications Security Staff, in developing policy for the DOJ on computer hackers and computer security issues. He also founded CIBIR Corporation, a private investigations company and he still maintains a Private Investigation license. Joe also spent 10 years at the Central Intelligence Agency, working in computer-related assignments. He can be reached at 703-310-3688 or jseanor@avaya.com.

[14]
BUSINESS CONTINUITY
AND DISASTER RECOVERY
POST 9/11

Do you have a plan that will keep your business operating after a cataclysmic event? If the Twin Towers nightmare taught us anything, it's the need to resist complacency and prepare for the worst.

"WE TRIED TO SPARE EFFORT, AND MET DISASTER"

- Marshal Henri Petain, after France fell to the Nazis

by DR. JIM KENNEDY

Corporate managers routinely take precautions to protect their companies against the statistical probabilities of various acts of God — tornadoes, floods and earthquakes. What companies have not sufficiently prepared for are assaults against their data and operational systems, either in the form of cyberterrorism or a massive terrorist event.

THE BIPOLAR WORLD OF OPPOSING ARMIES MASSED IN FIXED FORMATIONS ON BATTLEFIELDS IS INCREASINGLY A RELIC OF A BYGONE ERA. WARFARE TODAY IS "ASYMMETRICAL," WHEREBY LOW-TECH, LOW-BUDGET GUERILLA FIGHTERS CAN CAUSE DISPROPORTIONATE DAMAGE AGAINST A COUNTRY'S MILITARY OR ECONOMIC INFRASTRUCTURE. YOUR COMPANY MUST NOW PREPARE FOR MORE INSIDIOUS ATTACKS THAT ARE CHEMICAL, BIOLOGICAL, RADIOLOGICAL, NUCLEAR OR EXPLOSIVE (CBRNE).

For most people, the term "fallout" connotes physical destruction and radioactivity from a nuclear explosion, conjuring stark images from the 1950s of bomb shelters and "duck-and-cover" exercises in school. In today's post September 11 world, fallout tends to mean the mass effect of an adverse event on a company's business functions. If a computer network is shut down, scores of employees are debilitated and other people who tangentially depend on that network are debilitated as well.

In the old days of mutually assured destruction, strategic assets like ICBMs were protected in concrete silos. These days, business and information systems are the greatest strategic assets of all, and you must protect them with business continuity and disaster recovery planning.

Business continuity planning is the process of developing advance arrangements and procedures that enable an organization to cope with the fallout of a disaster, allowing critical business functions to continue. Disaster recovery planning is the information technology aspect of business continuity planning and deals with the recovery of technical infrastructure.

Business continuity planning generally covers all aspects of the business: its people, its processes, its technology, its facilities and its infrastructure. All of these pieces must be in place to at least continue critical operations after an event. An event could be anything from a major snowstorm where you can't get to the facility to a power outage or a bomb threat.

The bipolar world of opposing armies massed in fixed formations on battlefields is increasingly a relic of a bygone era. Warfare today is "asymmetrical," whereby low-tech, low-budget guerilla fighters can cause disproportionate damage against a country's military or economic infrastructure. Your company must now prepare for more insidious attacks that are chemical, biological, radiological, nuclear or explosive (CBRNE).

Consider this fact: the terrorist attacks of September 11, which wreaked incalculable damage to America's society and economy, were perpetrated by a handful of religious fanatics armed with little more than box cutters. The CIA estimates that the entire terrorist incident, including the attack on the Pentagon, cost al Qaeda a grand total of $500,000. Compare this dollar figure to America's annual military budget of nearly $400 Billion.

Case in point: a "dirty bomb" of radioactive materials (e.g., stolen medical waste) wrapped around a few sticks of dynamite is cheap and easy to make. Detonating one in the subway system of, say, Washington, DC, would result in scant physical damage. However, the ensuing psychological terror would sow mayhem and effectively shut down the nation's capital. Is your company ready for such an event? If not, read on.

THE FOUR STAGES OF BUSINESS CONTINUITY

There are four stages that characterize business continuity, from response to the initial event to restoration:

❶ **Response:** the reaction to an adverse event or incident to assess the damage or impact and to determine the required level of response, containment and control activity. Response not only addresses matters of life, safety and evacuation, but also the policies, procedures and actions to be followed in the event of an emergency. It is the first step that immediately follows a disaster event.

Insider Notes: Business continuity planning generally covers all aspects of the business: its people, its processes, its technology, its facilities and its infrastructure. All of these pieces must be in place to at least continue critical operations after an event.

❷ **Resumption:** the process of planning for, and implementing the restarting of, mission critical business operations following an event or disaster. The most critical or time-sensitive functions are addressed first. The process continues along a planned sequence to address all identified areas. This step is usually taken after the impacted infrastructure, data communications and environment have been successfully reestablished at an alternate location (a warm or hot site).

❸ **Recovery:** where business continuity focuses on implementing expanded operations to address less time-sensitive business operations immediately following the interruption or disaster. In this stage, the process to restore overall business and technology at the restored, or a new, location is initiated. If this event will last longer than a week or so, a hot or warm site will no longer satisfy a company's needs. Therefore, the focus is to either restore the original site, if possible, or to look for a location where the business can regroup and provide its necessary business functions for a protracted period of time. This move from initially failed sites to a more permanent location is restoration.

❹ **Restoration:** the process of planning for and implementing procedures for the repair or relocation of the primary site and its contents, and for the restoration of normal operations at the primary site.

For example, a company experiences a major fire that renders its operation uninhabitable. The company has properly planned for such an occurrence and has a "hot site" (an alternative location which has all of the necessary systems, space for personnel and infrastructure to perform its critical business functions for a limited time frame, usually 5 to 10 days). The company exercises it contingency plan and moves its operations down the street to its "hot site." At the same time, the business has deployed personnel who are responsible to assess damage and to plan for the restoration of business operations back to the original facilities.

HOW 9/11 CHANGED EVERYTHING

Since September 11, businesses and contingency planners have had to change the way they think and plan for adverse events. Indeed, 9/11 was the beginning of the new thought process. The power blackout that affected much of the Northeast in 2003 also reinforced the notion that nothing could be taken for granted. Before these disastrous events, companies took for granted the availability of public infrastructures, such as telephones, power and utilities, and transportation.

Thinking was a little more proactive in places like Florida, where hurricanes are a seasonal threat, and on the West Coast, where earthquakes have long been a fact of life. But in the cities from the Midwest to the Northeast, the acceptable planning strategy was merely to ensure that the phone system and other critical infrastructures kept working.

Then, on a beautiful September morning, Islamic fascists flew airliners into the World Trade Center, a savage act that forever changed the government and corporate status quo. The attacks took out a tremendous amount of physical infrastructure for a protracted period of time. The first change in thinking was where to locate alternate sites.

The devastation of 9/11, and the dark area of the 2003 power failure, established the need to select sites farther away from the event. Relocating 10-15 miles, or even to an adjacent borough or town, would no longer prove adequate. In fact, one suggestion from the SEC's post-9/11 commission report is to move recovery sites more than 150 miles away. There's been some reluctance from New York authorities to follow that recommendation, because of political pressures to keep the recovery sites near Wall Street. Nevertheless, the first lesson is to assume a 100-mile radius as the area of "fallout," and from that point look farther out for placement of alternative sites.

Another major change in contingency plan thinking was the type of adverse event to anticipate. Most of the planning prior to 9/11 was centered on natural or technological risks, such as earthquakes, or power failures or hurricanes. These continue to occur and should be considered in any planning. However, we now must consider the aforementioned CBRNE.

Insider Notes: There is an old saying in business continuity that "the plan is not complete until you test it, and when you're done, you need to test it, and when you're all finished — test it." Until the plan is tested, it can't be considered usable.

THERE HAS NOT BEEN A PROPORTIONATE AMOUNT OF WORK DONE BY COMPANIES TO REVISE THEIR STRATEGIC THINKING ABOUT POTENTIAL RISKS AND TO UPDATE AND TEST THEIR BUSINESS CONTINUITY PLANS WITH CBRNE SCENARIOS IN MIND. THAT IS ONE OF THE ISSUES THAT COMPANIES MUST IMMEDIATELY ADDRESS.

When you deal with chemical, biological and radiological events, the impact not only affects the building and infrastructure, but the availability of people. In most cases, contingency plans assumed an ability to move people and have them available when, and where, needed. CBRNE has a wider impact on a company.

There has not been a proportionate amount of work done by companies to revise their strategic thinking about potential risks and to update and test their business continuity plans with CBRNE scenarios in mind. That is one of the issues that companies must immediately address. Have they incorporated new thinking into their business continuity or disaster recovery plans, and have these new threats been included?

Companies must be sure that they have a plan. Most major financial institutions probably have plans due to strict regulations, but surveys taken over the last three years have shown that organizations in other industries are severely lacking in any coordinated planning. If something were to happen, they would improvise, but the fact is that something should already be in place. Call trees should exist; action plans governing how people should react in certain scenarios are needed; and the systems should be tested.

There is an old saying in business continuity that "the plan is not complete until you test it, and when you're done, you need to test it, and when you're all finished — test it." Until the plan is tested, it can't be considered usable.

RECONSIDER EXISTING, OUTDATED PLANS

The world is divided into two eras: pre- and post-9/11. Pre-9/11, many companies relied upon contingency plans that assumed that critical infrastructures would have the necessary redundancy and would be in place. Most plans of that time made a basic assumption that they would be able to recover within a few hours.

When the blackout of 2003 occurred, and the power failure lasted more than a day, it severely hampered organizations because their recovery strategies never took into account a power failure that would last longer than a few hours. Even the telecommunications carriers, which are usually very prepared, had considerable problems. Many critical cell sites run on an eight-hour battery backup. After eight hours, they assume the power is back on and that they can be recharged. This was not the case during the blackout, and people lost cell phone use for a protracted period of time. In New York City, after the 9/11 event, the city had no power, no cell phones, no landline phones, water was interrupted, physical access by transportation was affected, and in many cases, especially in the first few days, necessary recovery resources were not immediately available. Therefore, the common mode of thinking — that a firm could redistribute people to another location — was impossible because they couldn't get people in, or out, of the city.

Companies today must examine each and every piece of infrastructure that they need, not only their own, but also the public infrastructure, to make sure that they have contingencies for them in case they are no longer available. If there is a chemical or biological event, it might not be widespread, but it could take a company down for a long period of time.

Insider Notes: The world is divided into two eras: pre- and post-9/11. Pre-9/11, many companies relied upon contingency plans that assumed that critical infrastructures would have the necessary redundancy and would be in place. Most plans of that time made a basic assumption that they would be able to recover within a few hours.

CASE STUDY: THE HORRORS OF 911

The Company: a Fortune 500 multinational

The Problem: All that could go wrong...

At the time of the 9/11 disaster, many firms believed that their business continuity plans were adequate, and some had even been tested to further remove any fears of business interruption by an unplanned event.

Shortly after the collapse of the first tower, all fears of business interruption resurfaced and many Fortune 500 corporations were in a fight for their very existences. One in particular believed that it had performed its due diligence and that everything that it needed for the continuity of its critical data and telecommunications operations, on which it heavily relied, had been taken care of. It was wrong. The company had employed redundant carriers for its long distance and data communications circuits, redundant facilities and diversity routing to their local telecommunication's central offices. This redundancy and diversity routing proved not enough for what it was about to encounter. In fact, it was to find that the city's own regulations would be the cause of several failures that even carriers were not prepared for.

In New York City it is difficult, if not impossible, to obtain permits for permanent backup generators. These generators are needed to restore utility power if it is disrupted for a protracted period of time. Power, water, natural ga and other critical utilities were cut off, as a result of the immense loss of critical infrastructure due to the collapse of the World Trade Center's two towers. As a result, numerous unforeseen problems were encountered with this firm's traditional business continuity plan.

The first was a prolonged loss of power. Even those carriers that had circuits and services not directly affected by this disaster were affected by the loss of infrastructure. Many carriers incorporate batteries in their central office facilities. These batteries are used to provide power to the data and telecommunications equipment, so their clients can continue operations.

However, these batteries only provide power for a period of about eight hours. This had always been enough time for utility companies to correct power problems in the event of a failure, but 9/11 and the subsequent power blackout of August 2003 proved this theory wrong. After eight hours, the batteries began to fail. Without utility power or any backup power generators, the central offices ceased to function and data and telecommunications circuits and services went down, bringing with it telephone service and links to corporate networks.

Where services were being supplied prior to the collapse, they were now slowly becoming inoperative. Consequently, the redundant routing and diversity of carriers, all prudent and long-proclaimed business continuity planning standards, proved insufficient to handle this event.

This same company had defined within its business continuity plan an alternative site directly across the river in New Jersey to handle its business in the event that its primary facilities became unavailable. However, this also proved ineffective.

The next problem encountered by this firm was the inability to get its employees to its alternate site. The NYPD almost immediately started to lock down certain areas of the financial district and, ultimately, the entire city. All tunnels and bridges were blocked and it was about 24 hours before a plan was in effect to allow inbound and outbound traffic on a restricted basis.

Those utility company employees already in the city were immediately pressed into service, assessing the damage and preparing plans for recovery. However, employees not in the city found it extremely difficult to get in. By 5 a.m. the next morning, police, fire, telephone, power, water and gas workers were allowed in, as long as they had proper ID. Later in the morning, other essential service personnel were allowed in, again, as long as they could state their business and possessed IDs.

Any company that had relied on an alternative processing facility in Manhattan or within a 10-15 mile radius of Manhattan found it extremely difficult to resume operations in a timely manner. Those firms that opted for recovery facilities within the 50-150 mile range fared considerably better. There is a school of thought that recovery sites should be closer, rather than farther away. That school of thought is now defunct. Recovery sites must be far enough outside of the zone of impact to make recovery possible.

As police began to ask people to show identification that they work for a specific company, those companies with no, or loosely enforced, picture ID processes found that their employees could not get back into their offices. These employees were denied access to help the company with its contingency efforts. The second planning failure was not knowing police policy in a situation like this.

At the same time, as firms were encountering access problems for their employees, they were also having a hard time getting critical assets and non-people resources to their sites. Police were restricting the movement of equipment. Many companies failed to produce the proper paperwork to pass through these restrictions. This brought the company down hard and limited its ability to recovery quickly.

This particular firm was rendered somewhat ineffective for almost a week because of the problem that occurred both during 9/11, and subsequently, for several days during the 2003 blackout. This institution has now begun to reengineer its business continuity infrastructure and planning as follows:

- Redesigned technical infrastructure, to ensure routing through different carriers and central offices that are resilient enough to successfully continue operating during an extended power outage
- Ensuring that all employees and contractors have picture IDs with an expiration date
- Implementing an alternative site far enough out of the reach of a potential impact zone to ensure that its employees feel safe going there, and that the facilities and infrastructure are available and safe for them when they arrive

Companies may be unable to enter their facilities because the police or other public safety organizations won't allow entry until they deem them safe. This could take time, as was the case with the anthrax contamination at postal facilities and the U.S. Senate office buildings in Washington DC. Even after the buildings were declared safe for reentry, there was lingering fear among workers and many did not immediately return to work. This prolonged the period of operational recovery.

Moreover, contingency planners need to consider how to respond to CBRNE events, what to look for and how to perform that immediate assessment prior to an event occurring. Then plans need to address such methods as, in case of a chemical event, how to block off air intakes for A/C, or with biological events, how to monitor personnel to ensure that the biological agents are not allowed into non-affected locations. New thinking, new strategies and new methods must be understood and utilized, as appropriate.

Contingency planning is planning for adverse situations so that the necessary people, processes, systems, forms and everything required for running the business day to day are available, especially those things that are mission critical to the company. Companies need to expand and extend their thinking and plan more about what happens when critical infrastructure is lost for a longer period of time.

While 9/11 represented a worse trauma and larger loss of life, the power failure of 2003 adversely affected more companies over a wider area. Many companies were completely unable to conduct business for two or three days. Subsequently, there have been additional power failures. Indeed, the country's power grid is aging and vulnerable, and it represents a continual source of concern.

> **Insider Notes:** Equipment that had been kept offline in storage might not be damaged in the traditional sense, but might be rendered unusable by electromagnetic pulses from a radiological weapon, or become contaminated from a biological weapon. Even simple paper forms might become "hot" and unusable in certain types of events.

WHILE 9/11 REPRESENTED A WORSE TRAUMA AND LARGER LOSS OF LIFE, THE POWER FAILURE OF 2003 ADVERSELY AFFECTED MORE COMPANIES OVER A WIDER AREA. MANY COMPANIES WERE COMPLETELY UNABLE TO CONDUCT BUSINESS FOR TWO OR THREE DAYS.

ACTION ITEM CHECKLIST

- **If your company does not have a plan in place, start working on one.** In today's uncertain and strife-torn world it's not if, but when that plan will be needed. If there's a plan in place, make sure it is regularly updated and provides contingencies for the potential of CBRNE and other protracted failures or events that could take your company out of business longer than anticipated.
- **Carefully plan for employees' needs in an emergency.** Obstacles may prevent employees from taking part in the recovery phase because of personal or location issues. Consider bringing in alternate resources from other locations, or train people to perform tasks outside of their normal job function.
- **Rigorously test your plans.** The time to test the plan isn't after an event has occurred. With the added stress of recovery, mistakes are often made. Only regular planning and execution of plans can ensure that procedures are followed.

Testing should also be built in. Testing probably is the least most practiced portion of a business continuity or disaster recovery plan. Testing often seems irrelevant, and it is also difficult in some cases to test in today's 24/7/365 world. This has made testing much more difficult, but also more necessary.

Some companies use a high availability strategy in which a failure of one system automatically "fails-over" (transfers functions in the event of failure) to another geographically distant site. For example, a call center in New York may fail-over to a call center in Arizona. That's fine, and that works very well, but too many companies wait until the last minute to test their fail-over plans. A non-tested plan can fail to consider that Phoenix is two hours behind New York, so a failure in New York early in the morning means people in Phoenix will not be at the call center site and will have to be called in earlier than normal.

After 9/11, it became clear that larger organizations need to coordinate disaster recovery planning with public services people: police, fire, office of emergency management, etc. to make sure that it understands how those services will react to an event. For example, the police, in the event of a bomb scare, may be required by law to evacuate the building. It may not release the building back to the organization for several hours. Therefore, a company needs to work with public services to understand their chain of command and cooperate in letting them help a company to quickly get back into its facilities.

THE TRADITIONAL APPROACH

The traditional approach to business continuity, as forwarded by organizations such as the Disaster Recovery Institute in the U.S. and the Business Continuity Institute in the U.K., begins with performing a Business Impact Assessment (BIA). This study inventories and examines all the processes and systems the organization uses in its operations, and identifies and prioritizes the components based on their mission critical nature. These components are often assigned Recovery Time Objectives (RTOs) and Recovery Point Objectives (RPOs) that best describe how long a business can afford to be without the component before suffering an unacceptable adverse impact.

RTOs are often measured with parameters such as immediate recovery, recovery within a few hours, recovery within 24 hours or recovery over time as resources permit, based on their level of business importance. RPO

Insider Notes: The traditional model of the IT department solely in charge of business continuity and disaster recovery is gone forever. Making IT responsible for these areas has never been a good idea, but that's especially true today. Continuity and recovery is now solidly the responsibility of senior management, landing squarely on the shoulders of the CEO. That's where the buck stops now.

A TRADITIONAL DISASTER PLAN ASSUMES THAT PEOPLE WILL BE AVAILABLE TO IMPLEMENT ITS RECOVERY STRATEGIES. RECENT TRAUMAS DEMONSTRATE THAT THIS MAY NO LONGER BE THE CASE. PEOPLE MAY FLEE THE AREA, FOR THEIR OWN SAFETY OR TO RECONNECT WITH FAMILY. TRAVEL MAY BE SEVERELY RESTRICTED, BY QUARANTINES, LOCK-DOWNS, GROUNDING OF AIRLINES, UNAVAILABILITY OF CARS AND THE FAILURE OF PUBLIC TRANSPORTATION THROUGH DESTRUCTION OR IMPENETRABLE GRIDLOCK.

refers to the point where the company must get back to following a "last loss" known transaction, etc.

In conjunction with the Business Impact Assessment, companies will also perform a Risk Analysis (RA). Organizations such as the National Institute for Science and Technology (NIST) have published documents that cover in detail what this entails. NFPA 1600, a document published by the National Fire Protection Association, a federation of diverse insurance companies, is also commonly used as guidance in performing a Risk Analysis. A Risk Analysis identifies all potential risks, human, environmental and technological, determines the probability of those risks, and then, based on the prioritization provided by the BIA, determines what the potential impact would be on mission critical items if, and when, the identified risk were to actually occur. Potential impacts can be very diverse, and can include financial, contractual, legal, public relations and customer confidence.

Once the BIA and RA are completed, the organization has a clearer picture of where they are vulnerable. The next step is to decide which risks to accept, which to manage through insurance, which to reduce through the use of alternate technologies and which to mitigate by developing a Business Continuity Plan (BCP), which outlines how a company will respond, to and recover from, threats to identified assets.

The BCP traditionally covers such details as identifying the people and teams responsible for addressing, leading and performing specific tasks, and the processes and technologies they will use. The plan also will address alternate facilities, which are usually broken down into three possibilities:

- **Hot sites** are fully loaded with all necessary equipment and are always standing by, ready to go with the flip of a switch. The hot site might be an alternate location owned by the company or a space pre-contracted and reserved with a third-party. By their nature, hot sites are expensive and temporary, allowing the company to buy time while longer term recovery plans are put into place.
- **Warm sites** are general facilities with basic amenities standing by, but not necessarily including all the equipment that the business will need to fully operate.
- **Cold sites** represent a shell, a physical place to move, if needed.

Senior management signs off on the BCP, which should be tested in real-world conditions and further refined. That often means simulating an event, at least on a limited basis, to ensure that every contingency has been considered and that the plan works as anticipated. An example would be to suddenly switch over a call center, re-routing all calls to test the efficacy of the backup plans, and the people, processes and technologies needed to ensure a transparent result in the case of an adverse event. The various Business Continuity organizations suggest that this test be done on at least an annual basis, and, for financial institutions, twice a year.

The BCP must also account for the fact that today's businesses are changing fairly rapidly. The days when people, processes and technology remain stable for years are far behind us. Therefore, the plan needs to be dynamic. It is never finished and must be constantly reconsidered in light of changes in the business. The recommended maintenance cycle is a minimum of six months, but many businesses should consider a three-month

Insider Notes: The phrase "management by walking around" takes on great importance in the context of disaster preparedness. Senior managers must see firsthand how business continuity and disaster recovery plans are proceeding and be keenly aware of their effectiveness.

CASE STUDY: A POWER FAILURE EQUALS SECURITY FAILURE

The Problem: a Florida-based services firm

This South Florida-based company experienced a prolonged power failure due to a series of severe thunderstorms.

The problems encountered were as follows:
- Improper access by unauthorized personnel
- Inability to use cell phones in the restoration of services
- Difficulties in getting critical employees to recovery site

In the first case, when management arrived to assess the damage to facilities, they found that it was completely open and that "homeless" and others seeking shelter from the storm had gained access to restricted facilities.

The Reason: Florida fire codes require all automatic locks to fail in the open position, so egress is not denied to anyone who might be in the building when power failed or the fire alarms were activated. That's a good and safe rule. However, for this company, it proved to be a security issue. The company's security team should have been aware of this situation and developed a plan that would dispatch security guards immediately upon power failure to secure the building.

The fact that this was not done increased the amount of time it took critical personnel to enter the building. These employees feared for their safety and waited for removal of non-company personnel before they entered to start restoration procedures.

Although internal doors remained locked, these people were able to wander within the facilities and certainly had the opportunity to commit serious damage. It is a well-known fact that the best time to attempt to breach an organization's physical or cyber security is when it is in recovery mode, because it probably didn't prepare for both physical and cyber security in its recovery planning.

Once the building was accessible, the next problem was encountered. The company had relied upon cell phones as its backup, in case of a telecommunications failure. However, this proved problematic. Cell phone towers rely upon utility power and batteries to supply power to critical circuits, enabling the cell site to function properly. Since the power had been off in excess of eight hours, cell sites were failing. This made it difficult, if not impossible, for people to use their cell phones.

Lastly, this firm found that, due to the storm's damage, many employees opted to stay at home and make sure that their families and property were properly protected. Since they were not available, the restoration plan was failing due to a lack of human resources. If the firm had thought this out in preplanning exercises, it would have been able to identify and use other recovery team members outside of the impacted area. They did not, and critical time was lost.

cycle, reviewing the plan, and confirming that the people, processes and technologies highlighted are still relevant.

KEY DIFFERENCES WITH THE NEW APPROACH

This is the way business continuity and disaster planning is performed, and this "status quo" framework continues to have merit. The key difference, in the post-9/11 world, is that the universe of potential threats has expanded greatly. Whereas before, the typical threat might have been a limited, short-term power failure brought on by weather-related conditions, today's threats are significantly more ominous and include CBRNE events.

To date, there has been little accounting for these new threats in the key documents, such as NFPA 1600 or NIST Business Recovery literature. These reports still assume traditional business impacts and recoveries. These strategies will likely suffice if your company uses the "garden variety" scenario that its facility will be unavailable and it will just cut over to a new one. But 9/11 and the 2003 Northeast blackout have vividly demonstrated that impacts can be more widespread and can adversely affect an organization's recovery sites, as well.

DATA SNAPSHOT

Most organizations exist in an ever-changing environment. Threats we would have never considered pre-9/11 have become commonplace throughout the world. It is short-sighted thinking that these threats will not once again reach the U.S. Plans to at least consider CBRNE threats and vulnerabilities should be undertaken, at minimum, by multi-

Have your business continuity plans been revised since 9/11 to reflect potential chemical, biological, radiological, nuclear or explosive threats to your organization?

YES: 19% | | **NO: 81%**

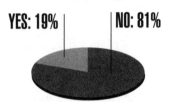

national corporations to protect their employees and assets. We should not succumb to the "ostrich effect" type of thinking and not review and revise BC & DR plans to meet CBRNE challenges.

Download the complete research study for free at www.blackbooksecurity.com/research
Source: 2005 Larstan / Reed Infosecurity Survey

A traditional disaster plan assumes that people will be available to implement its recovery strategies. Recent traumas demonstrate that this may no longer be the case. People may flee the area, for their own safety or to reconnect with family. Travel may be severely restricted, by quarantines, lockdowns, grounding of airlines, unavailability of cars and the failure of public transportation through destruction or impenetrable gridlock.

Another assumption that may no longer be valid is that certain technologies and capabilities will be readily available. No one anticipated during the terrorist strikes of 9/11 that both landlines and cell phone communications would be unavailable in a wide area for an extended period. Even when cellular communications are, at least initially, available, how do they fare in an extended period of power outage? These observations point to new considerations for any Business Recovery Plan.

Companies now need to consider that, in a CBRNE attack, a zone of impact might be dozens of miles wide, depending on wind conditions and other factors. Businesses may need to balance logistical convenience with a need to locate hot sites well outside any reasonably anticipated zone of impact.

Moreover, personnel might not be able to reach the hot site, so new personnel may need to be allocated in a recovery scenario. Businesses should realize that post-traumatic stress syndrome may dampen employee productivity for months, or years, after the disastrous event.

New threats also mean new actions. Years ago there might not have been a reason to shut down air intakes and restrict use of air conditioning, but today you need to look at those possibilities, among others, under many types of threat scenarios.

Another new aspect in the post-9/11 world is that backup equipment might not be available. Equipment that had been kept offline in storage might not be damaged in the traditional sense, but might be rendered unusable by electromagnetic pulses from a radiological weapon, or become contaminated from a biological weapon. Even simple paper forms might become "hot" and unusable in certain types of events.

Today's businesses need to understand the convergence of security and business continuity. Some forward-thinking organizations are combining the functions under the umbrella of business assurance, which is fast becoming the new paradigm. In the old days, if power was out because of severe weather, heightened security was not a major issue. Now, if a building is targeted and employees move to an alternate building, the new building must have security levels that are as strong as, or stronger than, that of the original building.

Insider Notes: Companies can't take the availability of infrastructure as a given. They must cast a hard look at utilities, power, telecom and fiber optic services from private carriers. They must determine how these services might be harmed during an event and what their backup will be.

BUSINESS CONTINUITY AND DISASTER RECOVERY ALSO REPRESENT A PUBLIC WELFARE ISSUE: IN THE EVENT OF DISASTER, PEOPLE NEED ACCESS TO THEIR MONEY AND TO HEALTHCARE INFORMATION, WHICH MEANS DATA MUST BE AVAILABLE WITHOUT A GLITCH.

Resumption scenarios must include and incorporate security equal to that afforded to the original primary systems, processes and people. Terrorists count on weaknesses in the recovery plans to launch secondary attacks to gain access to valuable information and company intellectual property.

These new threats also point to the need for new assessment capabilities. That means access to new types of monitoring equipment, and the training to use and understand it. In a radiological attack, how does one determine a clear area versus an area of impact? What does one look for, and how does one measure it? The company might need to take these questions into account. Companies also must consider the development and training of in-house HAZMAT teams, to allow company access to knowledgeable people who can provide information from which senior management can make decisions during times of crisis.

Another key action that companies need to take that they didn't need to in the past is to include the efforts of public utilities and public authorities to determine what their response will be under certain scenarios, and include these impacts in their own planning processes. How will a fire department respond to a chemical spill? Will they lock the building down, and for how long? Most cities have plans in place, and, of course, some aspects are kept confidential for security reasons. But a proactive company needs to learn all it can to most effectively plan for resumption and recovery.

A contemporary approach to business continuity and disaster recovery may still make use of the traditional Business Impact Assessment and Risk Analysis tools, but the scope must be significantly widened to take into account the new threats suggested by the events of 9/11. The net results of these events will prompt proactive businesses to expand on the vision within the framework of traditional tools.

Senior managers in all business functions must be aware of a new universe of risks to the health of their businesses and provide support for business assurance programs. They must support allocating the resources necessary to plan and continuously review strategies, to make sure that they provide the proper level of protection for the enterprise.

BEST PRACTICES

Over the past three to four years, there has been a tremendous proliferation of new federal and industry regulations affecting business continuity and disaster recovery. This has caused a great deal of anxiety among business leaders, and, it seems, with good reason.

Even though these regulations don't spell out business continuity and disaster recovery as a process, their demands for a guarantee of information availability can only be fulfilled through effective business continuity and disaster recovery efforts.

Business continuity and disaster recovery also represent a public welfare issue: in the event of disaster, people need access to their money and to healthcare information, which means data must be available without a glitch.

And yet, complacency abounds. Surveys taken since the events of 9/11 and the 2003 Northeast blackout show very clearly that these events alone have not sharpened the focus on business continuity. The surveys show that, with the exception of minor increases in budgets, efforts remain business as usual, with no obvious increase in creating, revising and testing disaster plans. In particular, there is an alarming disconnect between plans and testing them.

> **Insider Notes:** The dynamics of a business change every three to six months, so continuity plans must be updated just as often, to include any new threats and risks. The need to plan more quickly and efficiently, as well as more often, changes the manner in which planning is conducted. Protracted, bureaucratic planning efforts must be replaced with workshops.

Part of the problem is that there is still a tremendous amount of confusion as to what the regulations say and what the auditors require. However, the crux for most of them, including Sarbanes-Oxley, Gramm-Leach-Bliley, HIPAA and California Public Law 1386, is to ensure that information is adequately protected and available when needed.

The traditional model of the IT department solely in charge of business continuity and disaster recovery is gone forever. Making IT responsible for these areas has never been a good idea, but that's especially true today. Continuity and recovery is now solidly the responsibility of senior management, landing squarely on the shoulders of the CEO. That's where the buck stops now.

I don't mean to disparage IT personnel. They don't necessarily lack the skills, but their focus tends to be on the mechanics of effective hardware and software, and not on the primary business mission. The responsibility for business continuity and disaster recovery needs to reside in an area that has more of a focus on overall business operations, a group that can understand the operation of the business lines, as opposed to only the technology tools that support them.

The formal mantel of responsibility differs from company to company. Some enterprises establish an organization led by a chief business assurance officer or chief business security officer. Others put a chief information security officer or chief security officer in charge. Still others tap an executive with the more traditional title of chief financial officer or chief information officer. Regardless, what they all should have in common is the "Chief" designation because they should be reporting directly to the CEO. This is a big change, and any company that is not organizing the function in this way probably isn't providing the top-level focus necessary to successfully protect their operations, information and intellectual property assets.

All of the regulations demand that the CEO fully understands where the company stands, and that he is able to report this status in a concise manner to the regulatory agencies to which he is responsible. This is a significant change. Before, there was a mandate from senior management saying

"IT, this is your responsibility, take care of it." They'd say, "Let me know if there are any problems, or if you need people or budget," otherwise they didn't really want to hear about it. But now that they have to put their names on the bottom line, it is a very different story.

The impact of the regulations must ultimately be to get senior management to plug into business continuity and disaster recovery programs and to lead them in a more proactive oversight manner, ensuring that they are complete and comprehensive in every way. Contemporary CEOs need to understand that they must personally ensure that what they think is being done, is actually being done. They need to see the test results and the frequency of testing, and all of the metrics, so they are comfortable facing the auditors and attesting to the success of their programs. This is the type of effort that can't come to life from a memo or an email or a policy. It will only come to fruition if it is driven from the top.

The phrase "management by walking around" takes on great importance in the context of disaster preparedness. Senior managers must see first hand how business continuity and disaster recovery plans are proceeding, and be keenly aware of their effectiveness. These executives also need to be perceived at all levels of the organization as champions of the effort, providing the resources necessary and demonstrating their personal interest in the results. They can't afford to assume that they will fully recover in two hours in the case of an event. They need to see the hard proof of testing for them to understand what is realistic and what is not. This is the level of due diligence senior management needs to bring to the table today.

It can't be emphasized enough that CEOs must ensure that their plans cover all the aspects of the business that are associated with regulations. They are the ones that must attest to this fact and show an auditor that

Insider Notes: Telecommunications providers are now regularly requested to demonstrate that they have taken precautions to ensure that data and voice networks will be available if an incident occurs. Even if it the data is compromised while in transit, or becomes unavailable, the data owner is ultimately responsible if it didn't perform the due diligence necessary to protect it.

TO BUILD AN OPTIMAL "FAIL-OVER" SITE, A COMPANY MUST UNDERSTAND WHICH OF ITS SYSTEMS AFFECT THE AVAILABILITY OF CRITICAL BUSINESS OPERATIONS. THIS BEGINS TO MOVE THE ISSUE OF BUSINESS CONTINUITY INTO THE REALM OF SYSTEMS SECURITY; THOSE TWO AREAS ARE NOW CONVERGING.

this is the case. The way they show that is to put the plan in the auditor's hands, provide evidence of testing, and that the testing achieved desired outcomes. As business stewards, CEOs must ensure that all mission critical and business critical services, processes and functions will be continued after an adverse event occurs. The definition of what this entails is constantly changing, and plans need to reflect these changes.

NEW TECHNOLOGIES

In addition to new regulations, the availability of new technologies also significantly affects the way leading companies move forward with their business continuity and disaster recovery efforts. This hardware derives directly from the concept of CBRNE threats, the threats of extended power outages and the realization that these types of events are a real possibility.

One such technology that many companies are using to great effect allows for a replication of data in a remote area, one outside the potential zone of impact. For example, a New York City-based financial company might have a processing center in Texas, Arizona or the Midwest, where every keystroke is automatically duplicated. If the link between New York and the remote location is severed, it is a trigger for the primary processing to be picked up there.

For example: If the business is magazine subscriptions and someone subscribing online presses the "send" button, and at that moment the New York processing facility goes down, the data, which also had been written at the remote location, now will be seamlessly processed from there, as well. The business does not lose data or much time in processing it appropriately.

The ability to direct processing over great distances is also leading some companies to move their processing outside of large cities altogether, even though their physical offices might remain there. Processing might no longer be in the same physical location as the business, and no longer needs to be.

Businesses are also looking at servers and other types of equipment that utilize technologies that draw less power, and are investigating how they can operate for longer periods in conditions of low or no grid power availability. Extended outages are now a real possibility. Small and medium-sized businesses are creating a better battery-backup type of environment, and larger businesses are increasingly relying on alternate sites outside of their immediate geographic area.

Companies can't take the availability of infrastructure as a given. They must cast a hard look at utilities, power, telecom and fiber optic services from private carriers. They must determine how these services might be harmed during an event and what their backup will be.

Companies might need to dig deeper into the portfolio of technologies, and perhaps investigate alternatives such as microwave communications between business locations and the processing centers. Overall, there needs to be a rethinking of how technologies are used, how they will be affected by a new universe of event possibilities, and how, even in the worst of circumstances, top management can best guarantee that they can get back in business quickly, regardless of the event's severity.

THE EMERGENCE OF BUSINESS ASSURANCE

Over the last decade, emergency preparedness and crisis management have influenced an overall evolution in continuity planning. Businesses today have much less tolerance to prolonged outages than they had five or ten years ago, with recovery now being expected in hours, even minutes, not days. Companies have hot site fail-over systems where no recovery is required at all because it is done automatically by the systems.

To build an optimal "fail-over" site, a company must understand which of its systems affect the availability of critical business operations. This begins

PERPETRATORS WILL UNDOUBTEDLY USE ANY PERCEIVED WEAKNESSES IN AN ORGANIZATION'S OPERATION TO LAUNCH AN ATTACK; THE ILL-PREPARED WILL SUFFER THE CONSEQUENCES.

to move the issue of business continuity into the realm of systems security; those two areas are now converging.

Confidentiality, integrity and availability are the three high-level precepts of a good security program. Availability, which one can quickly see, is an area covered by both security and business continuity. The loss of a system, whether due to a power failure or a denial-of-service cyber attack, is no less a loss of critical business function.

Another aspect of this convergence is protection of the critical systems or processes that are operated out of hot or warm sites. The business continuity planner must make sure that all security precautions taken for operations during normal conditions are not made any less stringent for those that are operated in recovery mode. Perpetrators will undoubtedly use any perceived weaknesses in an organization's operation to launch an attack; the ill-prepared will suffer the consequences.

Planners now need to be more attuned to the dependencies their companies have on technology, and make sure that they protect their systems availability. In response to this, business continuity and security are migrating from being two separate planning disciplines into one combined discipline called business assurance, chartered with the total protection of mission critical assets and operations. Regardless of the type of disaster, whether it is denial-of-service attacks, viruses, natural disasters or an act of terrorism, "business assurance" means making sure that the business processes, people and systems are in place and operational when they are needed to provide goods and services.

CONTINUITY PLANNING IN THE NEW ENTERPRISE

There is a change in the way companies consider business continuity. Recovery time requirements are continuously shrinking in this "eContinuity" world. There is also the need to include in continuity planning the standard threats of human intervention, technological failure, and natural disaster, as well as the threats imposed by cyberterrorism and information warfare (viruses and denial-of-service attacks), to make sure that the critical business infrastructure is protected. Plans must encompass all of these things, and do so in an efficient manner. Risk and impact assessments must be done more frequently, accomplished more quickly and with more accuracy.

The dynamics of a business change every three to six months, so continuity plans must be updated just as often, to include any new threats and risks. The need to plan more quickly and efficiently, as well as more often, changes the manner in which planning is conducted. Protracted, bureaucratic planning efforts must be replaced with workshops.

In these workshops, planning staff should sit down with managers responsible for specific business areas and together complete an impact and risk assessment, focusing on how their business will be impacted, the cost of that impact, requirements for recovery, optimal recovery time and a definition of recovery point objectives. These can then be identified and translated into mitigation strategies.

The business network also must be included in any disaster recovery or business continuity plan because the networks are an all-inclusive part of any of today's business operations. Most companies operate in a dispersed or a non-centralized manner, with their clients and employees located in a wide variety of places, making the network the entryway into business systems and processes. Consequently, the network must be considered in any continuity plan.

Another key area is privacy, which is becoming increasingly important as regulations are passed that relate not only to the privacy of information, but also to the assurance that information be accurate and available when needed, and not subject to compromise. A continuity plan now must include security mechanisms, to make sure that when a plan is implemented it does

DATA SNAPSHOT

The Business Continuity Institute, in its planning guides, indicates that: "The development of a Business Continuity Management competence and capability is achieved only through a structured and consistently applied exercise program." What this means is that without regular testing the plans cannot be considered as ready for use.

Has your business continuity or continuuity of operations plan been tested in the last year?

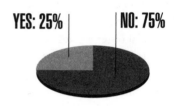

YES: 25%   NO: 75%

Download the complete research study for free at www.blackbooksecurity.com/research
Source: 2005 Larstan / Reed Infosecurity Survey

not leave the company at risk and all appropriate security measures are in place at the fail-over site. There must be no security compromises at the moment when a company is most vulnerable.

CBRNE: THE DARK THREAT

Every plan must consider and evaluate a CBRNE risk if the operation has a high profile — or is located in an area where there's a likelihood of such an event. An example would be a highly populated city or a place of a high concentration of governmental activities. If so, then appropriate plans for it must be included. These plans must detail how the company should react to those attacks, and also consider how public entities like the police, fire and other public organizations will respond.

COORDINATION WITH MAJOR PARTNERS OR SUPPLIERS

Responsible management will ensure that its own operations are capable of surviving an adverse event. It is also of the utmost importance, however, that any third-party business providers continue to provide the company with services and goods if it is adversely impacted by an event. One growing trend for companies that use third-party providers for services and goods is to require proof that these providers are taking due diligence and care in protecting information and the flow of data, and ensuring that those goods and services will be available on a continuous basis. Some organizations are actually requesting a letter of compliance that business continuity plans are in place, and require copies of an audit, like an SAS 70 audit, to make sure that they can rely on that provider.

Telecommunications providers are now regularly requested to demonstrate that they have taken precautions to ensure that data and voice networks will be available if an incident occurs. Even if it the data is compromised while in transit, or becomes unavailable, the data owner is ultimately responsible if it didn't perform the due diligence necessary to protect it.

There have been occurrences where ISPs or application service providers have been compromised because their security or their business continuity has not been adequately taken into account. Under regulations such as SOX, GLBA and HIPAA, it is still the responsibility of the owner of the data to make sure that it is properly protected and is available when needed.

Telecommunications carriers have another challenge — ensuring data separation. In many cases, competitor's data are traveling across the same circuits using the same routers or switches, and it's the ultimate responsibility of both these businesses and the carrier to make sure that any data that traverses this network is separate from all other customers.

TESTING THE BUSINESS CONTINUITY PLAN

Regardless of the type of plan or business, it's imperative to continually review and test what the plan is supposed to accomplish. One type of test is the "desk tests" conducted while building the plan, under which managers walk through it to make sure that its sounds feasible and that it provides the levels of recovery required.

Then there are physical walkthroughs, also a desktop exercise, which involves the recovery teams and makes sure that the time frames for recovery are doable, and the people are reachable. A simple test of a call out tree to the various recovery teams might uncover lapses that would be disastrous during an event that requires immediate remediation. When an event occurs, employees are highly stressed, which impedes their ability to adequately synthesize information and make appropriate decisions quickly. Testing is an absolute requirement.

There also is a requirement for periodic and regular testing as part of the regulations, and the audits that are being performed against those regulations. Financial institutions tend to test twice a year; telecom carriers and other business operations may test once a year. The point is that without testing, a company doesn't know if the plan will work. The best thing to do is test the plan, then test the plan, and, when that's all finished, test the plan! With this done, a company can be confident that it has completed all the due diligence it can. This won't necessarily provide 100% proof that it will work precisely the same way when an event occurs, but the probability is much higher that the recovery will be more successful if a test is undertaken ahead of time.

Testing is an ultimate conclusion of the overall planning cycle. Test results are then used to revise the plan to address inadequacies, and the cycle starts all over. Unfortunately, testing is one of those things that are unpopular and not done often enough. This needs to change. Potential threats are getting more complex and expected recovery times are becoming much shorter. Companies must be able to respond more rapidly to do their jobs when an event does occur, and the only way that can happen is through adequate testing.

Larger companies that utilize fail-over hot sites have an opportunity to run the test in parallel with their regular day-to-day operations, which would not be an impact on them at any point in time during their 24x7 operation. This would certainly be expensive, but not as expensive as being out of business for a protracted period of time because the plan failed.

Testing the call-out tree to make sure it's still valid is a very simple test that doesn't require too much time or cost, doesn't impact a large amount of people and can provide a fairly good feeling that the people will be there when you need them. If a company thinks out-of-the-box and looks at what it is trying to accomplish, there is probably a way to conduct desktop exercises, structured walkthroughs and partial fail-overs to test pieces of the system, which, if done creatively, can eventually test the entire system with a minimum of disruption. But, no matter how testing is accomplished, it needs to be done.

The military is a good example of how testing can improve outcomes. The military is able to carry out complex operations with high rates of success because it continually tests; businesses should do the same. To rephrase a famous Clausewitz dictum: economics is the continuation of war by other means.

In the global economy, business security and national security have become one and the same. A mere glance at the morning newspaper shows that security threats are omnipresent and growing. Your company stands a good chance of encountering disaster — if not yesterday or today, then definitely tomorrow. Prepare now, or pay a heavy price.

■ ■ ■

Dr. Jim Kennedy is Distinguished Member of Consulting Staff in the Security and Business Continuity Practice of Lucent Worldwide Services. In this position, Dr. Kennedy provides consulting services in information security and business continuity to a wide range of clients all over the world.

Dr. Kennedy has over 25 years experience in the business continuity and disaster recovery fields and holds numerous certifications in network engineering, security and business continuity. He has developed more than 30 recovery plans, planned or participated in more than 100 BC&DR plan tests and has helped to coordinate three actual recovery operations during his 25 year career. He has worked in the telecommunications, manufacturing, pharmaceutical, consulting and chemical industry sectors.

Before rejoining Lucent in 2003, Dr. Kennedy held senior IT and network engineering, operations and business assurance management roles with AM International, Exxon, EDS and Pfizer. Dr. Kennedy can be reached at 973-386-2223 or jtkennedy@lucent.com.

GLOSSARY

ACL   Access Control List

BASEL II   International standard requiring banks to implement enterprise risk management policies that align capital adequacy assessment with underlying credit risk, market risk and operational risk

BCP   Business Continuity Plan

BIA   Business Impact Assessment

BGP   Border Gateway Routing Protocol

BS7799   A Uniform Security Management Standard

BSM   Business Services Management

CBRNE   Chemical, Biological, Radiological, Nuclear, or Explosive

CC   Common Criteria for Information Technology Security Evaluation

CCEAL   Common Criteria Evaluation Assurance Level

CCTA   Central Computer and Telecommunications Association (UK-based)

CEO   Chief Executive Officer

CERT   Computer Emergency Response Team

CFO   Chief Financial Officer

CIA   Confidence, Integrity and Availability

CMS   Call Management System

CIO   Chief Information Officer

CISO   Chief Information Security Officer

COBIT   Control Objectives for Information and Related Technology — A reference model for IT governance

COBRA   Consultative, Objective, and Bi-functional Risk Analysis

COO   Chief Operating Officer

CRAMM	Risk Assessment and Management Method
CRM	Customer Relationship Management
CSO	Chief Security Officer
CXO	A Company Senior Executive Officer
DAC	Discretionary Access Control
DARPA	Defense Advanced Research Projects Agency
DLLS	Window Files
DMCA	Digital Millennium Copywrite Act
DMZ	Demilitarized Zone — Small network that separates a company's private network and the outside public network
DNS	Domain Name System
DRM	Digital Rights Management
DSL	Divided Services Line
DSS	Decision Support System
EDI	Electronic Data Interchange
EDPA	European Data Protection Act
ERP	Enterprise Resource Planning
FSTC	Financial Services Technology Consortium
FTP	File Transfer Protocol
GLBA	Gramm-Leach-Bliley Act
HAZMAT	Hazardous Materials
HIPAA	Health Insurance Portability and Accountability Act
HR	Human Resources
HTML	Hypertext Mark-up Language
HTTP	Hypertext Text Transfer Protocol

IAM	Identity and Access Management
IDM	Identity Management
IDMEF	Intrusion Detection Message Exchange Format
IDP	Intrusion Detection and Prevention
IDS	Intrusion Detection System
IE	Internet Explorer
IETF	Internet Engineering Task Force
IIS	Internet Information Services
IM	Instant Message
IMAP	Internet Message Access Protocol
IP	Intellectual Property
IPS	Intrusion Protection System
IPSEC	Intellectual Property Security
IRC	Internet Relay Chat
ISAC	Information Sharing and Analysis Center
ISO	International Organization of Standardization
ISO 17799	Reference Model for IT Security Governance
ISP	Internet Service Provider
IT	Information Technology
IVR	Interactive Voice Response
MAC	Media Access Control
M&A	Merger and Acquisition
MLS	Multi-level Security
MP3	Digital Music Format
MRD	Market Requirements Document

NDR   Network Disaster Recovery

NFPA 1600   Risk Analysis Guidance from the National Fire Protection Association

NFS   Network File System

NIST   National Institute of Science and Technology

OCTAVE   Operationally Critical Threat Asset and Vulnerability Evaluation

ODS   Operational Data Store

OSPF   Open Shortest Path First Routing Protocol

P2P   Peer to Peer Communication

PBX   Private Branch Exchange

PDA   Personal Digital Assistant

PGP   PGP — Pretty Good Privacy — Email encryption technology

PIN   Personal Identification Number

PKI   Public Key Infrastructure

POP3   An email Protocol

RAID   Redundant Array of Independent Drives

RFP   Request for Proposal

RMO   Risk Management Organization

ROI   Return on Investment

RPO   Recovery Point Objective

RTO   Recovery Time Objective

SAN	Storage Area Network
SARA	Simple to Apply Risk Analysis
SAS70	Financial Audit for IT Controls
SB 1386	California Breach Information Act
SCM	Source Code Management
SD CARDS	Secure Digital Cards
SEC	Security and Exchange Commission
SIM	Security Information Management
SIP	Session Initiation Protocol
SLA	Service Level Agreement
SMTP	Simple Mail Transfer Protocol
SNMP	Simple Network Management Protocol
SOHO	Small Office Home Office
SOX	Sarbanes-Oxley
SPRINT	Simplified Process for Risk Identification
SQL	Sequential Query Language
SUS	Software Update Services
TCO	Total Cost of Ownership
TCP/IP	Transmission Control Protocol/Internet Protocol
UDP	Universal Data Protocol
URL	Universal Resource Locate
USB PORT	Universal Serial Bus
VOIP	Voice Over Internet Protocol
VLAN	Virtual Local Area Network
VPN	Virtual Private Network

SECURITY RESOURCE APPENDIX

Organizations, Companies & Products That Will Help Keep Your IT Infrastructure Safe

To be included in the next edition, apply at
www.blackbooksecurity.com/appendixregister

Company Name:	Avaya Inc.
Address:	211 Mount Airy Road
City:	Basking Ridge
State:	NJ
Zip:	07920
Phone:	908-953-6000 or 800-784-6104
Web Site:	www.avaya.com

DESCRIPTION:

Avaya Inc. designs, builds and manages communications networks for more than 1 million businesses worldwide, including 90 percent of the FORTUNE 500®. Focused on businesses large to small, Avaya is a world leader in secure and reliable Internet Protocol (IP) telephony systems and communications software applications and services. Driving the convergence of voice and data communications with business applications — and distinguished by comprehensive worldwide services — Avaya helps customers leverage existing and new networks to achieve superior business results.

SERVICES:

- Security Assessment, Planning & Policy Development
- PBX Security Services
- Security Hardening Services
- Business Continuity/Disaster Recovery
- Secure Access and Control
- Managed Security Services for Voice
- Managed Security Services for Data

For more information, please visit www1.avaya.com/security/

Company Name:	BMC Software, Inc.
Address:	2101 City West Blvd
City:	Houston
State:	Texas
Zip:	77042
Phone:	+01-713-918-8800
Web Site:	www.bmc.com/identitymanagement

DESCRIPTION:

Founded in 1980, BMC Software, Inc. [NYSE:BMC] is a leading provider of enterprise management solutions that empower companies to manage their IT infrastructure from a business perspective. BMC Software's Business Service Management (BSM) strategy and in particular its Identity Management Solution, CONTROL-SA, are aligned with business needs to ensure that the challenges of today's IT environments are successfully addressed. With BMC Software, the IT organization can manage what matters at a business-service level. A strategic advantage of BSM is the ability to lower the total cost of IT and business operations, comply with regulatory issues and even enhance revenue opportunities.

SERVICES:

BMC Software has collaborated with customers and partners during the past year to build common implementation approaches tied to immediate business needs. BMC Software identified the eight most common implementation approaches that emerged, forming what the company now refers to as Routes to Value™.

Routes to Value provide a clear, competitive differentiator and facilitate customer engagements by simplifying the value of BSM with very clear deployment processes. The Routes to Value are: Infrastructure and Application Management; Service Impact and Event Management; Service Level Management; Capacity Management and Provisioning; Change and Configuration Management; Asset Management and Discovery; Incident and Problem Management; Identity Management.

Starting with one or more of these Routes to Value, companies are able to address immediate IT needs while at the same time follow a clear roadmap for full Business Service Management implementation.

SPECIAL OFFERINGS:

To take advantage of a BMC Software special offer for readers of Corporate Security, please visit us at www.bmc.com/identitymanagement/blackbook and enter code bbCS2004. *(estimated value of the offer is $50)*

Company Name:	CERT Coordination Center (CERT/CC)
Address:	CERT® Coordination Center
	Software Engineering Institute
	Carnegie Mellon University
City:	Pittsburgh
State:	PA
Zip:	15213-3890
Phone:	412-268-7090
Web Site:	www.cert.org/nav/index_main.html

DESCRIPTION:

The CERT Coordination Center (CERT/CC) is located at the Software Engineering Institute (SEI), a federally funded research and development center at Carnegie Mellon University in Pittsburgh, Pennsylvania. Following the Morris worm incident, which brought 10 percent of Internet systems to a halt in November 1988, the Defense Advanced Research Projects Agency (DARPA) charged the SEI with setting up a center to coordinate communication among experts during security emergencies and to help prevent future incidents.

While we continue to respond to major security incidents and analyze product vulnerabilities, our role has expanded over the years. Along with the rapid increase in the size of the internet and its use for critical functions, there have been progressive changes in intruder techniques, increased amounts of damage, increased difficulty of detecting an attack, and increased difficulty of catching the attackers. To better manage these changes, the CERT/CC is now part of the larger SEI Networked Systems Survivability Program, whose primary goals are to ensure that appropriate technology and systems management practices are used to resist attacks on networked systems and to limit damage and ensure continuity of critical services in spite of successful attacks, accidents, or failures ("survivability").

The CERT/CC is now also part of US-CERT, a joint effort with the Department of Homeland Security's National Cyber Security Division. US-CERT complements and enhances CERT/CC capabilities of preventing cyber attacks, protecting systems, and responding to the effects of cyber attacks across the internet.

SERVICES:

Vulnerability Analysis and Incident Response; Survivable Enterprise Management; Education and Training; and Survivable Network Technology

Company Name:	Columbia University, Computer Science Department
Address:	450 Computer Science Building
City:	New York
State:	NY
Zip:	10027
Phone:	212-939-7000
Web Site:	www.cs.columbia.edu
	www.cs.columbia.edu/ids

DESCRIPTION:

The Computer Science Department of Columbia University is ranked amongst the top academic institutions in computer security research, as well as other disciplines. Several faculty are members of the IETF, consult for industry, and conduct research supported by numerous agencies and corporations.

SERVICES:

Basic and applied research in computer security supported by government and industrial Grants and contracts.

Company Name:	Computer Associates International, Inc.
Address:	One CA Plaza
City:	Islandia
State:	New York
Zipcode:	11749
Phone:	631-342-6000
Website:	www.ca.com

DESCRIPTION:

As the management software experts for more than 28 years, Computer Associates International Inc. (NYSE:CA) recognizes that security management doesn't exist in isolation. It's part of an overall IT infrastructure that covers many disciplines. CA's vision is that disciplines which are traditionally considered distinct — operations, storage, security, life cycle and service management — should be integrated tightly to optimize the performance, reliability and efficiency of enterprise IT environments

CA's eTrust™ Security Management solutions, applies its considerable expertise in management software to today's security management issues. eTrust Security Management solutions protect information assets and resources; provides appropriate access to employees, customers and partners; secures content through proactive protection against attacks; and centrally manages security-related administration. eTrust solutions are grouped into three areas: Identity and Access Management, Threat Management and Security Information Management. These solutions address virtually every aspect of an organization's security, seamlessly integrated and can operate with your existing security infrastructure — helping to cut costs and enhance security.

SERVICES:

CA's breadth of security technology is enhanced by its dedication to customer service. The CA Technology Services team helps ensure access to our knowledgeable technical skills throughout all stages of the project life cycle and CA Education courses that help organizations derive the most value from their CA investment. CA's FlexSelect Licensing, the industry's most flexible software purchasing and payment plan, allows customers to base agreements on meaningful business metrics and derive greater value from their software investments.

SPECIAL OFFERINGS:

Please visit http://ca.com/security/ to read the Security Management White Paper: A New Model to Align Security With Business Needs.

Company Name:	Fortinet, Inc.
Address:	920 Stewart Drive
City:	Sunnyvale
State:	CA
Zip:	94085
Phone:	408-235-7700
Web Site:	www.fortinet.com

DESCRIPTION:

Fortinet is the leader in providing ASIC-based Antivirus Firewall systems designed to provide real-time network protection against the latest generation of network based threats. Fortinet security systems detect and eliminate the most damaging, content-based threats from e-mail and Web traffic such as viruses, worms, intrusions, inappropriate Web content and more in real time — without degrading network performance. Fortinet's products have received many awards including the winner of the 2003 Networking Industry Awards Firewall Product of the Year and the 2004 Security Product of the Year Award from Network Computing Magazine. Named as IDC's leader in their Unified Threat Management category, Fortinet security systems are the only security products that are quadruple certified by the ICSA (antivirus, firewall, IPSec, NIDS).

SERVICES:

Fortinet systems deliver a full range of network level and application-level services in integrated, easily managed platforms. Fortinet solutions provide Stateful Firewall, IPSec VPN, Antivirus, IDS & IPS, Web Content Filtering, Anti-Spam, and Bandwidth Shaping to create a unique approach to solving customer's security issues. Fortinet's Dynamic Threat Prevention System provides a much higher detection and blocking rate over single function security platforms and offer customers better value.

Company Name:	Information Systems
	Security Association (ISSA)®
	ISSA Headquarters
	7044 S. 13th Street
	Oak Creek, WI 53154
Phone:	414-908-4949
Toll Free in U.S.:	800-370-ISSA
Fax:	414-768-8001
Web Site:	www.issa.org

DESCRIPTION:

The Information Systems Security Association (ISSA)® is a not-for-profit, international organization of information security professionals and practitioners. It provides educational forums, publications and peer interaction opportunities that enhance the knowledge, skill and professional growth of its members.

SERVICES:

Member benefits include:

- Professional Networking
- Education
- Conferences
- Webcasts
- Subscription to The ISSA Journal monthly magazine

Company Name:	Infosecurity/Security Leadership Conference Series (jointly produced by (ISC)²® and Infosecurity)
Address:	383 Main Avenue
City:	Norwalk
State:	CT
Zip:	06851
Phone:	203-840-5651
Web Site:	www.infosecurityevent.com
	www.securityleadershipseries.com

DESCRIPTION:

Infosecurity heightens the sharing of information critical to a more secure and compliant information infrastructure through the delivery of a highly balanced, quality educational program for security professionals, practitioners and business leaders. Infosecurity is committed to advancing the knowledge of emerging threats and vulnerabilities, solutions to mitigate these dangers and best practices in the effort to protect both private and public networks.

SERVICES:

Educational programs, CPE offerings towards CISSPs (courtesy of (ISC)²), new product sourcing, a full spectrum of security products, systems, solutions

FEE:

$200 off any Infosecurity or Security Leadership Full Conference registration fee of $995.

Company Name:	ISACA®
Address:	3701 Algonquin Road, Suite 1010
City:	Rolling Meadows
State:	Illinois
Zip:	60008
Phone:	847-253-1545
Web Site:	www.isaca.org

DESCRIPTION:

ISACA is a pace-setting global organization for information governance, control, security and audit professionals. Its IS auditing and IS control standards are followed by practitioners worldwide. It administers the globally recognized Certified Information Systems Auditor' (CISA) certification and the new Certified Information Security Manager" (CISM™) certification. ISACA publishes a leading technical journal — the Information Systems Control Journal — and it hosts a series of international conferences. Together, ISACA and its affiliated IT Governance Institute lead the information technology control community and serve its practitioners by providing the elements needed by IT professionals in an ever-changing worldwide environment.

SERVICES:

- Membership
- ISACA Bookstore
- Global Conferences and Educational Programs
- K-NET
- Information Systems Control Journal
- Discussion Forums
- Leadership
- Access to Standards, Guidelines and Procedures
- Research
- Certification

Company Name:	$(ISC)^2$
Address:	33920 US 19 North, Suite 205
City:	Palm Harbor
State:	Florida
Zip:	34684 USA
Phone:	727-785-0189

DESCRIPTION:

Based in Palm Harbor, Florida, USA with offices in London, Hong Kong and Tokyo, the International Information Systems Security Certification Consortium, Inc. $(ISC)^{2®}$ is the premier organization dedicated to providing information security professionals around the world with the standard for professional certification based on $(ISC)^2$'s CBK®, a compendium of industry "best practices" for information security professionals. Since its inception in 1989, the non-profit organization has certified more than 28,000 information security professionals in 120 countries. $(ISC)^2$ awards the Certified Information Systems Security Professional (CISSP®) and the Systems Security Certified Practitioner (SSCP®) credentials. The CISSP, the Gold Standard in information security certifications, is the first information technology credential to meet the requirements of ISO/IEC 17024, a global benchmark for certification of personnel. More information about $(ISC)^2$ is available at www.isc2.org.

SERVICES:

- Maintaining the CBK® for information security (IS),
- Certifying industry professionals and practitioners under an international IS standard,
- Providing education,
- Administering certification examinations, and
- Ensuring the continued competence of credential-holders, primarily through continuing education.

SPECIAL OFFERINGS:

Get the latest information on trends and issues affecting you — the information security professional. Send your email request for a copy of the $(ISC)^2$/IDC 2004 Global Information Security Workforce Study to wkfstudy@isc2.org.

Company Name:	The Global CSO Council
Address:	4616 Henry Street
City:	Pittsburgh
State:	PA
Zip:	15213
Phone:	412-268-6755
Web Site:	www.csocouncil.org

DESCRIPTION:

The Global Council of CSOs is a think tank comprised of a group of influential corporate, government and academic security experts dedicated to raising the awareness of online security issues. The Council encourages dialogue and action to meet the new challenges of online security. The Council focuses on defining the role CSOs should take in corporate, national security, and future technology development.

SERVICES:

The Council is the first step in providing senior public and private sector leadership with the following five objectives:

1. Bring together CSOs to address online security challenges in an ever-changing environment, with a focus on business issues rather than technological issues;
2. Define the proper role, background, and reporting arrangements for CSOs within business organizations;
3. Define the role of the CSO in implementing The National Strategy to Secure Cyberspace;
4. Determine the appropriate times and means for CSOs to communicate with government on cyber security issues; and
5. Communicate candidly with technology vendors on a regular basis, to help define security related business needs and offer suggestions on how technology can be used to minimize risks.

Carnegie Mellon University's newly formed CyLab, a comprehensive research and education center led by Pradeep K. Khosla and Rich Pethia, will act as the Council's Executive Secretariat. This role supports CyLab's mission of creating a partnership between academia, government and industry-based organizations to create technologies for improving the nation's capabilities in response, prediction, education and development of new technologies for addressing the threats to the cyber infrastructure.

Company Name:	Lucent Technologies
Address:	600 Mountain Ave.
City:	Murray Hill
State:	NJ
Zip:	07974
Phone:	908-582-8500 (corporate headquarters)
	For Products, Services, and General Information, visit
	www.lucent.com or call:
	1-888-4-LUCENT (1-888-458-2368)
	Outside the United States call collect: 512-434-1523
Web Site:	www.lucent.com

DESCRIPTION:

Lucent Technologies designs and delivers the systems, services and software that drive next-generation communications networks. Supported by Bell Labs research and development, Lucent uses its strengths in mobility, optical, software, data and voice networking technologies, as well as services, to create new revenue-generating opportunities for its customers, while enabling them to quickly deploy and better manage their networks. Lucent's customer base includes communications service providers, governments and enterprises worldwide. For more information on Lucent Technologies, which has headquarters in Murray Hill, N.J., USA, visit www.lucent.com.

SERVICES:

Lucent Worldwide Services-one of the industry's most experienced and knowledgeable network services organization. With technicians, network designers, consultants and engineers, LWS serves the world's largest service providers, enterprises and government institutions in more than 49 countries and 6 continents. LWS' four lines of business include Professional, Managed, Maintenance and Deployment Services. LWS's Reliability & Security Services portfolio includes:

- Network Security Assessment Service
- Security Penetration Testing
- Security Policy Development
- Security Program Development
- Security Incident Response Process
- Security Awareness Programs
- Security Design & Implementation
- Business Continuity Services
- Reliability Analysis
- Managed Security Services

Lucent's Integrated Network Solutions (INS)—Delivers optical, data and voice networks and network operations software to the world's leading wireline service providers, which include long-distance carriers, incumbent local service providers, public telecommunications providers, emerging service providers, backbone builders and large enterprises.

Lucent's Mobility Solutions group—Provides networks for the world's mobile service providers to help them design, deploy and tap the revenue potential of third-generation (3G) networks. Lucent is the global market leader in spread-spectrum technology, which is the basis for the world's two predominant 3G standards: CDMA2000 and UMTS.

Company Name:	Schlumberger Information Solutions
Address:	5599 San Felipe, Suite 1700
City:	Houston
State:	TX
Zip:	77056
Phone:	713-513-2000
Web Site:	www.sis.slb.com

DESCRIPTION:

Schlumberger Information Solutions (SIS), an operating unit of Schlumberger, is organized in four business segments: Software Technologies, Information Management, Infrastructure Services and Business Consulting. These integrated segments are designed to provide a set of complete solutions and capabilities that support oil and gas industry core operational processes. Through its globally distributed professional and expert staff, SIS delivers unparalleled support, industry-leading software and the right information, delivered securely through a private network, to enable real-time operations.

SERVICES:

Software Technologies: SIS delivers an ever-expanding suite of software tools for finding, understanding and managing increasingly complex petroleum reservoirs and providing timely access to information needed for E&P decision-making.

Information Management: SIS next generation E&P information solutions ensure that the right data is available to the right people at the right time, with appropriate levels of quality and security. These solutions support key business processes and bring quantifiable value by reducing the cost to locate and access critical information.

IT Infrastructure Services: SIS provides infrastructure services that securely link the field to the office. The key components of this offering are secure global connectivity, both terrestrial and via satellite; petro-technical computing infrastructure solutions; a broad range of security services including identity and access management; and real-time data and collaboration solutions.

Business Consulting: The SIS Business Consulting group, a global organization that combines deep industry experience with strong business consulting expertise, spans the other SIS business segments.

FEE:

Security white papers as they become available — $ 495 each.

Company Name:	Security Risk Solutions, LLC
Address:	280 Round Swamp Road
City:	Melville
State:	New York
Zip:	11747
Phone:	(Office) 631-692-5175
	(Cell) 516 -680-4349

DESCRIPTION:

Steve Katz, CISSP is the founder and President of Security Risk Solutions (SRS). SRS is an information security company that provides strategic consulting to security product and service companies; helping them to position their product messages and helping them offering their products to the Financial Services sector. SRS also advises venture capital companies; helping them to evaluate potential investments in companies offering information security products and services.

Company Name:	Tablus, Inc.
Address:	155 Bovet Road, Suite 610
City:	San Mateo
State:	CA
Zip:	94402
Phone:	650-572-1515
Web Site:	www.tablus.com

DESCRIPTION:

Tablus, a leading provider of enterprise class software solutions, ensures peace of mind for senior G2000 business executives by monitoring and securing the transmission of high value information across network boundaries. Its patent-pending technology helps organizations accurately identify, investigate and proactively respond to security policy violations that could damage brand equity, reduce shareholder value, erode company revenue, result in non-compliance penalties and other negative consequences. Tablus management and engineering teams bring together extensive experience in security, knowledge management, networking and database technology. The Company is funded by Menlo Ventures, one of Silicon Valley's oldest and most prominent venture capital partnerships. For more information, please visit www.tablus.com.

SERVICES:

Content Alarm™ is a security solution that uses a patent-pending linguistic analysis engine and automated file crawler technology to continually monitor and accurately identify when high-value information is transmitted outside network boundaries allowing companies to effectively manage their security policies.

SPECIAL OFFERINGS:

Complimentary copies of Tablus white papers:
  Managing Liability Risks
  Protecting Trade Secrets and Confidential Information in the Internet Age

Company Name:	Trend Micro Incorporated
Address:	Shinjuku MAYNDS Tower, 30F 2-1-1 Yoyogi, Shibuya-ku
City:	Tokyo
State:	JAPAN
Zip:	151-0053
Phone:	+03-5334-3600
Web Site:	www.trendmicro.com

DESCRIPTION:

Trend Micro, Inc., a global leader in network antivirus and Internet content security software and services, led the migration of virus protection from the desktop to the network server and the Internet gateway, and is today pioneering antivirus technologies at the network layer. Trend Micro focuses on helping customers prevent and minimize the impact of network viruses and mixed-threat attacks through its award-winning Trend Micro™ Enterprise Protection Strategy. Headquartered in Tokyo, Japan, Trend Micro has grown into a transnational organization with worldwide operations, represented in over 30 countries. Its stock trades on the Tokyo Stock Exchange and the NASDAQ.

SERVICES:

Desktop and Client Security; Outbreak Management; Network Layer Security; e-Mail and Groupware Security; Internet Gateway Security; File Server and Storage Security.

Trend Micro provides several industry-unique services that complement Trend Micro's award-winning products, including information deployment and attack-specific policies and cleaning templates that help minimize the impact of network viruses, network vulnerabilities, and mixed-threat attacks. Trend Micro offers a range of services, backed by timely knowledge and expertise from TrendLabs to help customers manage all phases of the virus outbreak lifecycle. Including Trend Micro™ Vulnerability Assessment; Trend Micro™ Outbreak Prevention Services; Trend Micro™ Virus Response Services; Trend Micro™ Damage Cleanup Services.

Virus Response Service Level Agreement: An industry unique offering, Trend Micro™ Virus Response Service Level Agreement guarantees customers that fully tested virus pattern files will be delivered within two hours from the time a virus case is submitted or Trend Micro will pay a penalty fee.

Premium Support program: Trend Micro's Premium Support Program provides customers with timely assistance that combines rapid response times with technical and computer security expertise to quickly address customer issues.

Company Name:	United States Computer Emergency Readiness Team (US-CERT)
Address:	1110 North Glebe Road
City:	Arlington
State:	VA
Zip:	22201
Phone:	888-282-0870
Web Site:	www.us-cert.gov/

DESCRIPTION:

US-CERT is a partnership between the Department of Homeland Security and the public and private sectors. Established to protect the nation's Internet infrastructure, US-CERT coordinates defense against and responses to cyber attacks across the nation.

Established in September 2003, US-CERT is a public-private partnership charged with improving computer security preparedness and response to cyber attacks in the United States. US-CERT is responsible for analyzing and reducing cyber threats and vulnerabilities, disseminating cyber threat warning information and coordinating incident response activities.

US-CERT also provides a way for citizens, businesses, and other institutions to communicate and coordinate directly with the United States government about cyber security.

US-CERT is the operational arm of the National Cyber Security Division (NCSD) at the Department of Homeland Security (DHS). The NCSD was established by DHS to serve as the federal government's cornerstone for cyber security coordination and preparedness, including implementation of the National Strategy to Secure Cyberspace.

SERVICES:

The National Cyber Alert System provides valuable cyber security information to all users. You can subscribe to free email lists through the US-CERT web site. The system sends alerts and other cyber security information that provide guidelines and actions to help you to better secure your portion of cyberspace. You can receive any or all of the following document through email.

- **Cyber Security Alerts** — Sign up at www.us-cert.gov/cas
- **Cyber Security Tips** — Sign up at www.us-cert.gov/cas
- **Cyber Security Bulletins** — Sign up at www.us-cert.gov/cas

Company Name:	VeriSign, Inc.
Address:	487 East Middlefield Road
City:	Mountain View, CA 94043
State:	California
Zip:	94043
Phone:	650-961-7500
Web Site:	www.verisign.com

DESCRIPTION:

VeriSign, Inc. (Nasdaq: VRSN) delivers intelligent infrastructure services that make the Internet and telecommunications networks more reliable and secure. Every day VeriSign helps thousands of businesses and millions of consumers conduct commerce and communications with confidence. Additional news and information about the company is available at www.verisign.com.

SPECIAL OFFERINGS:

Reports:

- VeriSign® Internet Security Intelligence Briefing (ISIB) (November 2004, July 2004, January 2004 and October 2003)
- Gartner North American Managed Security Services Provider (MSSP) Magic Quadrant

White Paper:

- Security Intelligence and Control^{SM} Services: The New Age of Information Security
- TeraGuard: VeriSign's Information Management Architecture
- Effective Strategies for Risk Management
- Managing Application Security in Business Processes
- Securing the Merchant Supply Chain
- Understanding Network Vulnerabilities

SERVICES:

SSL Services: Email Security Services; Managed Security Services; Global Security Consulting; PKI and Authentication; Code Signing; Payment Services. **VeriSign Communications Services:** Intelligent Database Services; Content and Application Services; Billing and Payment Services; Connectivity and Interoperability. **Naming and Directory Services:** Naming Services; Directory Services; Digital Brand Management Services.

Company Name:	WholeSecurity
Address:	5001 Plaza on the Lake; Suite 301
City:	Austin
State:	TX
Zip:	78746
Phone:	(512) 874-7426
Web Site:	www.wholesecurity.com

DESCRIPTION:

WholeSecurity is the leading provider of behavioral endpoint security solutions. Our products and services protect users' PCs from worms, Trojan horses, keystroke loggers, and phishing attacks. WholeSecurity's products leverage patent-pending behavioral technology to identify and eliminate these threats, whether they are known or unknown, on both managed and unmanaged PCs. Based in Austin, Texas, WholeSecurity's customers include Deutsche Bank, Comerica, eBay, Raymond James and Cambridge Health Alliance.

SERVICES:

WholeSecurity offers three types of software solutions to meet the needs of their customers:

- On-demand endpoint security for companies who need to protect anytime, anywhere access via SSL VPN, Citrix®, or web mail technologies;
- Always-on endpoint security for companies who require strong threat protection on their LANs or IPSEC VPNs;
- Consumer identity theft prevention for companies who want to ensure that their customers' PCs are protected against eavesdropping and phishing threats.

LARSTAN'S THE BLACK BOOK™ ON

CORPORATE SECURITY

LARSTAN's
THE BLACK
BOOK™ ON
CORPORATE
SECURITY

UPCOMING SECURITY BLACK BOOKS:

Larstan Publishing is looking for qualified subject matter experts to work with us to author sections in a number of books we are publishing in 2005-2006. Titles include:

- **The Black Book on Business Continuity & Disaster Recovery** (Summer 2005)
- **The Black Book on Government Security** (Fall 2005)
- **The Black Book on Corporate Security 2006** (Winter 2006)

Larstan is now accepting author applications. To be considered, please complete your author application which can be found at www.blackbooksecurity.com. To learn more, contact Publisher Eric Green directly at 914-244-0160 or eric.green@larstan.net.

NEW 2005 TECHNOLOGY BLACK BOOKS:

Larstan's influential **The Black Book Series™**, is looking for experienced "thought leaders" to contribute to a number of new books we are publishing in 2005. Larstan is now accepting author applications for these and other upcoming titles, including:

- **The Black Book on Government Technology**
- **The Black Book on Healthcare Technology**
- **The Black Book on Financial Services Technology**
- **The Black Book on Retail Technology**
- **The Black Book on Transportation & Logistics**
- **The Black Book on Manufacturing Technology**

For more information on these or other titles, Larstan Publishing or The Black Book Series, please contact Group Publisher Mike Wiebner at 301-637-4591 x903 or mwiebner@larstan.net.

The Corporate Security Resource Center @

www.BlackBookSecurity.com

ead to our website at www.BlackBookSecurity.com and find an
ray of free informational resources at your disposal. Items include:

Daily Security News Feed
Newsletters by World Class Security Experts
"Ask the Experts" — Get Your Questions Answered
Market Research
White Papers
Case Studies
Vendor & Association Resource Guide
Educational Seminars & Webcasts

e'd love to hear about your successes, challenges and comments
n the book. Email us at comments@blackbooksecurity.com. If you
end it, we will read it!

www.BlackBookSecurity.com

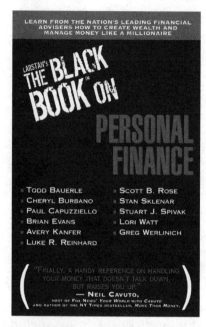
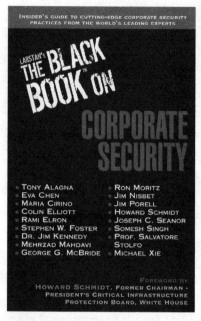